All in One®

Recommended by Teachers
Trusted by Toppers

ENTREPRENEURSHIP
Class 11

AF889471

EVERYTHING YOU NEED TO SCORE

- Simplified Theory
- All Types of Exam Pattern Questions
- CBQs; MCQs, A-R, Case Based
- Sample Question Papers

CBSE Exams 2026

Author
Shruti Manglik

arihant
SUCCESS AND NOTHING LESS

arihant
SUCCESS AND NOTHING LESS

ARIHANT PRAKASHAN
(School Division Series)

卐 *ADMINISTRATIVE & PRODUCTION OFFICES*

Regd. Office

'Ramchhaya' 4577/15, Agarwal Road, Darya Ganj, New Delhi -110002
Tele: 011- 47630600, 43518550; Fax: 011- 23280316

卐 *Head Office*

Kalindi, TP Nagar, Meerut (UP) - 250002, Tel: 0121-7156203, 7156204

卐 *SALES & SUPPORT OFFICES*

Agra, Ahmedabad, Bengaluru, Bareilly, Chennai, Delhi, Guwahati, Hyderabad, Jaipur, Jhansi, Kolkata, Lucknow, Nagpur & Pune.

PO No : TXT-XX-XXXXXXX-X-XX

Published By Arihant Publications (India) Ltd.

For further information about the books published by Arihant, log on to www.arihantbooks.com or e-mail at info@arihantbooks.com

Follow us on

卐 *PRICE* ₹250.00

PRODUCTION TEAM

Publishing Managers Mahendra Singh Rawat & Keshav Mohan	*Cover Designer* Salman Shaikh	*Inner Designer* Ankit Tyagi
Project Head Saurabh Gupta	*Page Layouting* Amit Bansal	*Proof Reader* Apoorvi

Index *cum* Study Planner

Studied | Revised | Exam ready

One Book- Endless Features

to Help you Succeed

CHAPTER 02

An Entrepreneur

In this Chapter...

- Why be an entrepreneur?
- Ethical entrepreneurship
- Values
- Attitude
- Motivation
- Intrapreneurship

In this Chapter

At the start of each chapter, all the topics of the chapter have been listed, so that students may know what they are going to study.

Competencies of an Entrepreneur

Competency is a set of defined behaviour that provides a structured guide enabling the identification, evaluation and development of the behaviours in an individual. Competency basically refers to skills and inner strength that an individual possesses.

A budding entrepreneur should have necessary competencies, so that he/she can venture into forming an enterprise and also be successful in it.

The necessary entrepreneurial competencies can be classified under the following categories

Complete Theory

Each chapter has Complete, Easy to Understand and Simplified theory covering latest syllabus and CBSE Textbook. Theory is developed in such a way that it is suitable for all types of learners.

CHECK POINT 01

1. Define fabian entrepreneur.
2. What do you mean by drone entrepreneurs?
3. What are industrial entrepreneurs?
4. Which type of entrepreneurs start their own business with their innovative skills and expertise?
5. Who is considered as pure entrepreneur?
6. State any one characteristic of an entrepreneur.

Check Points

A set of 4-6 Questions given in between the text, helps students to remain connected with the text while studying. They can instantly assess themselves for their understanding.

EXAM PATTERN EXERCISE

Objective Type Questions (1 Mark)

Multiple Choice Questions

1 .... entrepreneurs usually copy or adopt suitable innovations made by innovative entrepreneurs.
(a) Imitative (b) Fabian
(c) Drone (d) Go-getters

Ans (a) Imitative

2 .... entrepreneurs are also known as pure entrepreneurs.
(a) Spontaneous
(b) Induced
(c) Motivated
(d) None of the above

Ans (a) Spontaneous

Short Answer Type I Questions (2 Marks)

1 Entrepreneurs can be classified on a number of basis. State them.

Ans Entrepreneurs can be classified on the basis of their socio-cultural backgrounds, scale or potential of operations, generation of venture creation or personality characteristics exhibited by them.

2 Name the types of entrepreneurs according to Danhof. CBSE TBQ

Ans According to C Danhof, entrepreneurs are classified into following types
(i) Innovative Entrepreneurs
(ii) Imitative Entrepreneurs
(iii) Fabian Entrepreneurs
(iv) Drone Entrepreneurs

Exam Pattern Exercise

To make students completely prepared for examination, this Exercise contains Exam Pattern Questions. This exercise covers all types of questions, like; MCQs, Case Based Questions, Assertion-Reason, SA & LA Type Questions. All the questions are fully explained helping students to understand, how to write the answers to get full marks in the exam.

One Book- Endless Features

to Help you Succeed

Case Studies

Case studies are given at the end of the chapter to facilitate the understanding of the practical aspect of the topic discussed, i.e, real life implications.

CASE STUDIES

Case 1

Carefully read the case study given below and answer the questions that follow

Steve Jobs and Apple

At 20, he and a friend (Steve Wozniak) started a company in a garage on 1st April, 1976. Later that year, the duo debuted the Apple I at the Homebrew Computer Club in Palo Alto, California. A local store offered to buy 50 machines and to finance the production, the duo had to sell their most expensive possessions. Jobs sold his Volkswagen van while Wozniak sold his Hewlett-Packard scientific calculator.

Jobs named their company - Apple in memory of a happy summer, he had spent as an orchard worker in Oregon.

By 1982 however, his company sales sagged in the face of competition from IBM's new PC. Jobs and Wozniak unveiled their new creation, Lisa to increase the company's bottom line, only to be another expensive failure.

When Jobs heard of the message he said, 'You've probably had somebody punch you in the stomach and it knocks the wind out you and you cannot breathe. The harder you try to breathe, the more you cannot breathe. And you know that the only thing you can do is just relax, so you can start breathing again.'

Jobs sold over $20 million of his Apple stock, spent days bicycling along the beach, feeling sad and lost, toured Paris and journeyed on to Italy.

Recalling this publicly heart-breaking episode, Jobs said,

'I didn't see it then, but it turned out that getting fired from Apple was the best thing that could have ever happened to me.

The heaviness of being successful was replaced by the lightness of being a beginner again, less sure about everything. It freed me to enter one of the most creative periods of my life'.

During the next five years, he started two companies – NeXT Step and Pixar.

Sample Question Papers

To make students practice of examination in real sense, there are 3 Sample Question Papers at the end. All these Sample Questions Papers are exactly prepared on the latest syllabus & pattern of examination.

CHAPTER ASSESSMENT

Objective Type Questions (1 Mark)

1 Economists view entrepreneur as
(a) investment (b) factor of production
(c) Both (a) and (b) (d) None of these

2 An entrepreneur is
(a) an innovator
(b) a job and wealth-generator
(c) Both (a) and (b) (d) None of the above

3 Entrepreneurial functions of an entrepreneur include
(a) innovation (b) risk-taking
(c) organisational building
(d) All of the above

4 Planning and organising are ………… functions of entrepreneur.

5 ………… develop from need and want.

6 An entrepreneur is an inventor. State true or false.

7 Entrepreneurship is an abstract process. State true or false.

10 Explain briefly two features of enterprise.

11 Highlight the inter-relatedness between entrepreneurship, entrepreneur and enterprise.

12 Differentiate between entrepreneur and entrepreneurship.

Short Answer Type II Questions (3 Marks)

13 What are the three entrepreneurial functions of an entrepreneur?

14 What are the three promotional functions of an entrepreneur?

15 Discuss any three managerial functions of an entrepreneur.

16 Explain three commercial functions of an entrepreneur.

Long Answer Type Questions (5 Marks)

17 Why is entrepreneurship necessary for the economy? Explain any four points.

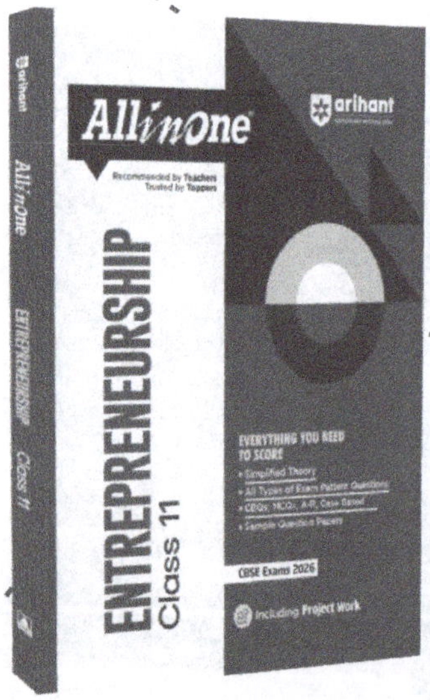

Chapter Assessment

Complete Test of Chapter in Exam format.

Sample Paper 1

A Highly Simulated Sample Question Paper for CBSE Class XI Examination

Entrepreneurship

General Instructions

Read the following instructions carefully and follow them

1. This question paper contains 34 questions. All questions are compulsory.
2. This question paper is divided into four sections—Section A, B, C and D.
3. Section A : Questions number 1 to 18 are Multiple Choice Type Questions. Each question carries 1 mark.
4. Section B : Questions number 19 to 24 are Short Answer Type-I Questions. Each question carries 2 marks. Write answer to each question in 30 to 40 words.
5. Section C : Questions number 25 to 29 are Short Answer Type-II Questions. Each question carries 3 marks. Write answer to each question in 50 to 70 words.
6. Section D : Questions number 30 to 34 are Long Answer Type Questions. Each question carries 5 marks. Write answer to each question in 120 to 150 words.
7. There is no overall choice. However, an internal choice has been provided in Section B, C and D of question paper. A candidate has to attempt only one of the alternatives in such questions.

Time : 3 hours **Max. Marks : 70**

Section-A

1. Mr. Kumar is working in a well-known company in Gujarat. He is responsible for providing assistance services such as book-keeping, typing, office support, etc. He is a part of (1)
I. managerial staff
II. trained technical manpower
III. professional manpower
IV. administrative manpower
Codes
(a) I and II (b) Only IV
(c) I and IV (d) I, II and III

8. Anil is the manufacturer of footwear and has a shop in the local market of Aligarh. He manufactures and sells same types of footwear to different retailers.
The retailers then sell the footwear to customers. The channel of distribution involved in this sale is (1)
I. direct II. one-level
III. two-level IV. three-level
Codes
(a) Only II (b) I and II
(c) Only III (d) All of these

Latest Course Structure

Paper : One **Time : 3 Hours** **Max. Marks : 70**

S. No.	Unit	Marks
1.	Entrepreneurship : Concept and Functions	15
2.	An Entrepreneur	
3.	Entrepreneurial Journey	20
4.	Entrepreneurship as Innovation and Problem Solving	
5.	Understanding the Market	15
6.	Business Finance and Arithmetic	20
7.	Resource Mobilization	
	PROJECT WORK	30
	Total	**100**

UNIT 1

Entrepreneurship: Concept and Functions

Competencies - Vision, Decision making, Logical, Critical and Analytical Thinking, Managing Skills

CONTENTS

- Entrepreneurship – Concept, Functions and Need
- Why Entrepreneurship for You
- Myths about Entrepreneurship
- Advantage and Limitations of Entrepreneurship
- Process of Entrepreneurship
- Entrepreneurship – The Indian Scenario

UNIT 2

An Entrepreneur

Competencies : Need Achievement, Motivation, Ethics, opportunity seeking, Passion, Independence

CONTENTS

- Why be an Entrepreneur
- Types of Entrepreneurs
- Competencies and characteristics
- Entrepreneurial Values, Attitudes and Motivation
- Intrapreneur: Meaning and Importance

UNIT 3

Entrepreneurial Journey

Competencies : Scanning the environment; Information seeking; creativity; Innovativeness; divergent thinking; Perseverance

CONTENTS

- Idea generation
- Feasibility Study and opportunity assessment
- Business Plan: meaning, purpose and elements
- Execution of Business Plan

UNIT 4

Entrepreneurship as Innovation and Problem Solving

Competencies : Risk taking; Determination; Initiative; problem solving ability; Adaptability to changing technologies

CONTENTS

- Entrepreneurs as problem solvers
- Innovations and Entrepreneurial Ventures – Global and Indian
- Role of Technology – E-commerce and Social Media
- Social Entrepreneurship - Concept

UNIT 5

Understanding the Market

Competencies : Task oriented, Opportunity seeking, resourcefulness, organizational skills, Analytical and logical reasoning

CONTENTS

- Market : Concept, Types
- Micro and Macro Market Environment
- Market Research - Concept, Importance and Process
- Marketing Mix

UNIT 6

Business Finance and Arithmetic

Competencies : Arithmetic skills, critical analysis, decision making, self-confidence, problem solving

CONTENTS

- Unit of Sale, Unit Price and Unit Cost - for single product or service
- Types of Costs - Start up, Variable and Fixed
- Break Even Analysis - for single product or service

UNIT 7

Resource Mobilization

Competencies : Resourcefulness; Collaboration; Managing Risk; Organizational Skills; Informed Decision Making

CONTENTS

- Types of Resources –Physical, Human, Financial and Intangible
- Selection and utilization of human resources and professionals like Accountants, Lawyers, Auditors, Board Members, etc

Project Work (Any Two Files)

- 10 Marks each for 02 Projects
- 5 Marks for Numerical Assessment
- 5 Marks for Viva Voce

Topics for the project

1. Visit of the District Industries Centre and prepare a report of activities and programs undertaken by them
2. Conduct a case study of any entrepreneurial venture in your nearby area.
3. Field Visit: Visit any business firm near your locality; interact with the owner of the business firm and prepare a field report on parameters like: type of business, scale of business, product/service dealing in, target customer, problems faced and measures to solve the faced challenges.
4. Learn to Earn
5. Know your State Handicraft and Handlooms as a means of economic activity for the livelihood of people and intellectual property rights attached to them for the promotion of local specific skills.

Note : Students need to complete two projects. Guidelines for project are given in the CBSE Textbook.

CHAPTER 01

Entrepreneurship: Concept and Functions

In this Chapter...

- Entrepreneurship
- The concept of entrepreneurship
- Functions of an entrepreneur
- Need for entrepreneurship
- Why entrepreneurship for you?
- Myths of entrepreneurship
- Advantages and disadvantages of entrepreneurship
- Process of entrepreneurship
- Entrepreneurship – The Indian Scenario

Entrepreneurship

Entrepreneurship is the act of identifying opportunities and exploiting them to one's advantage. It is the process of systematic innovation which consists of the purposeful and organised search for changes and a systematic analysis of the opportunities, that such change might offer for economic and social transformation.

According to **Jaffrey A Timmons**, "Entrepreneurship is the ability to create and build something from practically nothing. Fundamentally, it is a human creative activity, finding personal energy by initiating, building and achieving an enterprise or organisation rather than by just watching, analysing or describing one. It requires the ability to take calculated risk and to reduce the chance of failure. It is the ability to build a founding team to complement the entrepreneur's skills and talents. It is the ability for sensing an opportunity where others see chaos, contradiction and confusion.

It is the know how to find, marshall and control resources and to make sure that the venture does not run out of money when it is needed most".

So, it can be concluded that entrepreneurship can be viewed as a creative and innovative response to the environment and an ability to recognise, initiate and exploit an economic opportunity.

It is the freedom to do what one likes to do, with all its attendant profits and risks. It is a passion pursued by its followers and is defined by results and not by attributes.

Vegetable Vendor, Newspaper Distributor, Laundry Service provider — Are they Entrepreneurs?

To a large extent, they are also risk takers. They may not be innovative, but they take risks upto their own potential and level. So, they are entrepreneurs.

Evolution of Entrepreneurship

The process of entrepreneurship has evolved through the centuries and had been viewed differently by the management thinkers, based on the prevailing market conditions in the world.

Richard Cantillon, an Irishman was the first to use the term 'entrepreneur' in 1734 to refer to economic activities.

He defined an entrepreneur as a person, who buys factor services at a certain price to sell at uncertain prices in future.

In 1803, **JB Say**, defined it as, "The process of entrepreneurship is the one which brings together the resources needed for a venture".

So, the early management thinkers associated entrepreneurship with accumulation of resources. Then with the passage of time, this concept became more product-based, i.e. manufacturing activities of toys, cars, two-wheelers, etc., came under it's purview.

In the present era, this concept has now become idea-centric. Today, the key to success in a business is not just inheritance, it is the creation of more wealth and the constant innovation from the prevailing conditions to the next best practices.

With the middle income group becoming more affluent and determined to spend more, a lot of idea-centric and need-based companies are mushrooming all over the world, e.g. Mumbai's Dabbahwalaah, creches, ready to eat food, instant noodles, etc. So, the new age business ventures are more idea-centric and not just product-based.

Thus, now entrepreneurship is defined as a creative and innovative response to the environment.

The Concept of Entrepreneurship

Entrepreneur →	Entrepreneurship →	Enterprise
↓	↓	↓
Person (Subject)	Process or action (Verb)	Outcome (Object)

An entrepreneur is a person who starts an enterprise. The process of such creation is called entrepreneurship. The entrepreneur is the **actor** and entrepreneurship is the **act**. The outcome of the actor and the act is called **enterprise**.

Concept of Entrepreneur

The word *entrepreneur* is derived from the French word *entreprendre* which means *to undertake*. Thus, individual who undertake the risk of a new enterprise is referred to as entrepreneur. He/She is a person responsible for setting up a new business. He/She has the initiative, skill for innovation and converts a situation into an opportunity.

He/She is a catalytic agent of change and puts up new green field projects that create wealth, opens up many employment opportunities and leads to the growth of other sectors.

According to **Richard Cantillon**, "Entrepreneur is a person, who pays a certain price for a product to resell it at an uncertain price, thereby making decisions about obtaining and using the resources while consequently admitting the risk of enterprise".

According to **Adam Smith**, "Entrepreneur is an individual, who undertakes the formation of an organisation for commercial purposes by recognising the potential demand for goods and services and thereby acts as an economic agent and transforms demand into supply".

According to **Joseph Schumpeter**, "Entrepreneurs are innovators, who use the process of entrepreneurship to shatter the status quo of the existing products and services, to set new products and new services". He describes entrepreneurs as innovators.

According to **Peter F Drucker**, An entrepreneur is one who always searches for changes, responds to it and exploits it as an opportunity.

He/She believes in increasing the value and consumer satisfaction. Thus, a professional manager who mobilises resources and allocates them to make a commercial gain from an opportunity, is also called an entrepreneur.

In simple words, an entrepreneur is someone who perceives opportunity, organises resources needed for exploiting that opportunity and exploits it.

On the basis of the above definitions, it can be concluded that an entrepreneur is a person who

- Develops and owns his/her own enterprise.
- Is a moderate risk taker and works under uncertainty for achieving the goal.
- Is innovative.
- Is a persuader of deviant pursuits.
- Reflects a strong urge to be independent.
- Persistently tries to do something better.
- Is dissatisfied with routine activities.
- Is prepared to withstand the hard life.
- Is determined, but patient.
- Exhibits a sense of leadership.
- Exhibits a sense of competitiveness.
- Takes personal responsibility.
- Is oriented towards the future.
- Tends to persist in the face of adversity.

Concept of Enterprise

An enterprise is the business organisation that is formed to provide goods and services, creates jobs, contributes to national income, exports and also towards the overall economic development of a country. It may be defined as, 'an undertaking or adventure involving uncertainty and risk and requiring innovation'.

Enterprise serves as the framework within which decisions concerning what to produce, how much to produce, when to produce and how to produce are taken by the owner.

The **essential features** of an enterprise are as follows

- An enterprise consists of people who work together primarily for the purpose of making and/or selling a product or a service.
- An enterprise makes use of several inputs like men, material, machine, etc to produce a given output.
- An enterprise is assumed to be a continuing entity.

Entrepreneur Vs Entrepreneurship

Both 'entrepreneur' and 'entrepreneurship' are different terms, which are like two sides of a coin, i.e. both the terms are co-related.

An *entrepreneur* is a person who bears the risks, unites various factors of production and carries out creative innovations. He/She could be an individual or institution, who tries to create something new.

An entrepreneur always tries to bring about change in terms of factor proportions, known as innovations.

On the other hand, *entrepreneurship* is the set of activities performed by an entrepreneur. It is the process of identifying opportunities in the market place and to mobilise the resources to achieve long-term gains.

The differences between entrepreneur and entrepreneurship is tabulated below

Entrepreneur	Entrepreneurship
Entrepreneur is a person responsible for setting a new enterprise. He/She converts an idea into an opportunity and takes steps to exploit that opportunity to create wealth.	Entrepreneurship is the process by which an entrepreneur establishes his business.
Entrepreneurs are tangible people.	Entrepreneurship is an abstract process.

CHECK POINT 01

1. Why is vegetable vendor considered as an entrepreneur?
2. Name the person who first used the term 'entrepreneur'.
3. Define entrepreneur.
4. State any one quality of an entrepreneur.
5. Mention any one feature of an enterprise.

Functions of an Entrepreneur

Rajesh Marwaha and JS Mehandipur, in their book "*Entrepreneurship and Small Business*" have defined the following functions of an entrepreneur

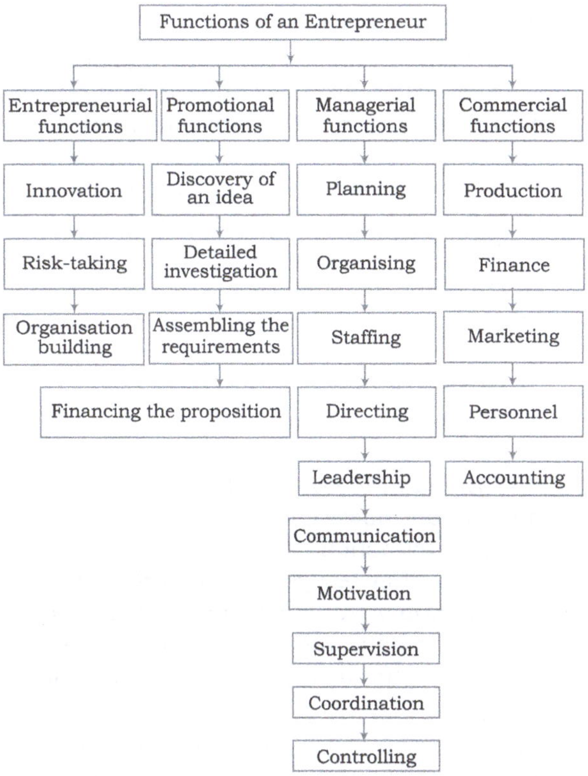

Entrepreneurial Functions

These functions are related with identification of an idea and readiness to undertake risk. The various functions to be performed by an entrepreneur under this head are as follows

1. **Innovation** It means an act of doing something new. The entrepreneur does not live with 'status-quo'.

He/She works to change the environment in accordance of his/her personal vision and values.

As an innovator, an entrepreneur has to

- Introduce new combinations of the means of production.
- Introduce a new product.
- Introduce a new market for an existing product.
- Identify a new source of raw material.

Thus, it can be concluded that entrepreneurs introduce something new in any branch of economic activity and try to exploit profit from it.

Examples of innovative products are I-pod, smart phones, induction cooker, LED television, LED lamps, etc.

2. **Risk Taking** It refers to taking responsibility for a loss that may occur due to unforeseen circumstances in the future. An entrepreneur has to take calculated risks because he/she faces uncertainty. However, he/she can minimise the uncertainties by planning to diversify his/her investment.

   He/She is a self-confident and highly optimistic person, willing to assume the risks involved in innovations, new ventures and expansion of an existing ventures.

   e.g. Dhirubhai Ambani was shown a piece of unfertile land in Jamnagar. He came to know that the land is not suitable for mango production, however he took the risk of mango production on the same piece of land and after few years, 6,000 tonnes of mango crop were harvested on an area of 2,000 acres and now the area is famous for the production of 'Alphonso', a variety of mango.

3. **Organisation Building** Organising and management are the main functions of an entrepreneur. It refers to bringing together the various factors of production to carry out the production activities.

   The main purpose is to allocate the production resources in order to minimise the losses and to reduce the production cost.

   Every decision regarding an enterprise is taken by an entrepreneur himself/herself, whether it is related to lines of business to expand or to employ more capital.

   Hence, we can say that an entrepreneur is the final judge in the conduct and operation of his/her business.

Promotional Functions

These functions are related to putting an idea into action. Various functions to be performed under this head are as follows

1. **Discovery of an Idea** An entrepreneur tries to visualise an opportunity for a particular type of business which can run profitably. He/She then develops the idea along with the experts in the field, and if they are convinced, then he/she can go ahead with more comprehensive analysis.

   e.g. Karsan Bhai Patel, the creator of 'Nirma washing powder', who was working as a factory chemist in Gujarat Mineral Development Corporation, started making detergent powder in his kitchen for poor rural women of Gujarat, after identifying their problem of non-affordability of established brands.

   Today, Nirma is one of the world's biggest detergent powder manufacturers. The brand sells over 8 lakh tonnes annually, capturing 40% of Indian market of detergents.

2. **Detailed Investigation** The entrepreneur estimates the total demand for a particular product in the market.

   After determining the prospective levels of demand for goods, he/she will then start to arrange the finances for the unit, along with the availability of power, labour, raw materials, machinery and other resources.

   The work of estimation becomes complicated if it is a new line of business. These estimates should be based on proper data and careful analysis of various factors over different periods of time.

3. **Assembling the Requirements** After making sure that the idea of enterprise is practical and profitable, the entrepreneur proceeds to assemble the requirements.

   He/She persuades some more people to join him/her on board. They may also be required to acquire some patent rights if they have invented something new and innovative.

The entrepreneur decides on the factory site, plant and machinery and contact the suppliers of the raw materials. Preliminary contracts are finalised and project is set to begin.

4. **Financing the Proposition** An entrepreneur has to decide about the capital structure of the enterprise. The requirements of finances are estimated first and then the sources from which money will come up are determined.

   Long-term and short-term financial requirements are estimated and the type of sources of funds are also decided like shares, bonds, debentures, loans, etc.

Managerial Functions

These functions relate to the day-to-day working of an enterprise. Functions to be performed under this head are as follows

1. **Planning** It is the basic managerial function of an entrepreneur which helps in determining the course of action to be followed to achieve various entrepreneurial objectives.

   It is concerned with the mental state of the entrepreneur and involves decision-making in advance, what to do, when to do, how to do and who will do a particular task.

2. **Organising** Every business enterprise needs the services of a large number of persons to look after its different aspects. An entrepreneur sets-up a goal which is to be achieved by its personnel.

   The function of organising is to arrange, guide, co-ordinate, direct and control the activities of the factors of production, so that the group objectives can be achieved.

3. **Staffing** This function involves making appointments for the positions created by the organisational process. It is concerned with the employment of human resources of an enterprise.

   In other words, it consists of human resources, manpower planning, recruitment, selection and placement of manpower, human resource development, promotions transfers, appraisals and determination of remuneration of the employees.

4. **Directing** It is concerned with carrying out the desired plans. It initiates organised and planned action.

   Through directing, entrepreneur guides, instructs, motivates employees and ensures their effective performance towards the accomplishment of group activities.

5. **Leadership** It is the process by which an entrepreneur directs/guides and influences the work of others in choosing and attaining specified goals by mediating between the individuals and the organisation in such a manner that both will get the maximum satisfaction.

6. **Communication** It is one of the most important functions of an entrepreneur and also a cause of concerns if not performed effectively. Communication refers to the exchange of ideas, feelings, emotions, knowledge and information between two or more persons.

   It has been observed that entrepreneurs spend about 75% to 90% of their working time communicating with others. It should be kept in mind that nothing happens in management until effective communication takes place.

7. **Motivation** It refers to the psychological process of creating an urge among the subordinates to do certain things or behave in a desired manner. The importance of this term can be realised from the fact that the performance of a worker not only depends upon his skills or ability but also on motivation.

   A sound motivational system must be productive, competitive, comprehensive and flexible, only then it will be able to help an organisation to achieve the required goals. Also it must consider the psychological, social, safety, egoistic and economic needs of the worker.

8. **Supervision** It refers to the job of overseeing subordinates at work to ensure the maximum utilisation of resources, to get the required and directed work done and to correct the subordinates whenever they go wrong.

9. **Coordination** It is one of the most important functions, as it is essential to channelise the activities of various individuals in the organisation, for the achievement of common goals.

The entrepreneur has to make sure that the work of different segments is going according to pre-determined targets and corrective measures have to be initialised if there is any deviation. Coordination is considered to be the essence of management.

10. **Controlling** It is the process which enables the entrepreneur to get his/her company's policies implemented and take corrective action if performance is not according to the pre-determined standards.

    The process begins with establishing standards of performance, measuring actual performance, comparing the actual performance with the standard, finding variations and finally, taking corrective action.

Commercial Functions

These functions are aimed at making the venture a success and to increase its profit earning capacity. An entrepreneur performs the following functions under this head

1. **Production** It is the creation of goods and services. It consists of manufacturing, ancillary and advisory activities. The activities of production are independent of the size of the undertaking.

   In a small concern, one person may be responsible for undertaking this function, whereas, in large organisations, this activity may be undertaken by various individuals or separate teams.
2. **Finance** It is the most important aspect in all organisations. The development and expansion of an enterprise needs more commitment for funds.

   It remains a focus of all business activities, as the need for money is continuous and it is the duty of the entrepreneur to look and analyse into the various sources of finance and appropriately arrange for them as and when required.
3. **Marketing** It is concerned with the movement of goods and services from the producers to the ultimate consumers. It is directed towards the satisfaction of consumer wants. Marketing plays a significant role in promoting the well-being of the business enterprise, by making the products popular among the consumers.
4. **Personnel** This function is concerned with employment, development and compensation for the personnel, the provisions of working conditions and welfare measures to maintain a good workforce in the organisation.
5. **Accounting** It is defined as a systematic recording of entrepreneurial transactions of an enterprise, so as to depict a clear picture of the financial position of the enterprise. The entrepreneur should look into the records of all the transactions which takes place in the organisation, so that, he/she is aware of his/her financial position.

CHECK POINT 02

1. Who defined the various functions of an entrepreneur?
2. Which function of an entrepreneur is related with identification of an idea and readiness to undertake risk?
3. Promotional functions of an entrepreneur are related to ....
4. State any two managerial functions of an entrepreneur.
5. What do you mean by controlling?

Need for Entrepreneurship

Economic development is the main reason behind the need for entrepreneurship in any country. Economic growth depends on the rate of innovation, which in turn, depends on the number and quality of entrepreneurs in the society. Thus, entrepreneur is an agent of progress in the society.

The need for entrepreneurship can be highlighted on the basis of following points

Need for Entrepreneurship

- Lifeline of a nation
- Provides innovation
- Adapting to change
- Increased profits
- Employment opportunities
- Social benefits

1. **Lifeline of a Nation** Entrepreneurship is the yardstick to measure the level of development of a country. No country can progress without the development of entrepreneurship.

Every country is trying to develop an environment which is conducive for the growth of entrepreneurs, so that the economic development of the nation is ensured.

2. **Provides Innovation** Entrepreneurship provides new ideas, imagination and vision to the enterprise. An entrepreneur is an innovator as he/she tries to find new technology, products and markets.

   He/She increases the productivity of various resources and stands at the centre of the whole process of economic development by indulging himself/herself in the process of innovation.

3. **Adapting to Change** (Inclusive growth) An enterprise operates in the changing environment and entrepreneur adopts these changes. Such changes made by entrepreneurs in their enterprises initiate the changes in the society as well as economy.

   Use of automation and advanced technology by enterprises brings growth in the enterprises as well as economy at large.

4. **Increased Profits** Profit is the excess of revenue over cost. It can be increased either by increasing revenue or by reducing cost. Increase in sales revenue is beyond the control of the enterprise, hence profit can be increased by reducing cost of production, which is possible only with the endeavour of an entrepreneur. Increase in profits increases the opportunities for future growth and development.

5. **Employment Opportunities** Entrepreneurship and its activities provide the maximum employment opportunities. Large number of persons are employed in the entrepreneurial activities in the country. The growth in these activities bring more and more employment opportunities.

6. **Social Benefits** An entrepreneur provides various good quality products and services at lowest possible price which indeed raises the standard of living and thereby, increases social benefits along with private benefits. An entrepreneur uses the scarce resources in the best possible way to bring peace and prosperity in the society.

Why Entrepreneurship for You?

One should become an entrepreneur or choose entrepreneurship due to the following reasons

Reasons to Choose Entrepreneurship

- Confidentiality
- Individual profit recipient
- Maintenance of flexibility
- Personal satisfaction
- Direct contact with the customers
- Individual and effective control
- Suitable for small scale business

1. **Confidentiality** The sole proprietor is not legally compelled to publish his accounts or share his secrets with others. A proprietor has all the decision-making powers. As a result, confidentiality or secrecy can be maintained easily.

2. **Individual Profit Recipient** All the profits which are earned from the business are to be enjoyed by the sole owner or proprietor himself/herself.

3. **Maintenance of Flexibility** As all the decisions are taken by the proprietor himself, so quick and prompt actions will be possible which brings flexibility of operations and quick adaptability of business to the changing environment.

4. **Personal Satisfaction** A sole proprietor can have the personal satisfaction associated with working for oneself. The success in business also induce sense of accomplishment and confidence.

5. **Direct Contact with the Customers** As all the work is carried out by the proprietor himself, so direct contact can be maintained with the customers. It also facilitates necessary and quick changes in the products as per the requirements of the customers.

6. **Individual and Effective Control** As all the decisions are taken by the sole proprietor, so total control of the firm lies in the hands of him/her only which results in complete freedom of action.

7. **Suitable for Small Scale Business** Sole proprietorship firm is most suitable form for a small scale business. There is no need to formally register the business or notify federal or state offices.

Myths of Entrepreneurship

According to **Guy Kawasaki**, "Many new entrepreneurs believe a set of myths about entrepreneurship".

Some of the most common myths are given below

1. **Starting a Business is Easy** It is not true that starting a business is an easy task. Most people who start a company fail to get one up and running.

   Seven years after implementing the process of a business, only one-third of entrepreneurs have a new company with positive cash flows greater than the salaries to labours and expenses of the owner for more than three consecutive months. However, it is generally easier to start small businesses.

2. **It takes a Lot of Money to Finance a New Business** Successful entrepreneurs, who don't believe in the myths, design their enterprises to work with lesser money. They usually rent a building rather than buying it and they turn fixed costs into variable costs by paying employees' commission instead of salaries.

   The typical start-up required for a small business is ₹ 1.5 lakh. e.g. Infosys was started with only ₹ 10,000.

3. **Start-ups can't be Financed with Debt** It is not correct to say that a new business cannot be started with debt. Most of the enterprises get started with debt rather than equity.

   However, the composition of debt and equity in the overall capital structure of an enterprise should be given due deliberations.

4. **Banks don't Lend Money to Start-ups** Government has implemented many schemes in collaboration with banks to provide finance for budding entrepreneurs.

   Hence, it is not correct to say that banks do not provide finance to new enterprises. e.g. IDBI and SIDBI banks were especially established to finance new businesses.

5. **Most Entrepreneurs Start Businesses in Attractive Industries** It is not true that most entrepreneurs start their enterprises in attractive industries only.

   The correlation between the number of entrepreneurs starting businesses in an industry and the number of companies failing in the industry is 0.77.

   It means that most entrepreneurs are picking up industries in which they are most likely to fail.

   e.g. Mahima Mehra started 'Hathi Chaap', a totally new venture that makes handmade paper from elephant dung.

6. **The Growth of a Start-up depends more on an Entrepreneur's Talent than on the Business He/She Chooses** It is a myth that growth of an enterprise depends only on the talent of the entrepreneur.

   The industry chosen by them also plays a key role. e.g. various dotcom companies mushroomed all over the world during the Y2K problem in the year 2000, to cash on the growing popularity of information technology.

7. **Most Enterprises are Financially Successful** This is another myth that entrepreneurship creates a lot of wealth, but it is very unevenly distributed. The typical profit of an owner-managed business is ₹ 2.4 lakh per year and only a top 10% of entrepreneurs earn more money than employees.

   Most of the entrepreneurs earn less money in their ventures as compared to what they would have earned working for somebody else.

CHECK POINT 03

1. What is the main reason behind the need for entrepreneurship in any country?
2. How can profits be increased?
3. State any one reason to become an entrepreneur.
4. Mention any one myth of entrepreneurship.

Advantages and Disadvantages of Entrepreneurship

To everything in life, there are advantages and disadvantages, and entrepreneurship is no exception. It involves lot of risk taking, yet it can pay off very well with rewards such as profits, the opportunity to be your own boss and make your own decisions.

Advantages/Disadvantages of Entrepreneurship

Advantages
- Excitement
- Originality
- Independence
- Rational compensation
- Freedom

Disadvantages
- Irregular income
- Fewer benefits
- Work schedule
- Administration
- Incompetent staff

Advantages of Entrepreneurship

Some main advantages of entrepreneurship are as follows

1. **Excitement** Involvement of risk element in the business makes it quite an exciting avenue. e.g. Steve Jobs left his position in Apple Inc and in his excitement to do something new, started Pixar which later turned out to be a successful venture.
2. **Originality** Entrepreneurs feel that they can provide something new to the society which others cannot or in other words, which was not been provided before. e.g. I-pod, I-pad, etc. This increases their self-confidence.
3. **Independence** Some wish to be their own boss and make all the important decisions themselves. For such persons, entrepreneurship is the perfect answer.
4. **Rational Compensation** (Salary) Entrepreneurs feel that they are not being paid, what they are worth and would rather work on their own and earn the money they should be earning for their efforts.
5. **Freedom** Entrepreneurs can work on any idea which they feel will eventually turn out to be a successful venture.

   e.g. Richard Branson's idea of space mission. They are given the liberty of freedom of thought which the employees do not enjoy.

Disadvantages of Entrepreneurship

Some disadvantages of entrepreneurship are as follows

1. **Irregular Income** Starting-up an enterprise means that the person must be willing to give up the security of a regular source of income.
2. **Fewer Benefits** There will be undoubtedly fewer benefits, especially when a business has just been started.
3. **Work Schedule** One cannot predict the work schedule of an entrepreneur, an emergency can come up in a matter of a second and late hours may become the norm.
4. **Administration** In a business, all the decisions are required to be taken by the entrepreneur himself/herself. There is no one ranked higher on the chain of command and the entrepreneur might feel himself/herself being burdened by the thought of making a wrong decision.
5. **Incompetent Staff** Most of the time, an entrepreneur works with such people who do not have the experience of work. Also, employees are not willing to make extra efforts to learn the trade. Hence, an entrepreneur has to deal with all such employees which increases his/her burden.

Process of Entrepreneurship

It is true that every successful event works as a systematic process and even though enterprises are as unique as the entrepreneurs who create it, yet most of them appear to work through a process.

Let us now see the process of entrepreneurship using a flow chart that follows

Step 1 Self-Discovery

It includes learning what they enjoy doing, examining their strengths and weaknesses as well as work experience and relating it to potential opportunities.

↓

Step 2 Identifying Opportunities

It includes looking for needs, wants, problems and challenges that are not yet being met or dealt effectively.

↓

Step 3 Generating and Evaluating Ideas

It involves using creativity and past experience to devise new and innovative ways to solve a problem or meet a need, and then narrowing the field to one best idea.

↓

Step 4 Planning

It involves researching and identifying resources needed to turn the idea into a viable venture. Also, doing research in the form of a written business plan and preparing marketing strategies.

↓

Step 5 Raising Start-up Capital

It includes using the business plan to attract investors, capitalists and partners. This stage can involve producing prototypes or test-marketing services.

↓

Step 6 Start-up

It includes launching the venture, developing a customer base and adjusting marketing and operational plans as required.

↓

Step 7 Growth

It includes growing the business, developing and following strategic plans, adapting to new circumstances.

↓

Step 8 Harvest

It means selling the business and harvesting the rewards. For many entrepreneurs, this also means moving on to new venture and new challenges.

Entrepreneurship - The Indian Scenario

Entrepreneurs are driven to achieve success in their business along with the qualities of a leader, manager, dreamer, innovator, risk taker, continuous learner, decision-maker, etc.

There are a lot of examples of the entrepreneurs in India who are now called synonymous of 'success'.

The declaration of the new economic policy has been responsible for creating an upsurge in the number of entrepreneurs in our country.

Recognising the crucial importance of these start-ups in boosting the economy of the country, the Government of India has come up with various initiatives to support start-ups in India which are as follows

1. **Start-up India** This scheme was launched with the aim of supporting Indian entrepreneurs to create 10 lakh mobile app start-ups.
2. **Software Technology Park** This scheme was established to promote and export computer software and professional services through communication networks or physical media. This scheme solely emphasises on computer software.
3. **Exemption of Income Tax** No income tax to be paid by the entrepreneurs for first three years. It helps to revolutionise the pace with which start-ups would grow in the future.
4. **Credit Guarantee Fund Trust for Micro and Small Enterprises** (CGTMSE) This scheme was launched by the government to help business units in getting collateral free loans at a low rate of interest up to a maximum of ₹ 100 lakhs under a tie-up with SIDBI. It facilitates in promoting new businesses and relaunching the existing ones.
5. **Make in India Scheme** Government launched 'Make in India' scheme with the aim to attract investments from across the globe and strengthen India's manufacturing sector.

   It also aims to facilitate investment, foster innovation, enhance skill development, protect intellectual property and build best in class manufacturing infrastructure in the country.

6. **Government Inspection** No government inspection is to be done of start-ups regarding various company related compliance for first three years.
7. **Patent Examination** Under this, patent application of start-ups are fast-tracked for examination and disposal. Start-ups are also allowed to get an 80% rebate in filling of patents.
8. **The Venture Capital Assistance Scheme** This scheme plays a vital role in providing financial support in the form of an interest free loan provided by SFAC to qualifying projects in order to meet shortfall in the capital requirement for implementation of the project.
9. **ATAL Innovation Mission** This scheme was set up by Niti Aayog, to promote an innovative culture and the development to the spirit of entrepreneurship across India.

CHECK POINT 04

1. Write any one advantage of entrepreneurship.
2. State any one disadvantage of entrepreneurship.
3. Which is the first step of the process of entrepreneurship?
4. Harvest means ...... the business and harvesting the rewards.
5. Mention any one scheme offered by government to start-up projects.

EXAM PATTERN EXERCISE

Objective Type Questions (1 Mark)

Multiple Choice Questions

1 An activity undertaken to earn profit is called
(a) Business (b) Entrepreneurship
(c) Enterprise (d) None of these

Ans (a) Business

2 The word 'entrepreneur' is derived from the French word 'entreprendre' which means
(a) to undertake (b) to over done
(c) to represent (d) None of these

Ans (a) to undertake

3 'Entrepreneurship is a creative activity'. It is said by
(a) Frederick Harbison (b) BF Hoselitz
(c) B Higgins (d) Joseph Schumpeter

Ans (d) Joseph Schumpeter

4 Mohit Rajvanshi wanted to search for changes, responds to it and exploits it as an opportunity. So, Mohit is a good
(a) businessman (b) entrepreneur
(c) Both (a) and (b) (d) None of these

Ans (b) An entrepreneur is a person who converts a situation into an opportunity.

5 .... was the first to use the term 'entrepreneur' in 1734.
(a) Peter F Drucker (b) J B Say
(c) Richard Cantillon (d) Adam Smith

Ans (c) Richard Cantillon

6 Sociologists feel that certain communities promote entrepreneurship. In India, such communities are
(a) Punjabis and Rajputs
(b) Marwaris and Banias
(c) Jats and Brahmins (d) None of these

Ans (b) Marwaris and Banias

7 As an innovator, an entrepreneur
(a) introduces new combinations of means of production
(b) introduces a new product
(c) identifies a new source of raw material
(d) All of the above

Ans (d) All of the above

8 Production, finance, marketing, personnel and accounting are all components of
(a) entrepreneurial functions
(b) promotional functions
(c) managerial functions
(d) commercial functions

Ans (d) commercial functions

9 Manshukhbhai Prajapati launched 'Mitticool' fridge in 2002. This fridge is made from terracotta and runs without electricity. Which entrepreneurial function has been performed by him?

(a) Innovation (b) Risk taking
(c) Both (a) and (b) (d) None of these

Ans (a) Innovation

10 Functions related to putting an idea into action are called

(a) Managerial functions
(b) Promotional functions
(c) Entrepreneurial functions (d) None of these

Ans (b) Promotional functions

11 In a developing country which follows a mixed economy, which sector is important?

(a) Government sector (b) Private sector
(c) Both (a) and (b) (d) None of these

Ans (c) Both (a) and (b)

12 Profits can be increased by

(a) increasing revenues (b) reducing costs
(c) Both (a) and (b) (d) None of these

Ans (c) Both (a) and (b)

13 At present, Infosys is a millionaire MNC. But, it was started only with

(a) ₹ 10,000 (b) ₹ 20,000
(c) ₹ 35,000 (d) ₹ 1,00,000

Ans (a) ₹ 10,000

14 .... and .... banks were especially established to finance new businesses.

(a) ICICI (b) IDBI
(c) SIDBI
(d) Both (b) and (c)

Ans (d) Both (b) and (c)

15 Rohit considers that starting a business is very easy but it takes a lot of money to finance it. He is not right in his assumption because

(a) it requires a lot of determination and learning.
(b) it does not take a lot of money to finance a new business.
(c) Both (a) and (b)
(d) None of the above

Ans (c) Both (a) and (b)

16 Pranay works in an MNC and gets a monthly salary of ₹ 45,000. He is not happy with his job and wants to start his own business. His wife is not in favour of his idea and she says that there are many disadvantages associated with becoming an entrepreneur. The disadvantage(s) can be

(a) irregular income
(b) erratic work schedule
(c) fewer benefits
(d) All of the above

Ans (d) All of the above

17 The first step in the process of entrepreneurship is

(a) self-discovery
(b) identifying opportunities
(c) evaluating ideas
(d) generating ideas

Ans (a) self-discovery

18 Which of the following is not a disadvantage of entrepreneurship?

(a) Person must be willing to give up the security of regular source of income
(b) Involvement of risk element in business makes it an exciting avenue
(c) One cannot predict the work schedule of an entrepreneur
(d) Entrepreneur has to deal with such employees which increases his/her burden

Ans (b) Involvement of risk element in business makes it an exciting avenue

19 **Assertion** (A) An entrepreneur is a person responsible for setting up a new business.

Reason (R) He/She converts a situation into an opportunity.

Alternatives

(a) Both Assertion (A) and Reason (R) are correct
(b) Assertion (A) is correct, but Reason (R) is incorrect
(c) Assertion (A) is incorrect, but Reason (R) is correct
(d) Both Assertion (A) and Reason (R) are incorrect

Ans (a) He/She is a catalytic agent of change and puts up new green field projects that create wealth, opens up many employment opportunities and leads to the growth of other sectors.

20 **Assertion** (A) Organising is the basic managerial function of an entrepreneur.

Reason (R) Organising helps in determining the course of action to be followed to achieve various entrepreneurial objectives.

Alternatives

(a) Both Assertion (A) and Reason (R) are correct
(b) Assertion (A) is correct, but Reason (R) is incorrect
(c) Assertion (A) is incorrect, but Reason (R) is correct
(d) Both Assertion (A) and Reason (R) are incorrect

Ans (a) Both Assertion (A) and Reason (R) are correct

21 Given below are functions of entrepreneur in Column I and their features in Column II. Match them correctly.

Column I	Column II
A. Entrepreneurial functions	(i) Day-to-day working of an enterprise.
B. Promotional functions	(ii) Making the venture a success.
C. Managerial functions	(iii) Identification of an idea and readiness to undertake risk.
D. Commercial functions	(iv) Putting an idea into action.

Codes

	A	B	C	D		A	B	C	D
(a)	(iii)	(iv)	(i)	(ii)	(b)	(ii)	(i)	(iii)	(iv)
(c)	(iii)	(iv)	(ii)	(i)	(d)	(ii)	(i)	(iv)	(iii)

Ans (a) (iii) (iv) (i) (ii)

22 Given below are steps in the process of entrepreneurship in Column I and their features in Column II. Match them correctly.

Column I	Column II
A. Self-discovery	(i) Researching and identifying resources.
B. Identifying opportunities	(ii) Examining work experience.
C. Generating and evaluating ideas	(iii) Looking for needs, wants etc.
D. Planning	(iv) Using creativity and past experience to devise new ways.

Codes

	A	B	C	D		A	B	C	D
(a)	(iii)	(iv)	(i)	(ii)	(b)	(ii)	(i)	(iii)	(iv)
(c)	(ii)	(iii)	(iv)	(i)	(d)	(ii)	(i)	(iv)	(iii)

Ans (c) (ii) (iii) (iv) (i)

23

Identify the concept shown in the given figure.

(a) Evolution of entrepreneur
(b) Myths of entrepreneurship
(c) Process of entrepreneurship
(d) None of the above

Ans (a) Evolution of entrepreneur

24

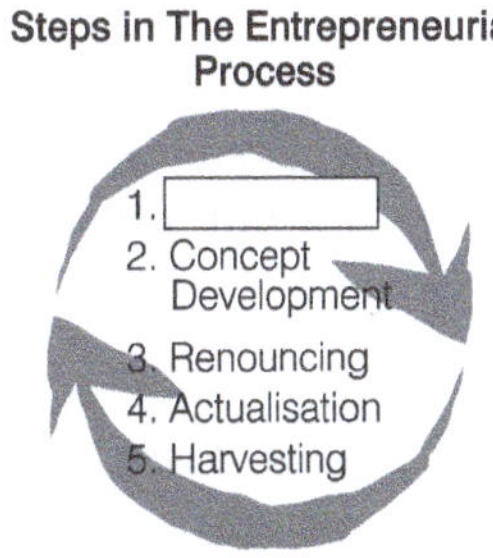

Identify the missing step in the given figure.

(a) Diagnosis
(b) Discovery
(c) Implementation
(d) None of these

Ans (b) Discovery

Fill in the Blanks

25 .... can be viewed as a creative and innovative response to the environment and an ability to recognise, initiate and exploit an economic opportunity.

Ans Entrepreneurship

26 Ritesh is a vegetable-vendor. He is also considered an entrepreneur as he also takes ....

Ans risks

27 The new age business ventures are more .... and not just product-based.

Ans idea-centric

28 Mithali is an entrepreneur who is ready to do something new. She does not live with 'Status-quo' and works to change the environment in accordance of her personal vision and value. So, Mithali is performing .... function of entrepreneur.

Ans entrepreneurial

29 The entrepreneur stands at the centre of the whole process of economic development by indulging himself/herself in the process of ....

Ans innovation

30 Mr. Patel is a creator of 'Shine washing powder' who worked as a factory chemist in Gujarat Mineral Development Corporation. He started making detergent powder in his kitchen for poor rural women of Gujarat. After sometime of struggle, he has become biggest detergent powder manufacturer. Mr. Patel performs the promotional function of ....

Ans discovery of an idea

31 .... is the main reason behind the need for entrepreneurship in any country.

Ans Economic development

32 According to ...., "Many new entrepreneurs believe a set of myths about entrepreneurship".

Ans Guy Kawasaki

33 The correlation between the number of entrepreneurs starting business in an industry and the number of companies failing in the industry is ....

Ans 0.77

State True or False

34 As a managerial function, staffing is concerned with the employment of human resources of an enterprise.

Ans True

35 An entrepreneur has to decide about the capital structure of the enterprise. This is a component of commercial functions to be performed by him.

Ans False. It is a component of promotional functions.

36 It has been observed that entrepreneurs spend about 50% of their working time communicating with others.

Ans False. They spend 75% to 90% of their working time communicating with others.

37 Mr. Mehta works in the business organisation that is formed to provide goods and services, creates jobs, contributes to national income, exports and also towards the overall economic development of a country. In this context, Mr. Mehta works in an enterprise.

Ans True

38 Kaushal Bhai identified the problem of poor rural women of Kerala and started making affordable bathing soaps for them under the brand name 'Auma'. The promotional function performed by him is 'Discovery of an idea'.

Ans True

39 Poorva wants to start her own business after completing her graduation. Poorva's parents refuse to finance her business. She is forced to give up her idea as she believes in, that start-ups cannot be started with debt. However, it is in reality a myth as most business are started with debt rather than equity.

Ans True

40 Entrepreneurs do not enjoy the liberty of freedom of thoughts.

Ans False. Employees do not enjoy the liberty of freedom of thoughts.

41 Entrepreneurs feel that business is exciting as it involves risk.

Ans True

42 The reason for slow progress of Indian economy during the first four decades of independence can be attributed to the lack of innovation shown by Indian entrepreneurs.

Ans True

Case Based Questions

43 Read the following article and answer the questions that follow

Ahab is an engineer and works in a MNC for a monthly salary of ₹ 55,000. He is not satisfied with his job, so he wants to quit and start his own venture. He has various ideas in his mind.

But his father refuses to his decision stating that there will be many disadvantages of this decision.

However, Ahab was determined to move forward to start a venture and left his job. With the savings and the fund he got from his company, Ahab was set to start his entrepreneurial journey.

Ahab was looking towards electrical products as he was an electrical engineer. He worked hard for several days and made a prototype of a bicycle for kids that self-balance without supporters. He showed the prototype to some of his friends and received a positive feedback. He made his first product with the help of some hired workers and launched the first sample in an entrepreneurial summit.

The bicycle received good appreciation and one of the popular investors showed interest in providing funding to Ahab. After some time, Ahab was able to start a manufacturing unit for his venture. With his determination and skills, Ahab was able to make his dream of owning a business come true.

(i) What are the disadvantages associated with Ahab's decision?

(a) Fewer benefits

(b) Irregular income

(c) Erratic work schedule

(d) All of the above

Ans (d) All of the above

(ii) Ahab played the function of a .... entrepreneur.

(a) planning

(b) employment

(c) entrepreneurial

(d) None of the above

Ans (c) entrepreneurial

(iii) Which of the following myths about entrepreneurship were busted by Ahab?

(a) It is very difficult to get money to start a new business

(b) Start-ups are very easy to establish

(c) Both (a) and (b)

(d) None of the above

Ans (c) Both (a) and (b)

(iv) Which of the following steps of the process of entrepreneurship were tapped by Ahab?

(a) Self-discovery

(b) Planning

(c) Identifying opportunities

(d) All of the above

Ans (d) All of the above

(v) "After some time, Ahab was able to start a manufacturing unit for his venture. With his determination and skills, Ahab was able to make his dream of owning a business come true."

Ahab will enjoy the following advantage of being an entrepreneur

(a) freedom (b) administration

(c) work schedule (d) All of these

Ans (a) Freedom

44 Read the following article and answer the questions that follow

Roohi is an enthusiastic individual with an aim of becoming a successful business woman. She studied artificial intelligence and application building and wanted to develop a mobile application for all girls that would track and record their movement if they are travelling alone or have some doubts about their safety at a specific place.

The idea in her mind was to develop the application with a feature of automatically calling an emergency number whenever the user strike the power button three times consecutively or just by speaking into the microphone 'HELP'.

Her idea was appreciated by fellow women and by joining hands with a women empowerment NGO, she was able to get enough funding through government schemes.

With the funds in her hand, Roohi employed several developers and coders to start working on the application.

After three months, they were able to develop the perfect application as per Roohi's vision. The application was launched and extensive marketing was done by the team. After some time, positive results came along as many users downloaded the application and used it for their safety. Roohi was awarded for this idea and product by the NGO.

(i) Which promotional function was performed by Roohi?
(a) Innovation
(b) Discovering an idea
(c) Planning
(d) Risk taking

Ans (b) Discovering an idea

(ii) "Her idea was appreciated by fellow women and by joining hands with a women empowerment NGO, she was able to get enough funding through government schemes."
Which government scheme is highlighted in the above statement?
(a) Start-up India
(b) Technology park
(c) Exemption of taxes
(d) Patent protection

Ans (a) Start-up India

(iii) "With the funds in her hand, Roohi employed several developers and coders to start working on the application."
Roohi performed .... managerial function.
(a) organising (b) staffing
(c) controlling (d) planning

Ans (b) staffing

(iv) "The application was launched and extensive marketing was done by the team. After some time, positive results came along as many users downloaded the application and used it for their safety."
Which of the following steps of entrepreneurial process is discussed above?
(a) Idea generation
(b) Growth
(c) Planning
(d) Harvest

Ans (d) Harvest

(v) Which entrepreneurial function was performed in developing the application?
(a) Innovation
(b) Organisation building
(c) Risk taking
(d) All of the above

Ans (d) All of the above

Short Answer Type I Questions (2 Marks)

1 "An enterprise may be defined as an undertaking or adventure involving uncertainty and risk and requiring innovation".

Keeping the given statement in mind, give the distinct features of an enterprise.

Ans The distinct features of an enterprise are as follows

(i) An enterprise consists of people who work together primarily for the purpose of making and/or selling a product or a service.

(ii) An enterprise makes use of several inputs like men, material, machine, etc. to produce a given output.

2 Differentiate between entrepreneur and entrepreneurship. **CBSE TBQ**

Ans

Basis	Entrepreneur	Entrepreneurship
Meaning	An entrepreneur is a person who bears the risks, unites various factors of production and carries out creative innovations.	Entrepreneurship is an activity of commencing a business usually a start-up company, offering distinct products and services to the target customers.
Represents	An innovator, who chased the dream, till it becomes true.	A procedure through which an innovation is done.

3 The role of private entrepreneurs increased tremendously after the economic reforms of 1991. Why?

Ans The role of private entrepreneurs increased after the reforms of 1991 due to the policies of liberalisation, privatisation and globalisation which removed all unnecessary restrictions on the private enterprise in the form of licenses, quotas, tariffs, trade restrictions between countries, etc.

4 Staffing is a difficult function for an entrepreneur. Do you agree?

Ans Yes, staffing is a difficult task for an entrepreneur.

It is the function of selecting the manpower to get the work done, hence, an entrepreneur has to find those people who are capable and skillful of doing that particular job.

An entrepreneur, thus has to search among a number of people to hire the right one.

5 Write a short note on controlling as a managerial function.

Ans Controlling is that managerial function through which an entrepreneur tries to implement his/her company's policies and also takes needed steps or corrective measures if a particular work has not been done, the way it should be. This has a chain of functions including establishing standards of performance, measuring actual performance, comparing the actual performance with the needed, etc.

6 What is the role of marketing in entrepreneurship?

Ans Marketing plays a major role in entrepreneurship. It is basically concerned with the movement of goods and services from the producers to its ultimate consumers and creating awareness about the product.

An entrepreneur works to earn revenue and this motive can be fulfilled by capturing larger share of market by using marketing tools such as advertisement, offers, discounts, etc.

7 Briefly explain finance as one of the commercial functions to be performed by an entrepreneur.

Ans Finance is the most important aspect in all organisations. The development and expansion of an enterprise needs more commitment of funds. It is the duty of the entrepreneur to look and analyse into the various sources of finance and appropriately arrange for them as and when required.

8 'Innovation is the weapon of success for an entrepreneur'. Justify.

Ans Yes, this statement is correct that innovation is very important for an enterprise.

An entrepreneur can be successful only when he/she innovates something new and creative. Entrepreneurs who enter into common businesses may not go a long way.

e.g. Facebook was an innovative concept of social networking started by Mark Zukerberg and achieved phenomenal success.

9 Shivi, a dropout from 10th is forced by her mother to start working as a domestic help. Shivi agrees on the condition to do only 'cooking' in 2-3 houses. One family turns out to be Punjabi, other Gujarati and the third one is Rajasthani. She cooked their three kinds of food for a year and to everyone's surprise, she expressed her desire to open up a small eating joint of her own.

All alone and determined, she finally opens 'Apna Bhoj', a small eating joint with her savings and it became a hot spot because of the fusion food platter being offered. Do you think Shivi is an entrepreneur? Give reasons for your answer. **CBSE TBQ**

Ans Yes, Shivi is an entrepreneur, as she has the desire to open her own enterprise, for which she arranged finance on her own (from her savings), also she took the risk and innovated different types of food products.

10 Karan, a rural boy, identifies the potential of organic farming in the village. He meets the zonal agricultural officer, who, looking at the determination of this 20 years old boy, helps him to arrange and procure multiple resources required for his farm land.

Then Karan takes a loan of ₹ 50,000 from SBI as his seed money of ₹ 10,000 is not enough to cater the requirement. Karan ties up with a nearby city's vegetable shop owner to sell his yield. His hardwork pays and the organic vegetables are a hit. This organic vegetable producer exhibits to be a good entrepreneur with good entrepreneurial skills. Do you agree? Justify giving reasons for your answer. **CBSE TBQ**

Ans Yes, this statement is justified as he first identified the opportunity and took the risk of starting organic farming, arranged finance for his venture and worked hard. His organic vegetables were a hit. This indicates that his entrepreneurial venture had been successful and that his hardwork has paid-off.

11 "Profit is the only motivational force behind every entrepreneur". Do you agree?

Ans No, profit is not the only motivational force behind every entrepreneur. Yes, it is true that it plays a major role in every business and also profits are required for further growth.

However, sometimes entrepreneurs work for social welfare also and not for profits only, especially in a socialist economy.

12 "Social benefits not only help the enterprise but also the society at large". How?

Ans Social benefits provided by an enterprise to the society not only help the enterprise in establishing its goodwill in the market, but it also raises the standard of living of the society by providing good quality products and services at the lowest possible cost. It also helps in efficient utilisation of scarce resources of the society.

13 Kamal, after completing his studies, wanted to start his own business. However, his father Mr Kishanlal discouraged him saying that it takes a lot of money to finance a new business. Is Mr Kishanlal justified in his view? Comment.

Ans No, Mr Kishanlal is not justified in his view. Successful entrepreneurs have designed their enterprises to work with lesser money. They usually rent a building rather than buying it and they turn fixed costs into variable costs by paying employees' commission instead of salaries. A survey has revealed that a typical start-up required for a small business is ₹ 1.5 lakh. He should also keep in mind that Infosys was started with only ₹ 10,000.

14 Explain any two advantages of being an entrepreneur. **CBSE TBQ**

Ans Two advantages of being an entrepreneur are as follows

(i) **Independence** Some people want to be their own boss and make all the important decisions on their own.

(ii) **Rational Compensation** Entrepreneurs are not being paid, what they are worth and would rather work on their own and earn the money they should be earning for their efforts.

15 Explain any two disadvantages of being an entrepreneur. **CBSE TBQ**

Ans Two disadvantages of being an entrepreneur are as follows

(i) **Irregular Income** Starting-up an enterprise means that the person must be willing to give up the security of a regular source of income.

(ii) **Fewer Benefits** There will undoubtedly be fewer benefits, especially when considering that a business has just been started.

16 An entrepreneur identifies a need that no existing businesses addresses and determines a solution for that need. Entrepreneurial activity includes developing and launching new businesses and marketing them, often with the end goal of selling the business to turn a profit.

An entrepreneur who regularly launches new businesses, sells them and then starts new businesses is a serial entrepreneur. Additionally, although the term 'entrepreneur' is often associated with startups and small businesses, any founder of a successful household-name business began as an entrepreneur.

If you want to become an entrepreneur but worry you don't have the money for it, your finances don't have to stop you from achieving your goals. Many entrepreneurs seek the initial funding for their pursuits from external sources such as angel investors, who may provide entrepreneurs with capital to cover startup costs (or, later, expansion costs).

If you can demonstrate a high growth potential for your business, you can also turn to a venture capitalist, who offers capital in exchange for receiving equity in your company.

Source *Max Freedman Business News Daily Contributing Writer Updated 2nd Dec, 2021*

(i) Which concept is highlighted in the above paragraph?

(ii) Mention any two functions of an entrepreneur.

Ans (i) Functions of an entrepreneur.

(ii) The functions of an entrepreneur are

(a) Innovation.

(b) Discovery of an idea.

17 The year 2021 has seen India make a mark for itself in the global entrepreneurial ecosystem. While the entire country saw a challenging time during the second wave of COVID-19 in May 2021, Indian entrepreneurs continued building for the country. Rapid digital transformation and adoption of tech during the lockdown led to unprecedented growth.

From being one of the emerging markets to consolidating its position as one of the fastest growing markets for emerging tech companies, this year has set the tone for what the next decade would look like for India.

2021 gave us nearly a decade's worth of unicorns in one year alone and 15 debutant IPOs with the likes of Zomato and Nazara Technologies that more than doubled from their issue price.

The acceptance of start-ups as a catalyst to the growth of the economy has encouraged not only foreign but also domestic investors to allocate capital to new-age companies.

As well-funded companies from the previous decade are entering a new phase of growth, they're generating cohorts of seasoned entrepreneurs and professionals starting up again with increasing maturity and resilience.

Source *By Pearl Agarwal, ET CONTRIBUTORS 22nd Dec, 2021*

(i) Which concept is highlighted in the above paragraph?

(ii) Mention any two needs of entrepreneurship.

Ans (i) Need for entrepreneurship.

(ii) Needs of entreprenership is as follows

(a) Adapting to change.

(b) Employment opportunities.

Short Answer Type II Questions (3 Marks)

1 Describe entrepreneurial functions of an entrepreneur. **CBSE TBQ**

Ans The entrepreneurial functions of an entrepreneur are

(i) **Innovation** It is the basic function of an entrepreneur. An entrepreneur should be the one who introduces something new and creative to the market. An entrepreneur should find new means of production, raw material, product, etc. e.g. smart phones.

(ii) **Risk Taking** It refers to ability of an entrepreneur to take risk, i.e. the responsibility for a loss that may occur due to unforeseen circumstances of the future.

(iii) **Organisation Building** It refers to bringing together the factors of production to carry out production activities. The main purpose is to allocate the productive resources in order to minimise the losses and thereby reduce the production cost.

2 Who is an entrepreneur? State the various functions required to be performed by an entrepreneur.

Ans Refer to topic 'concept of entrepreneur' on page 2 and 'functions of entrepreneur' on page 3.

3 What is the need of entrepreneurship in an economy? **CBSE TBQ**

Ans The need of entrepreneurship in an economy can be highlighted from the following points

(i) **Lifeline of a Nation** Entrepreneurship is the yardstick to measure the level of development of a country. No country can progress without the development of entrepreneurship.

Every country is trying to develop its trade, so that it can help in it's economic development.

(ii) **Provides Innovation** Entrepreneurship provides new ideas, imagination and vision to the enterprise. An entrepreneur is an innovator as he/she tries to find new technology, products and markets. He/She also increases the productivity of various resources.

(iii) **Inclusive Growth** An enterprise operates in a changing environment. The entrepreneur moulds the enterprise in such a changing environment. He/She moulds not only the enterprise, but also alters the environment itself to ensure the success of the enterprise.

Because of all such reasons, we can easily make out the need for entrepreneurship in the economic development. They innovate products, give employment, increase productivity and hence production.

4 Why are entrepreneurs called agents of progress for a nation? What role do they play in the Nation's development? **CBSE TBQ**

Ans Economic growth of any country depends on the rate of innovation in the economic field, and increases rate of growth in GDP, i.e. total value of goods and services (production) in an economy in a year, more production means the more number of entrepreneurs and quality of entrepreneurs in the society.

Country's economy progresses only when more number of entrepreneurs emerge in all fields.

Entrepreneur is the only person who bear the costs and risks of launching a new venture, developing a new product, commercialising an invention, adapting a technology and developing a new market, start a new enterprise.

More number of enterprise means more entrepreneurs, more entrepreneurs means increasing economic diversification and growth which is equivalent to progress of nation. Therefore, entrepreneurs are 'agents of progress' for a nation.

Entrepreneur plays important role in the nation's development

(i) Increase in the rate of growth in GDP (Total value of goods and services produced in an economy in a year).

(ii) Increasing productivity.

(iii) Providing employment opportunities.

(iv) Optimal use of available resources

(v) Continued innovation-in techno-managerial practices and finally international competitiveness.

(vi) Increasing economic diversification.

5 Explain why one should become an entrepreneur by giving any three reasons.

Ans One should become an entrepreneur or choose entrepreneurship due to the following reasons

(i) **Confidentiality** The sole proprietor is not legally compelled to publish his accounts or share his secrets with others. A proprietor has all the decision-making powers. As a result, confidentiality or secrecy can be maintained easily.

(ii) **Individual Profit Recipient** All the profits which are earned from the business are to be enjoyed by the sole owner or proprietor himself/herself.

(iii) **Maintenance of Flexibility** As all the decisions are taken by the proprietor himself, so quick and prompt actions will be possible which bring flexibility of operations and quick adaptability of business to the changing environment.

6 Explain briefly the following myths relating to entrepreneurship.

(i) Start-ups cannot be financed with debt.

(ii) Banks don't lend money to start-up.

Ans (i) **Start-ups cannot be Financed with Debt** It is not correct to say that a new business cannot be started with debt. Most of the enterprises get started with debt rather than equity.

(ii) **Banks don't Lend Money to Start-up** Government has implemented many schemes in collaboration with banks to provide finance for budding entrepreneurs. Hence, it is not correct to say that banks do not provide finance to new enterprises.

7 Meena Sharma started Hathi Chaap. It was totally a new venture where different raw materials were tried out to make handmade paper. After researching a lot, they found that elephant dung had more fibre content which made it easy to make handmade paper. This entrepreneur is an example to contradict the normal myth that exists in entrepreneurship. Identify the myth and explain it. Name any two more myths related with entrepreneurship.

Ans Myth contradicted in the given case is 'Most entrepreneurs start business in attractive industries'.

It is not true that most entrepreneurs start their enterprises in attractive industries only. The correlation between the number of entrepreneurs starting businesses in an industry and the number of companies failing in the industry is 0.77. It means that most entrepreneurs are picking up industries in which they are most likely to fail.

Two more myths related to entrepreneurship are

(i) Starting a business is easy.

(ii) It takes a lot of money to finance a new business.

8 Rahul is a renowned entrepreneur. His friend Rohit passed his MBA exam recently. As Rohit wanted to opt for a profitable career, so he asked Rahul to suggest some career options. Rohit suggest him to be an entrepreneur by explaining different advantages related to it. In context of the above situation, explain any three advantages of entrepreneurship.

Ans Some main advantages of entrepreneurship are as follows

(i) **Excitement** Involvement of risk element in the business makes it quite an exciting avenue. e.g. Steve Jobs left his position in Apple Inc and in his excitement to do something new, started Pixar which later turned out to be a successful venture.

(ii) **Originality** Entrepreneurs feel that they can provide something new to the society which others cannot or in other words, which was not been provided before. e.g. I-pod, I-pad, etc. This increases their self-confidence.

(iii) **Independence** Some wish to be their own boss and make all the important decisions themselves. For such persons, entrepreneurship is the perfect answer.

Long Answer Type Questions (5 Marks)

1 Briefly discuss the concept of 'entrepreneur' and also give the definitions given by prominent management thinkers.

Ans Refer to text on page 2.

2 "Innovation is the hallmark of entrepreneurship". Why is innovation referred as the basic function of an entrepreneur? **CBSE TBQ**

Ans Innovation is the first and foremost function of an entrepreneur. A successful entrepreneur is the one who has invented something new and innovative.

e.g. 'Zerox' was the company, who had invented photocopier machine for the first time and hence enjoyed a patent for over 25 years which helped it to become a market leader in the concerned industry.

So, innovation is a tool in the hands of entrepreneurs which enables them to dream big and achieve bigger. It inspires entrepreneurial thinking and helps them to exploit a business opportunity.

According to **Schumpeter**, also, the basic function of entrepreneur is to innovate.

According to him, an entrepreneur introduces something new in the economy and carries out new combinations of means of production.

An entrepreneur may innovate in the following ways

(i) Introduce new products.

(ii) Use a new method of production.

(iii) Find a new market for a product or a service.

(iv) Find a new use of a product/service.

(v) Improve an existing product or service.

The above mentioned innovations will help him to surge ahead of his competitors.

Therefore, innovation is referred as the basic function of an entrepreneur.

3 What is the need of entrepreneurship in an economy? Give atleast six benefits. **CBSE TBQ**

Or "Entrepreneurs, in their drive and pursuit to create something new, at times, results in causing major loss to the nation's natural resources". Shouldn't they be discouraged? Justify giving reasons for your answer. **CBSE TBQ**

Ans It is true to say that in the process of entrepreneurship, sometimes it leads to wastage of nation's resources, however it doesn't mean that they should be discouraged.

Suppose for example, if a student failed to get a good grade in a class, then should he stop studying. An entrepreneur provides many benefits like innovation, employment, growth, etc which cannot be ignored with few unsuccessful attempts.

In mixed economy like India, an entrepreneur plays a major role in economic development along with the government.

Need for Entrepreneurship Refer to text on page 6 and 7.

4 "With the change in government at the centre, Mr Narendra Modi, the Prime Minister of India, introduced several new incentives for entrepreneurs including the implementation of GST (Goods and Services Tax), saying that entrepreneurship is the need of the hour." Is Mr Modi's contention right? Justify your answer.

Ans Yes, Mr Modi's contention is right.
Need for Entrepreneurship Refer to text on page 6 and 7.

5 Differentiate between entrepreneurial functions and managerial functions of an entrepreneur. **CBSE TBQ**

Ans Both the functions of the entrepreneur are as important as the other. Entrepreneurial functions are the ones which start before the production of goods and services, i.e. to decide upon the type of goods to be produced which involve innovation, risk taking and building of an organisation.

On the other hand, managerial functions start after deciding upon the idea of the product, i.e. to make the idea a reality and hence are required for the accomplishment of production activity.

Differences between entrepreneurial functions and managerial functions are given below

Entrepreneurial Functions	Managerial Functions
(i) The various entrepreneurial functions are innovation, creativity, risk taking and organisation building.	The functions to be performed under this head are planning, organising, staffing, directing and controlling.
(ii) To perform these functions, an entrepreneur should possess technical knowledge and experience in innovative field.	To perform these functions, an entrepreneur should possess managerial knowledge and experience.

6 Mehak wants to start a textile unit near Gurgaon. Discuss the commercial functions which she will require to plan and perform for the same. **CBSE TBQ**

Ans Commercial functions that Mehak should perform are as follows (any four)

(i) **Production** It refers to the creation of goods and services or it is the process of transforming raw materials into something useful. It consists of manufacturing, ancillary and advisory activities.

(ii) **Finance** The second function that Mehak has to perform is to arrange finance for the enterprise because any enterprise can go a long way only with appropriate availability of finance or money.

So, she has to look for various opportunities to arrange for finance.

(iii) **Marketing** It plays a major role in an enterprise as through this process, goods and services are provided to the ultimate consumers for direct satisfaction of wants.

(iv) **Personnel** This is the function concerned with employment, development and compensation for the personnel and also the provision of working conditions and welfare measures.

(v) **Accounting** An entrepreneur should look in the record keeping of the entries of all transactions which takes place in the organisation, so that she is aware of her financial position.

7 Explain four promotional functions of an entrepreneur. **CBSE TBQ**

Ans Four promotional functions of an entrepreneur are as follows

(i) **Discovery of an Idea** An entrepreneur tries to visualise an opportunity for a particular type of business which can run profitably. Then the entrepreneur develops the idea with the experts, to make the idea a reality.

(ii) **Detailed Investigation** The entrepreneur estimates the total demand for a particular product in the market.

After deciding the product, the entrepreneur has to arrange finance and manpower and also required raw material to start production.

(iii) **Assembling the Requirements** Next step is to decide on the requirements and hence an entrepreneur persuades some more people to join him.

He may also be required to get patent rights if he has invented something new.

(iv) **Financing the Proposition** An entrepreneur has to decide about the capital requirement of the enterprise. The requirements of finance are decided initially and eventually he has to find out the sources of short-term and long-term finance like shares, bonds, debentures, loans, etc.

8 Explain any four managerial functions of an entrepreneur. **CBSE TBQ**

Ans Four managerial functions of an entrepreneur are as follows

(i) **Planning** It is the basic managerial function of an entrepreneur. It helps in determining the objective of an enterprise. Planning is concerned with the mental state of an entrepreneur. It is decision-making in advance.

(ii) **Organising** An entrepreneur sets-up a goal which is to be achieved by its personnel. The function of organising is to arrange, guide, coordinate, direct and control the activities of the factors of production.

(iii) **Staffing** It is concerned with employment of human resources. In other words, it consists of human resources, manpower planning, recruitment, selection and placement, development of human resources, etc.

(iv) **Directing** It is concerned with carrying out the desired plans. It initiates organised and planned action and ensures effective performance by subordinates towards the accomplishment of group activities.

9 Explain the following myths related to entrepreneurship

(i) Starting a business is easy.

(ii) Most entrepreneurs start a business in attractive industries.

(iii) Most entrepreneurs are financially successful.

Ans Refer to text on page 8.

10 Kareem, an engineering graduate from Coimbatore began a unit to produce submersible pumps. He started the enterprise with enthusiasm, but when he faced some difficulties in the execution of their plans, he lost confidence and finally gave up the business venture.

Identify the disadvantages of entrepreneurship which are faced by Kareem in the above situation.

Ans Disadvantages of entrepreneurship that Kareem may have faced are

(i) **Irregular Income** Starting-up an enterprise means that the person must be willing to give up the security of a regular source of income.

(ii) **Fewer Benefits** There will be undoubtedly fewer benefits, especially when a business has just been started.

(iii) **Work Schedule** One cannot predict the work schedule of an entrepreneur, an emergency can come up in a matter of a second and late hours may become the norm.

(iv) **Administration** In a business, all the decisions are required to be taken by the entrepreneur himself/herself.

There is no one ranked higher on the chain of command and the entrepreneur might feel himself/herself being burdened by the thought of making a wrong decision.

11 "Entrepreneurship is advantageous as well as disadvantageous". In the light of the above statement, discuss the advantages and disadvantages of entrepreneurship.

Ans Refer to text on page 9.

12 "Starting a venture is not an easy task. A series of activities needs to be planned and undertaken to create an enterprise". Discuss them briefly. **CBSE TBQ**

Or

Describe the process of entrepreneurship. **CBSE TBQ**

Ans The above statement is correct that starting a new venture is not an easy task. An entrepreneur has to arrange a number of things before starting a new business.

The process starts from the will to start an enterprise, to identifying the opportunity, then looking at the feasibility, arranging finance, manpower, etc., which is a long chain of activity and the success of an entrepreneur depends on the degree of innovation and ability to take risk.

So, it is not easy to be an entrepreneur.

Process of Entrepreneurship Process of entrepreneurship involves a step-by-step functioning of an entrepreneur. The flow chart given below describes the process of entrepreneurship

***Step* 1** **Self-discovery** First step is to learn what a person enjoys doing and examining their strengths and weaknesses.

***Step* 2** **Identifying Opportunities** This step relates to looking for needs, wants, problems and challenges that are not yet being met or dealt effectively.

***Step* 3** **Generating and Evaluating Ideas** This is concerned with using creativity and past experience to devise new and innovative ways to solve a problem or meet a need.

***Step* 4** **Planning** This is the plan phase which involves researching and identifying resources needed to turn the idea into a viable venture.

***Step* 5** **Arranging Start-up Capital** Next step is to attract new investors, venture capitalists and partners to arrange sufficient funds to start an enterprise.

Step 6 **Start-up** Launching the venture, developing a customer base and adjusting marketing and operational plans as required.

Step 7 **Growth** Next process is to make the enterprise growing by adapting to new circumstances.

Step 8 **Harvest** Last step is to sell the product in the market and earn the revenue to grow further.

13 Gautam, is a young underemployed youth belonging to the backward village of Rampur. His friend advise him to start a business saying that there are many government schemes launched for the development of entrepreneurs in the country.

Is the assertion of Gautam's friend correct? Also, explain three schemes which are offered by government to enterprises.

Ans Yes, Gautam's friend's assertion is correct. Government has taken an initiative to encourage entrepreneurship through providing various schemes.

Some of them are as follows

(i) **Start-up India** This scheme was launched with the aim of supporting Indian entrepreneurs to create 10 lakh mobile app start-ups.

(ii) **Software Technology Park** This scheme was established to promote and export computer software and professional services through communication networks or physical media. This scheme solely emphasises on computer software.

(iii) **Credit Guarantee Fund Trust for Micro and Small Enterprises** (CGTMSE) This scheme was launched by the government to help business units in getting collateral free loans at a low rate of interest up to a maximum of ₹ 100 lakhs under a tie-up with SIDBI. It facilitates in promoting new businesses and relaunching the existing ones.

14 Entrepreneurship is a consistent process of being inspired, adventurous and prepared. It plays a vital role in economic development and brings significant changes in the economies of market.

In the light of changing business scenario, earlier studies have shown certain factors that affect entrepreneurial development.

In the present study, an effort has been made to study those factors that affect entrepreneurial development in the wake of changing business scenario in Indian perspectives. The idea was to explore these factors for creating a platform for further research. It was observed that, many researchers have analysed entrepreneurial orientations, entrepreneurs' behaviour, their personality traits, leadership styles.

The impact of entrepreneurial education on youth, and various exogenous factors affecting entrepreneurial orientations (innovativeness, risk taking capacity of entrepreneurs, proactiveness, info-seeking behaviour) like, cultural/ethnic background, family businesses background and their Emotional Intelligence (EI) are also studied.

However, majority of these observations are from the studies conducted mainly in developed part of the world like USA, European Countries, Japan, and some of them from China.

A few studies have been identified in developing countries. Plethora of Indian studies rests around limited topics only. However, Indian perspectives were found missing. This literature review can create a platform for further study in Indian scenario.

Source *3rd Annual Commerce Convention on Leveraging Business: Discovering New Horizons At: School of Economics, New Delhi*

(i) Which concept is highlighted in the above paragraph?

(ii) Why is it important? Explain in detail.

Ans (i) Importance of entrepreneurship.

(ii) Refer to topic 'need for entrepreneurship' on page 6 and 7.

15 Entrepreneurship is discipline (Croci, 2016). Entrepreneurship is a distinct, being a discipline by its own right. Croci (2016) also defined entrepreneurship with autonomous discipline that can operate independently as well as interdisciplinary.

Other study defines entrepreneurship as "practice begins with action and creation of new organisation" (Barot, 2015). Barot (2015) also stated that entrepreneurship is a key to success and every individual that creates a new organisation of business means enter into a new paradigm of entrepreneurship.

Nevertheless, the entrepreneurship is an activity that shifted the old habits into the new one with fully discipline and independent.

Entrepreneurship is an art (Chang et al, 2015). Chang (2015) stated that "art entrepreneurship is relatively new topic of research and the focus area are exploring the management process of entrepreneurship such as creativity and autonomy, capacity for adaptability, and create artistic as well as economic and social value".

There are many definitions of entrepreneurship, some of them are seeing entrepreneurship as a process of successful organisation, and other define entrepreneurship as building mindset and skills. However, the final destination of entrepreneurship definition is generating jobs opportunities and lead to economic development (Barot, 2015) (Hessels, 2019).

Next, entrepreneurship must employ manpower resources with technical and skill labour and managerial talents (Barot, 2015) (Chang et al, 2015).

Source *August, 2020 Journal of Management Accounting and Economics 7 (Entrepreneurship): 2020-2383*

(i) Which concept is highlighted in the above paragraph?

(ii) Explain different myths associated with it.

Ans (i) Meaning of entrepreneurship.

(ii) Refer to text on page 8

CASE STUDIES

Carefully read the case study given below and answer the questions that follow

The Earth at this Innovator's Feet

Mansukhbhai Prajapati remoulded his family's struggling pottery business to produce the Mitticool range of ingenious earthenware, including a fridge that works without electricity.

Reporting on the devastation and thousands of lives lost during the 2001 earthquake in Gujarat, local newspapers had this intriguing headline describing the havoc wreaked at a potters' colony: 'Garibonna fridge no bhookon' (pieces of the poor people's fridge). Among the debris were the shards of hundreds of broken clay pitchers.

That headline proved to be a game-changer for Wakaner - based potter, Mansukhbhai Prajapati, who literally picked up the pieces to begin a fresh on a remarkably innovative idea-the Mitticool refrigerator, which is made of mud/clay and works without electricity.

Originally from Morbi village in Rajkot, South Gujarat, Prajapati, a tenth-standard dropout, began working at a tea-stall after his father discouraged him from entering the family's pottery business as the income was negligible. Later, he became a supervisor at a roof-tile manufacturing company and eventually, in 1989, returned to his passion for pottery by producing tavdi or tawa (frying pan) from clay.

Although, his father-in-law desired him to continue working at the roof-tile company, Prajapati's wife encouraged him to experiment with the family business all over again.

It was this abiding interest in innovation that led him to develop the Mitticool water filter, way back in 1997.

A lot of rigorous experimentation went into his work on the Mitticool refrigerator, which he launched in 2002.

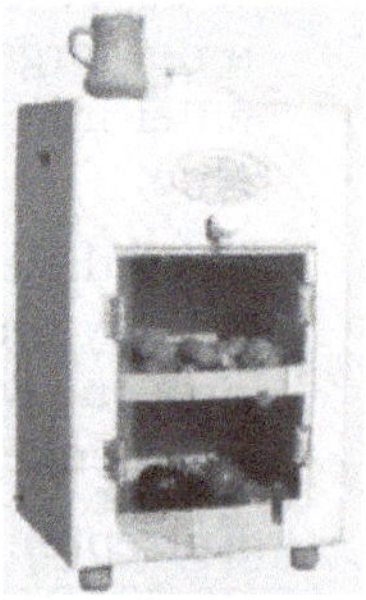

Besides a tank for cooling and storing 10 litres of water, the earthenware, refrigerator has two compartments for storing 5 kg of vegetables, fruits and other food.

It takes about seven days to make one Mitticool fridge. The special terracotta clay used is baked at 1,200 degree celsius to harden it. Like any clay pot used to cool water, the fridge too works by keeping the inside temperature 10 degrees lower than the outside. The natural cooling process keeps vegetables and fruits fresh for upto 5 days and milk products for upto 3 days.

Measuring 27 inches high and 15 inches wide, the fridge costs between ₹ 3,000 to ₹ 3,500. As it works without electricity, it is especially useful in villages that experience frequent power cuts.

1 "Entrepreneur is a person who is innovative". Keeping this statement in mind, identify whether Mansukhbhai is an entrepreneur or not? If yes, what was his innovation?

Ans Yes, Mansukhbhai is surely an entrepreneur, as he invented 'Mitticool' range of ingenious earthenware, including a fridge that works without electricity.

2 Which entrepreneurial functions were performed by Mansukhbhai? Quote the lines which indicate the functions being performed?

Ans Mansukhbhai performed the following functions

(i) **Innovation** Indicated from the line, "It was the abiding interest in innovation that led him to develop the Mitticool water filter way back in 1997".

(ii) **Risk** Indicated from the line, "A lot of rigorous experimentation went into his work on the Mitticool refrigerator, which he launched in 2002".

CHAPTER ASSESSMENT

Objective Type Questions (1 Mark)

1 Economists view entrepreneur as
(a) investment (b) factor of production
(c) Both (a) and (b) (d) None of these

2 An entrepreneur is
(a) an innovator
(b) a job and wealth-generator
(c) Both (a) and (b) (d) None of the above

3 Entrepreneurial functions of an entrepreneur include
(a) innovation (b) risk-taking
(c) organisational building
(d) All of the above

4 Planning and organising are .... functions of entrepreneur.

5 .... develop from need and want.

6 An entrepreneur is an inventor. State true or false.

7 Entrepreneurship is an abstract process. State true or false.

Short Answer Type I Questions (2 Marks)

8 Mention any two important definitions of an entrepreneur.

9 Who will be an entrepreneur? Mention any four points.

10 Explain briefly two features of enterprise.

11 Highlight the inter-relatedness between entrepreneurship, entrepreneur and enterprise.

12 Differentiate between entrepreneur and entrepreneurship.

Short Answer Type II Questions (3 Marks)

13 What are the three entrepreneurial functions of an entrepreneur?

14 What are the three promotional functions of an entrepreneur?

15 Discuss any three managerial functions of an entrepreneur.

16 Explain three commercial functions of an entrepreneur.

Long Answer Type Questions (5 Marks)

17 Why is entrepreneurship necessary for the economy? Explain any four points.

18 Mention any four reasons to become an entrepreneur.

19 Briefly describe advantages and disadvantages of entrepreneurship.

20 Elaborate the process of entrepreneurship.

For explanations scan the given QR Code

CHAPTER 02

An Entrepreneur

In this Chapter...

- Why be an entrepreneur?
- Ethical entrepreneurship
- Values
- Attitude
- Motivation
- Intrapreneurship

Why be an Entrepreneur?

Entrepreneurship allows entrepreneur to be innovative and follow his/her passion, event if it requires taking risks. Working on the passion and converting it into a reality is something that only entrepreneurs get to witness as they have the privilege to do business the way they want.

Though people may have different personal perception and motivation for going into entrepreneurship, there are a few common reasons why individuals be an entrepreneur

- It provides them an interested area to work upon.
- It provides them an opportunity to convert their unconventional ideas into reality.
- It allows them to be their own boss.
- It provides an opportunity to earn more money.
- It offers individuals flexibility.
- It helps to improve the standard of living.

Types of Entrepreneurs

Entrepreneurs can be of different types. They can be classified on the basis of their socio-cultural backgrounds, scale or potential of operations, generation of venture creation or personality characteristics exhibited by them.

Based on the above mentioned basis, the various types of entrepreneurs and their classification are discussed ahead.

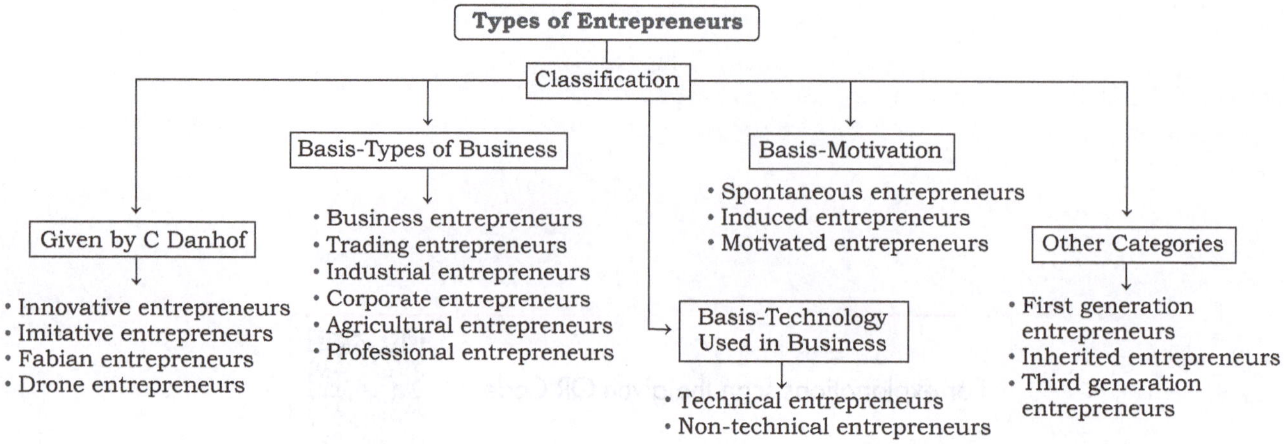

Classification Given by C Danhof

C Danhof has broadly classified entrepreneurs into four types, which are as follows

1. **Innovative Entrepreneurs** These entrepreneurs are those who introduce new products, new methods of production techniques, or discover a new market or a new service or reorganises the enterprise. They are aggressive in nature and exhibit cleverness and resourcefulness by putting attractive possibilities into practice.

   They are commonly found in developed countries where opportunities and resources are in abundance and they contribute towards building a modern capitalist economy, e.g. Walt Disney was an innovative entrepreneur, who started huge theme parks such as the Disney Land in America.

2. **Imitative Entrepreneurs** These entrepreneurs usually copy or adopt suitable innovations made by innovative entrepreneurs. They are adaptive and more flexible. They generally organise factors of production rather than creating them. The imitative entrepreneurs are also revolutionary and important.

   They are generally found in the underdeveloped economies, where facilities for research and development are not easily available. e.g. The local mobile companies generally use the same technology of big manufacturers and produce cheap mobiles.

3. **Fabian Entrepreneurs** These are usually second generation entrepreneurs in a family business enterprise. They are unwilling to take risks and hence, do not start a new venture.

   They follow the footsteps of their predecessors. They initiate only when they are confident that failure to do so would result in a loss of their relative position in the enterprise.

   These entrepreneurs are usually rigid, fundamental and cautious in their approach. They are also very shy and lazy. e.g. in India, coparceners in Joint Hindu Family Business.

4. **Drone Entrepreneurs** These are those types of entrepreneurs who refuse to accept the opportunities that come their way.

   They are generally traditional or conventional in their approach. They are not ready to make changes in their existing production methods, even if they suffer losses.

   They are also known as laggards. e.g. farmers using traditional methods of cultivation even after the developments in modern technology.

Classification on the Basis of Types of Business

Depending upon the nature, size and business types, entrepreneurs are divided into following categories, which are as follows

1. **Business Entrepreneurs** These entrepreneurs are those, who evolve an idea of a new product or service and then set-up an enterprise and arrange resources to convert that idea into reality.

   Most of the entrepreneurs belong to this category as majority of them is found in the field of small trading and manufacturing concerns.

2. **Trading Entrepreneurs** These are the ones who undertake trading activities either in domestic markets or in foreign markets. For this, they need to identify the potential market for their products by looking at the market demand and afterwards, they put many ideas to promote their business. e.g. Big Bazaar, Reliance Fresh, etc.

3. **Industrial Entrepreneurs** They essentially manufacture products and offer services, which have an effective demand in the market.

   They have the ability to transform economic resources and technology into a profitable unit. e.g. Hero Motocorp, Tata Industries, etc.

4. **Corporate Entrepreneurs** These entrepreneurs are the ones, who through their creative and innovative ideas and skills are able to organise, manage and control a corporate undertaking very effectively and efficiently.

   A corporate undertaking is one, which requires registration under existing laws such as joint stock companies and cooperative societies. e.g. Infosys, Reliance India Limited, etc.

5. **Agricultural Entrepreneurs** These entrepreneurs are those who undertake agricultural and allied activities as an area of business. They engage themselves in growing and marketing different crops, fertilisers and other inputs of agriculture, by employing new and modern techniques, machines, good quality seeds and irrigation facilities, etc. e.g. owners of coffee and tea plantations.
6. **Professional Entrepreneurs** They are the ones who start a business to sell it, when it is established. These people always look forward to develop or start an alternative project by selling the current running business. They are less interested in the management of an established business.

Classification on the Basis of Technology used in Business

On the basis of the use of technology, we can further divide entrepreneurs into following two categories

1. **Technical Entrepreneurs** They are the ones, who have the ability to develop new and improved quality of goods and services out of their own knowledge, skills and specialisation. They concentrate more on production than on marketing.
2. **Non-technical Entrepreneurs** They usually focus on developing alternative ways of marketing the goods or services in order to promote their business. They are not concerned with the technique of production but they concentrate more on marketing.

Classification on the Basis of Motivation

Based on motivational factors, entrepreneurs can be classified into three types, which are as follows

1. **Spontaneous Entrepreneurs** These entrepreneurs are motivated by their desire for self-fulfilment and to achieve their excellence in job performance.

   Their strength lies in their creative abilities. They undertake work for self-satisfaction in work, ego or status. They do not need any external motivation. They are also known as **pure entrepreneurs**.
2. **Induced Entrepreneurs** They emerge as entrepreneurs because of various supports from the government in the form of finance, incentives, concessions and other facilities.

   Many times, prospective entrepreneurs are induced or even forced by their special circumstances, such as loss of job or inability to find a suitable job according to their talent and merit to adapt to entrepreneurship.
3. **Motivated Entrepreneurs** These entrepreneurs are motivated to set-up an enterprise in order to use their technical and professional expertise and skills. They have enough confidence in their abilities. They are very ambitious and are normally not satisfied by the slow progress of their jobs.

   They enter the market because of the possibility of making and marketing of some new products or services and once the customers accept the product or service, then entrepreneurs are further motivated by reward in terms of profit.

Other Categories of Entrepreneurs

Other categories of entrepreneurs can be classified as

1. **First Generation Entrepreneurs** These entrepreneurs start their own business with their innovative skills and expertise. They usually combine different technologies to produce some goods or services. e.g. Infosys started by Narayan Murthy.
2. **Inherited Entrepreneurs/Second Generation Entrepreneurs** These entrepreneurs do not start an enterprise on their own rather they join their family business which has already been started by their father, i.e. they inherited an enterprise from their family.

   This form of business is very popular in India, known as Joint Hindu Family Business. e.g. Reliance Industries which had been started by Dhiru Bhai Ambani now had been passed on to Mukesh Ambani and Anil Ambani.
3. **Third Generation Entrepreneurs** These are those types of entrepreneurs wherein their grandparents have been original entrepreneurs (first generation), which has been passed onto their fathers (second generation) and then to themselves. e.g. Tata Industries.

Competencies of an Entrepreneur

Competency is a set of defined behaviour that provides a structured guide enabling the identification, evaluation and development of the behaviours in an individual. Competency basically refers to skills and inner strength that an individual possesses.

A budding entrepreneur should have necessary competencies, so that he/she can venture into forming an enterprise and also be successful in it.

The necessary entrepreneurial competencies can be classified under the following categories

Competencies of an Entrepreneur

- Basic competencies
- Initiative
- Creativity and innovation
- Risk taking and risk management
- Problem solving
- Leadership
- Persistence
- Quality performance
- Information seeking
- Systematic planning
- Persuasion and influencing others
- Enterprise launching competencies
- Enterprise management competencies

1. **Basic Competencies** These competencies are acquired by an entrepreneur for efficient running of business. They relate to the type of behaviour exhibited by entrepreneur while performing various tasks.

   Some of these competencies are latent (already existing but not being utilised) in the entrepreneur, which need to be identified, nursed and nurtured. Others are acquired through training and practice.

2. **Initiative** It is the most fundamental competency required in an entrepreneur. It is rather the first step in the enterprise. This is the competency of the entrepreneur relating to 'endeavour (start) something new'.

   An entrepreneur should be a keen observer of the society, the commercial trends, the product types, the change dynamics and the consumer trends.

   The entrepreneur can take right initiative by pursuing the following tasks

   - Complete knowledge of the area should be possessed by the entrepreneur, where he is planning to take initiative.
   - Entrepreneur should have the knowledge of needs, wants and desires of the consumers.
   - Entrepreneur must have information about the available products and services as per the present market situation.
   - Entrepreneur must have relevance of the new products to be introduced in the market.
   - Complete knowledge about the tools and techniques should be possessed by the entrepreneur.
   - Analysis should be done by an entrepreneur whether the area where he is planning to take initiative has been attempted by other persons and he must see their experiences.

3. **Creativity and Innovation** Competency in creativity and innovation are sometimes basic traits of certain individuals. An entrepreneur might not have any new ideas, but he/she may use creative ideas and innovative products and services to meet the challenges of a situation or take advantage of the utility of an idea or a product to create wealth. e.g. packing shampoos in small sachets.

4. **Risk Taking and Risk Management** An entrepreneur generally ventures into new ideas and new services.

   There are several factors which will affect the success of his venture, *viz.* demand and supply in the market, resources availability, acceptability of the product design and service, etc.

   All these factors are outside the control of the entrepreneur. Therefore, it can be said that an entrepreneur walks into the areas of uncertainty.

   So, an entrepreneur should have the competency of taking risks, i.e. he/she should not be a safe player and also when risk arises, he/she should be able to manage it. e.g. when Dhirubhai Ambani faced cash crunch, he took the risk of issuing shares in 1977 to the public, when there was not much awareness regarding the share market.

   Following functions can be performed by an entrepreneur to get the accuracy in calculation of risk and risk management

   - Proper planning of actions.
   - Planning for crisis management.
   - Anticipation of all the hindrances or difficult situations ahead.

- Various alternatives should be evaluated.
- Policies, programmes and situation should be analysed.
- Pre-preparation for possibilities of hijacking of ideas and services by other powerful individuals or systems.

5. **Problem Solving** Once an entrepreneur is aware that he/she has ventured in a new business and has taken certain calculated risks, he/she should also be prepared for many problems that are bound to come in the path of success of his venture. He/She should have the competency to evaluate alternative strategies or resources that would help to solve the problem, generate new ideas, products, services, etc e.g. Ratan Tata shifted the manufacturing plant of Nano cars from Singur to Sanand due to unforeseen complexities.

   An entrepreneur must do the following things to attain the competency to face problem with confidence and to take the right decision at the right time
   - Proper resources should be searched in order to solve the problem.
   - The root cause of the problem should be understood by the entrepreneur.
   - In order to prevent re-occurence of the similar problems, new ideas, products, vision, services etc. should be developed and reviewed at regular intervals.
   - An entrepreneur should work on the principle that says every problem has a solution.
   - He should understand that problem solving is a part of each project/venture.
   - He should be competent to find out the alternative solution to every problem.
   - Alternate strategy should be used till the solutions for problems are found.

6. **Leadership** An entrepreneur should also have leadership qualities, so that he/she is able to guide and motivate his/her entire team. Whenever a business faces a problem, it is the will power, effective business acumen and communication skills of a leader which oversees the success of the corporation.

7. **Persistence** Creating a demand in the market for the product/service of the business is one of the main requirements for the success of the business venture and this calls for intense perseverance on the part of the entrepreneur. Road-blocks in his endeavour to success should not discourage the entrepreneur.

   e.g. when Mahima Mehra brought out her product-Haathi Chaap, she had experimented on various other materials unsuccessfully before finally using elephant dung to manufacture handmade paper.

8. **Quality Performance** Since, entrepreneurs value outstanding performance, one of the competencies necessary is the sensitivity to and concern for the 'standards' and 'quality of work'.

   One should develop the skill of comparing the quality of the products/services with certain standards, which he/she himself/herself evolves or are set by others.
   e.g. Steve Jobs, the brain behind Apple and I-pod, is known to value quality in all the products introduced by the company.

9. **Information Seeking** Information plays a very crucial role at every stage of enterprise building and management, as it helps an entrepreneur to be aware of the changes taking place in the environment affecting the business.

   Entrepreneurs can get this information by
   - Personally conducting research.
   - Using feedback from previous related experience, etc.

   The quality and extent of information collected and their role in decision-making, by and large decides the success and failure of any entrepreneurial venture. Therefore, this is an important competency of an entrepreneur.

10. **Systematic Planning** Every entrepreneur has limited resources in terms of time, finance and manpower.

    They invest their life's savings and total energy in creating entrepreneurial ventures and therefore, before putting the whole enterprise into operation, they should develop a detailed blueprint through systematic planning. So, an entrepreneur should have the competency to plan.

11. **Persuasion and Influencing Others** One of the important functions of an entrepreneur is to influence the environment comprising of individuals and institutions, for

mobilising resources, obtaining inputs, organising production and selling products and services.

So, entrepreneur should have the competency of persuading and influencing others.

An entrepreneur should do the following things to influence others in the market

- The social and personal objectives practised by the firm should be explained properly.
- The technology used in the products should be explained by an entrepreneur.
- In order to make the products better than competitor's products, he/she should add value and innovative elements in his/her products and services.
- He/She should develop the feeling of trust and faith in the mind of customers by convincing them about the quality standard of the products.
- Special and distinct features of the product must be highlighted in order to differentiate it from the competitor's product.

12. **Enterprise Launching Competencies** A lot of opportunities exists in the environment, but not all people respond to them. Most of the individuals perceive only the apparent and traditional openings of earning. But, entrepreneurs respond to the opportunities existing in the environment.

    Also, resources are available to all the members of the society, but very few make efforts to ensure best use of these resources and these few are the entrepreneurs. So, entrepreneurs should have the competency to identify opportunities, avail and facilitate the resources needed to launch their enterprise.

13. **Enterprise Management Competencies** The enterprise may be small or big, but it demands management abilities on the part of its owner or manager. Various management functions such as production, marketing, finance, etc are crucial functions of an entrepreneur. These influence the result directly and are therefore, necessary determinants for the sustenance of an enterprise. So, an entrepreneur should have management competency.

Characteristics of an Entrepreneur

An entrepreneur should possess the following features or characteristics

1. **Efficient Risk-taker** An entrepreneur should possess the ability of taking risks with great efficiency.

   Entrepreneurs have an indifferent approach towards risks as they have confidence on their skills and an in-depth understanding of the situation which encourages them to bear risk courageously.

2. **Sufficient Knowledge** An entrepreneur should possess complete knowledge of his industry and market.

   With proper and appropriate knowledge, an entrepreneur can solve any problem and tackle any crisis.

3. **Creative Person** An entrepreneur is considered as a creative person who has the ability to generate new products, services, new methods of production, etc. He creates opportunity for innovation, experimentation and production.

4. **Passionate** Passionate attitude towards work helps an entrepreneur to overcome various hurdles and difficulties, and forge ahead towards the pre-planned goals.

5. **Empathy** A good entrepreneur should know the strengths and weaknesses of every employee who works under him. Without this feature or quality, an entrepreneur cannot reach the heart of employees nor the success he desires.

6. **Pre-determined Goals** Proper planning is an essential characteristic of a good entrepreneur which provides guidelines with minimum to no damage incurred to a business.

CHECK POINT 01

1. Define fabian entrepreneur.
2. What do you mean by drone entrepreneurs?
3. What are industrial entrepreneurs?
4. Which type of entrepreneurs start their own business with their innovative skills and expertise?
5. Who is considered as pure entrepreneur?
6. State any one characteristic of an entrepreneur.

Ethical Entrepreneurship

Ethics refers to well-founded standards of right and wrong, that prescribe what an individual ought to do, usually in terms of rights, obligations, benefits to society, fairness or specific virtues.

Ethics means those standards that impose reasonable obligations on an individual to refrain from social and moral evils such as stealing, murder, assault and fraud. Ethics also mean the continuous efforts on the part of an individual for the betterment of his/her own moral beliefs and conduct.

Business ethics basically mean to conduct business with a human touch in order to give welfare to the society. Business ethics comprises of the study of proper business policies and practices regarding controvercial issues such as corporate governance, insider trading, bribery, discrimination, corporate social responsibilities and fiduciary responsibilities.

Business ethics are often guided by law or provide a basic framework that businesses may choose to follow in order to gain public acceptance.

According to **Andrew Crane,** "Business ethics are the study of business situations, activities and decisions where issues of right and wrong are addressed".

Importance of Ethical Entrepreneurship

(Ethical Practices to be Followed by an Entrepreneur)

According to **Johan Wempe**, "Ethical entrepreneurship, in a nutshell, amounts to the achievement of ethical goals through entrepreneurship". An entrepreneur should not forget that for success to be long lasting, he/she will have to follow some ethical standards in their business practices.

Some practices to be followed by them are given below

- Providing quality and correct quantity of goods to consumers.
- Keeping in mind the environmental issues during production.
- Paying the minimum and correct wages to the workers.
- Not to use child labour in their production.
- Judicious use of natural resources.

Key Areas of Concern in Business Ethics

Key areas of concern in business ethics are as follows

1. **Corporate Governance** This essentially involves balancing the interests of many stakeholders in a company such as shareholders, management, customers, suppliers, government, etc.
2. **Insider Trading** It is defined by the **Black's Law Dictionary** as, "The use of material and non-public information in trading the shares of a company by a corporate insider or any other person who owes a fiduciary duty to the company".
3. **Corporate Social Responsibility** It means that a business should be socially responsible by being sensitive to the needs of a society. e.g. opening of charitable schools, hospitals, etc. by business houses.
4. **Fiduciary Responsibility** It exists with individuals or businesses who handle money or property for others. The term 'fiduciary' refers to a relationship in which one person has a responsibility of care for the assets or rights of another person.

Values

A civilised society considers qualities like honesty, truthfulness, integrity, etc, as important for happy and healthy living.

These set of beliefs that provide standards which guide behaviour is known as 'values'. Thus, value determines what people consider to be good or bad for a civilised society.

According to **Milton Rokeach**, values can be defined as, "Beliefs that guide actions and judgement across a variety of situations".

Entrepreneurial Values

In relation to business, social values define the objectives of the business, as well as, the manner in which business affairs should be conducted.

Entrepreneurs share some of these qualities that guide and direct them and hence, these values are referred to as 'entrepreneurial values'.

The various factors which influence entrepreneurial values are as follows

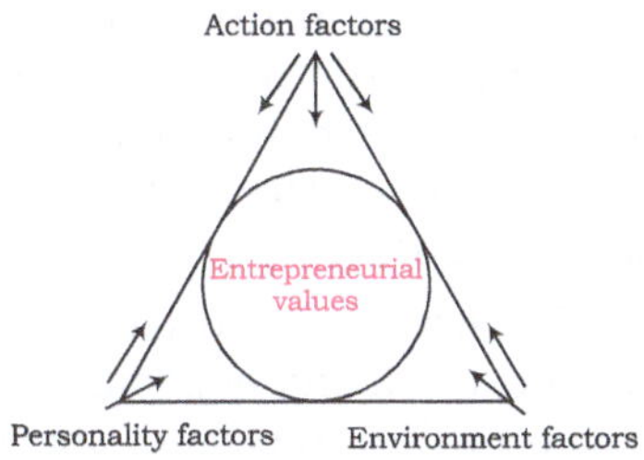

1. **Action Factors** These factors are those which arise due to the action of others or are a result of the influence of others on the entrepreneur.
2. **Environment Factors** These factors arise out of the environment in which an entrepreneur operates.
3. **Personality Factors** These factors depend upon the personality of the entrepreneur.

Collectively, all the three factors affect the core values of an entrepreneur.

Core Values

Core values are basic entrepreneurial values found in all entrepreneurs. Research studies have shown that there are basically four core values, that are generally possessed by dynamic entrepreneurs. These values are found in varying degrees in different entrepreneurs.

A brief discussion of core values is given below

Core Values
- → Innovation and creativity
- → Independence or ownership
- → Respect for work
- → Quest for outstanding performance

1. **Innovation and Creativity** These are the most important core values and found among most of the entrepreneurs. Creativity is the ability to see new ways of doing things and innovativeness is the ability to make it work in practice.

   Entrepreneurs are guided by these values when they come out with creative ideas, new products, services, processes, etc to solve specific problems of the society. e.g. earlier, hair oils and shampoos were available only in tins and bottles. Introducing them in small packs has become convenient for customers to carry and use them.

   This has helped in raising the revenues of the businesses. Innovativeness in an entrepreneur can be seen through various actions such as
   - Experimenting with new ideas, e.g. introduction of debit and credit cards in the banking sector.
   - Facing uncertainty in order to try out new ideas.
   - Not giving up or becoming upset when errors occur.
   - Finding problems to solve.
   - Finding new use for existing methods or equipment.
   - Demonstrating originality.
   - Introducing changes, e.g. induction cook tops.
   - Providing critical inputs for the new ideas.
   - Providing evaluation of proposed ideas.
2. **Independence or Ownership** (Self-reliance) Entrepreneurs drive great satisfaction in their sense of 'independence' or 'ownership'. They all have a very strong and positive ego drive which enables them to define their mission and achieve it through commitment, sense of complete identification, sincerity and hard work.

   e.g. in his quest for independence, Dhirubhai Ambani gave up his job in Yemen and returned back to India to start his own business.
3. **Respect for Work** The entrepreneurs have great respect for their work. Successful entrepreneurs believe that they can achieve anything through hard work. The biographies of all successful entrepreneurs reveal that they have achieved the pinnacle of success through hard work.

   This value provides goal direction, which encourages them to pursue a path and career in which the rewards and incentives are directly linked to the degree and quality of efforts made.
4. **Quest for Outstanding Performance** Dynamic entrepreneurs are guided by the value of outstanding performance.

   Challenges seem to stimulate and motivate them. As they have strong motivation to succeed, they value performance of a high order.

Thus, the entrepreneur, due to his/her quest for excellence, is an 'overcomer' who can resolve problems under pressure. They are persistent and hardworking when things go wrong.

e.g. Steve Jobs, always believed in outstanding performance. When Apple phone was launched, he took great care to make the package eco-friendly and light-weight with 3D images on it.

Attitude

Attitude may be defined as the way a person feels about something — a person, a place, a commodity, a situation or an idea. Attitude constitutes an important psychological attribute of individuals, which shape their behaviour.

e.g. A young man was passing through a site construction, where he saw three labourers working on the site. He went near to them and asked each one 'what are they doing'?

First one replied, "I am pulling in to earn a living. I am working and earning".

Second one replied, "I am constructing a wall".

Third one replied, "I am building a beautiful mansion".

All the three labourers were doing the same work, but what differentiated them was their attitude towards work.

Features of Attitude

Attitude generally exhibits the following features

1. **Affects Behaviour** People have a natural tendency to maintain consistency between attitude and behaviour. In the absence of external intervention, attitude leads to intended behaviour.
2. **Attitude is Invisible** Attitude is basically a psychological phenomenon, which cannot be directly observed. However, it can be interpreted by observing its consequences. e.g. if a person is highly productive, we may infer that he/she has a positive attitude towards his/her work.
3. **Attitude is Acquired** Attitude is generally learnt or acquired over a period of time. The process of learning attitude starts from childhood and continues throughout the life of an individual. In childhood, the family members have a greater influence on the attitude a child develops.
4. **Attitude is Pervasive** Attitude has their presence felt in all the aspects of society. It is formed in the process of socialisation and hence, may relate to anything in the world. For instance, a person may have positive or negative attitude towards religion, politics, politicians or countries.

Sources of Attitude

One of the features of attitude is that it is acquired. The thoughts, feelings and tendencies to behave are acquired or learned gradually, from the following sources

1. **Direct Personal Experience** The person gets direct experience while working which influences his attitude in several ways. e.g. if a worker finds his/her job challenging, but supervisors understanding and co-workers very cooperative, then he/she will have a positive attitude towards his/her job because of the quality of his/her direct experience with the job.
2. **Group Associations** People are influenced to one degree or another by other members of the group to which they belong. Several groups, including family, work and peer groups and cultural and sub-cultural groups are important in affecting a person's attitudinal development.
3. **Influential Others** A person's attitude can be formed and changed through personal contact with influential persons such as respected friends, relatives and experts. Opinion leaders also influence the attitudes and purchase behaviour of their followers.

   To capitalise on this type of influence, advertisers often use actors and actresses, who look similar to or act similar to their intended audiences.

Another application which advertisers use to influence audience attitudes is the so called 'slice of life' commercial. These advertisements show typical people confronting typical problems and finding solutions in the use of advertised brand. e.g. Kareena Kapoor using 'Head and Shoulders' shampoo for dandruff problem.

Essential Attitudes of an Entrepreneur

The following attitudes present in an entrepreneur will help him/her to achieve success in his/her venture

Essential Attitudes of an Entrepreneur

- Have passion for business
- Set an example of trustworthiness
- Be flexible, except with core values
- Don't let fear of failure hold one back
- Make timely decisions
- Major company asset is oneself
- Keep one's ego under control
- Believe in oneself
- Encourage and accept criticism
- Maintain strong work ethic
- Rebound quickly from setbacks
- Get out of comfort zone to pursue something important

1. **Have Passion for Business** An entrepreneur should have a passion for his/her business which will help him/her to overcome difficult moments, generate trust among people and persuade others to do business with him/her. However, passion cannot be taught, it is an in-born feeling.
2. **Set an Example of Trustworthiness** People have confidence in trustworthy individuals and want to work for them in a culture of integrity. The same is true for customers. They want to buy from entrepreneurs they trust. So, an entrepreneur should be trustworthy.
3. **Be Flexible, Except with Core Values** Flexibility is important for success in today's dynamic environment. So, plans and strategies are bound to change with changing times. However, no matter what the pressure for immediate profits, an entrepreneur should not compromise on core values.
4. **Don't let Fear of Failure hold One Back** Failure is an opportunity to learn. All things being equal, venture capitalists would rather invest money in an individual, who tried and failed founding a company than in someone who never tried.
5. **Make Timely Decisions** An entrepreneur should always take timely decisions based on his/her intuition. Planning and thought are good, but procrastination (delaying to a future date) leads one to miss opportunities.
6. **The Major Company Asset is Oneself** One should take care of oneself. One's health is more valuable than the most expensive machinery or computer software for the business.

   One doesn't have to choose between one's family or business, play or work. Maintain one's own health for balance and energy, which will, in turn, enhance one's outlook.
7. **Keep One's Ego under Control** An entrepreneur should not believe in show-off. He/She should not spend his/her profits on expensive gadgets to impress others. Instead, he/she should build a war chest for unexpected needs or opportunities. He/She should also hear out new ideas and suggestions from subordinates and peers, no matter how crazy they sound.
8. **Believe in Oneself** One needs to believe in one's own self, in one's company, and that one will be successful. One's confidence is contagious to one's employees, customers, stakeholders, suppliers and everyone, one deals with.
9. **Encourage and Accept Criticism Graciously, Admitting One's Mistake** Entrepreneurs are humans and are bound to make mistakes. However, they should learn to admit their mistake. Also, they should encourage their employees to give them their honest opinion, even if it is in conflict with their own opinion. This will help an entrepreneur to view his/her decision from a different perspective.
10. **Maintain a Strong Work Ethic** An entrepreneur should be the first to follow and maintain a strong work ethic, only then the employees will follow the lead. It will also help one to beat one's competitors by outworking them, particularly in case of similar products and services.
11. **Rebound Quickly from Setbacks** There surely will be plenty of ups and downs as one builds up the business. Learn from the setbacks and move on.

One can't change the past, but it should be remembered that future is definitely in our hands.

12. **Periodically Getting Out of One's Comfort Zone to pursue Something Important** Many times one feels uncomfortable while implementing a needed change in technology, people, mission, competition etc. For the business and the entrepreneur to grow personally, the entrepreneur should step out of his comfort zone and implement what is good for the business.

Motivation

Entrepreneurial motivation may be defined as a process that activates the entrepreneurs to exert a high level of effort for the achievement of their goals. It refers to the drive or forces within an entrepreneur that affects his/her direction, intensity and persistence of voluntary behaviour.

According to **Robert Dubin**, "Motivation is the complex force starting and keeping a person at work in an organisation. Motivation is something which moves the person to action and continues him in the course of action already initiated".

Process of Motivation

Motivation is essentially a process. It can be well expressed in the form of a model.

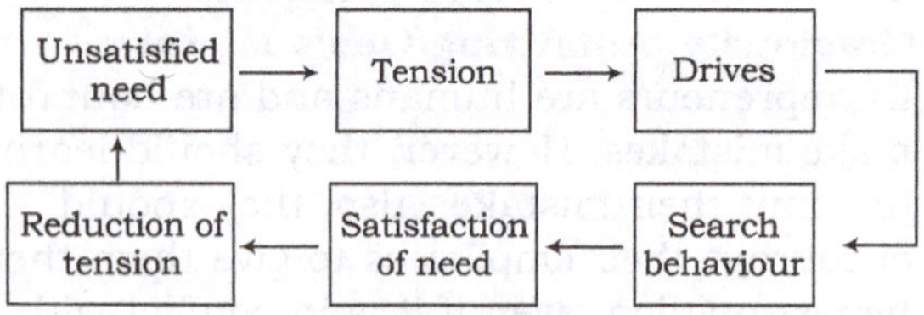

Motivation Process

The process of motivation starts with an unsatisfied need of an individual. Every individual possesses an urge or a need, or a multitude of needs, desires or expectations.

These unsatisfied needs lead to tension within the individual and motivates him/her to search for ways to relieve his/her tension. This leads one to certain drives and searching alternatives to achieve one's goal which will eventually reduce tension.

e.g. if a person is hungry, then this need will create tension and he/she will start thinking about ways to satisfy his/her need.

This will stimulate his/her drives, causing to search for different options (bread, sweets, biscuits, parantha, etc.) to satisfy his/her need.

Suppose an individual eats biscuit, then his/her need is satisfied and he/she is relieved of tension.

Motivation Theories

Several management thinkers have put forward motivation theories which encourage an entrepreneur to continue his/her work inspite of all odds. Two important theories which are discussed in this chapter are as follows

1. Maslow's Hierarchy of Needs Theory

This theory was proposed by **Abraham Maslow** and is based on the assumption that people are motivated by a series of five universal needs.

These needs are ranked, according to the order in which they influence human behaviour, in hierarchical fashion, as depicted below

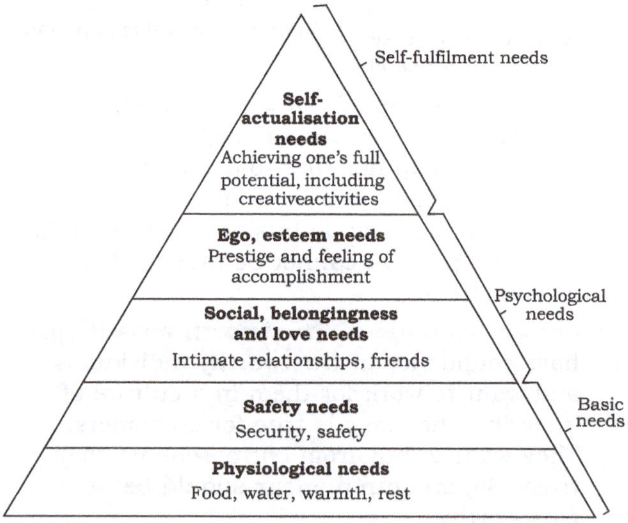

(i) **Physiological Needs** These needs are lowest in the pyramidical structure and are deemed to be the lowest level needs, such as the need for food and water. As long as physiological needs are unsatisfied, they exist as a driving or motivating force in a person's life.

A hungry person has a felt need. This felt need sets-up both psychological and physical tensions that manifest themselves in overt behaviours directed at reducing those tensions (getting something to eat).

Once the hunger is satisfied, the tension is reduced, and the need for food ceases to motivate. At this point (assuming that other physiological requirements are also satisfied), the next higher order need becomes the motivating need.

(ii) **Safety Needs** These needs are second in the pyramidical structure and emerge only after the physiological needs are fulfilled.

These needs include a desire for security, stability, dependency, protection, freedom from fear and anxiety, and a need for structure, order and law.

In the workplace, this need translates into a need for atleast a minimal degree of employment security, the knowledge that we cannot be fired on a whim and that appropriate levels of effort and productivity will ensure continued employment.

(iii) **Social Needs** These needs rank third in the pyramidical structure and emerge after the safety needs have been fulfilled. These needs include the need for belongingness and love. Being social creatures, humans have a need to belong.

In the workplace, this need may be satisfied by an ability to interact with one's co-workers and perhaps to be able to work collaboratively with their colleagues.

(iv) **Ego and Esteem Needs** These needs rank fourth in the pyramidical structure and emerge after the social needs have been fulfilled. Esteem needs include the desire for self-respect, self-esteem and the esteem of others.

When focused externally, these needs also include the desire for reputation, prestige, status, fame, glory, dominance, recognition, attention, importance and appreciation.

(v) **Self-actualisation Needs** These needs rank the highest in Maslow's pyramidical structure and emerge after the satisfaction of ego and esteem needs. These needs comprise of the need for self-realisation, continuous self-development and the process of becoming all that a person is capable of.

2. McClelland's Theory of Needs

According to **David McClelland**, regardless of culture or gender, people are driven by three motives

(i) **Achievement Needs** The need for achievement is characterised by the wish to take responsibility for finding solutions to problems, master complex tasks, set goals and get feedback on the level of success. People with achievement motives are motivated by standards of excellence, delineated roles and responsibilities and concrete, timely feedback.

(ii) **Affiliation Needs** The need for affiliation is characterised by a desire to belong, an enjoyment of teamwork, a concern about interpersonal relationships and a need to reduce uncertainty.

Those with affiliation motives are motivated when they can accomplish things with people they know and trust.

(iii) **Power Needs** The need for power is characterised by a drive to control and influence others, a need to win arguments, a need to persuade and prevail. The power motive is activated when people are allowed to have an impact, impress those in power, or beat competitors.

According to **McClelland**, "The presence of these motives or drives in an individual indicates a predisposition to behave in certain ways.

Therefore, from a manager's perspective, recognising which need is dominant in any particular individual affects the way in which that person can be motivated".

CHECK POINT 02

1. State any one area of concern in business ethics.
2. Mention the factors influencing entrepreneurial values.
3. Entrepreneurs drive great satisfaction in their sense of ...... or ....
4. State any one essential attitude of an entrepreneur.
5. Define motivation.

Intrapreneurship

This word was first used by management consultant **Gifford Pinchot** in the 1980s. The concept of 'intrapreneurship' requires that managers inside the company should be encouraged to be entrepreneurs within the firm rather than go outside. It is also termed as 'corporate entrepreneurship'.

Intrapreneur

Intrapreneurs are usually employees within a company, who are assigned a specific idea or project, with instructions to develop it in the same manner as an entrepreneur does.

Intrapreneurs are capable individuals having the resources of the company at their disposal. The intrapreneur's main job is to turn the specific project into a profitable venture. They can also be referred to as 'paid entrepreneurs' or 'inside entrepreneurs'.

So, it can be concluded that intrapreneur is someone who has an entrepreneurial streak but chooses to align his/her talents with a large organisation in place of creating his/her own organisation. Intrapreneurs are most successful when management empowers and supports them.

Importance of Intrapreneurship

Intrapreneurship is increasingly becoming a necessity in today's corporate world because of the below mentioned reasons

1. **Growth** Intrapreneurship helps organisations to generate new businesses thereby leading to their growth by widening their scale of operations.
2. **Innovation** Intrapreneurship provides an environment to support and sustain innovation over time.
3. **Change** Intrapreneurship enables organisations to effectively accelerate and manage change.
4. **Engagement** Intrapreneurship provides a platform to engage employees in work that is challenging and meaningful. This helps in retaining employees in the organisation and results in the growth of the business.

So, it can be concluded that, organisations that have embraced intrapreneurship, have achieved higher financial returns, increased productivity, more innovation and higher levels of employee engagement.

Intrapreneurship – Examples from the Corporate World

Through the Google Intrapreneurship Program, all the employees are empowered and encouraged to spend 20% of their time on projects that interest them and that they think will benefit Google and their customers.

The Google 'Innovation Time Off' Intrapreneurship Program has a formal process for the selection of entrepreneurial projects, for the formal evaluation process and the monitoring of each Google approved entrepreneurial project.

For a Google employee, to participate in the program, he/she needs to submit a project proposal with a timeline. It is critical to note that several of Google's newest products and services such as G-mail, Google news, Orkut and Adsense have all originated through this program.

In India also, Marico, manufacturers of Parachute Hair Oil, Saffola, Kaya Skin Clinic Industries have institutionalised innovation awards, where they receive 30-40 entries every year for innovations across the spectrum, including factories, brand, sales and human resource, virtually covering the whole organisation.

The company believes that there will be failures and unless one is ready to fail, one can never succeed.

Kinetic Engineering Limited is the flagship company of Firodia Group of companies, one of the pioneering groups in automobiles in India, founded in 1972 by **Mr HK Firodia**.

The company encourages employees to use their time efficiently for innovation in its upcoming products. The Kinetic Zing Model of bicycle was the idea of an employee working in the corporation.

Consequences of not Encouraging Intrapreneurship

A company not encouraging intrapreneurship may face the following consequences

- Difficulty in retaining innovative employees.
- Loss of profit generating ideas.

A classic case of entrepreneurs is that of the founders of Adobe, **John Warnock** and **Charles Geschke**. They both were employees of Xerox. As employees, they were frustrated because their new product ideas were not encouraged.

They quit Xerox in the early 1980s to begin their own business. Currently, Adobe has an annual turnover of over $ 3 billion.

Difference between Entrepreneur and Employee

Broadly, the difference between entrepreneur and employee is that an entrepreneur is the owner of the enterprise and an employee is in the services of the enterprise and both work for the interest of the enterprise.

The following are other basic differences

1. **Motive** The motive of an entrepreneur is to start a venture by setting up an enterprise. One undertakes the venture for his personal gratification, whereas the employee's job is to render one's services in the ongoing or new enterprise set-up by someone else.
2. **Status** An entrepreneur is the owner of the enterprise, whereas an employee is the servant in the enterprise owned by the entrepreneur.
3. **Risk Bearing** An entrepreneur being the owner of the enterprise assumes all risks and uncertainty involved in running the enterprise. He/she considers and thinks about his business 24 hours, whereas an employee, being a servant does not bear any risk. All that can happen is one may lose his/her job with or without some compensation. Employee is on duty for certain hours only.
4. **Rewards** The reward, an entrepreneur gets, for bearing risks involved in the enterprise is profit or at times handsome profit, which is uncertain, whereas an employee gets rewarded for his/her services rendered in the enterprise as salary which is fixed and certain as per appointment letter issued. In addition, employee gets a bonus as per prescribed rules and festival tokens, etc, in cash or kind, sometimes also based on performance.
5. **Innovations** The entrepreneur himself/herself thinks over what and how to produce goods and services. He/She has to bear in mind about meeting the changing demands of the customers. Hence, he/she acts as an innovator as well as a change agent, whereas employee executes the set plans as per the given schedule. Thus, employee's job is to meet up the targets decided by his/her employer.
6. **Qualification** An entrepreneur needs to possess qualities and qualifications like high achievement motive, originality in thinking, farsightedness, risk bearing abilities and much more, whereas an employee needs to possess qualifications as per the status in the enterprise which are pre-set and detailed in black and white, like an accountant can be CA/M.Com, etc and a manager may be an MBA in Marketing/Finance or Human Resource, etc as per the nature of the enterprise.

Difference between Entrepreneur and Intrapreneur

Basis	Entrepreneur	Intrapreneur
Meaning	Entrepreneur refers to a person who sets up his own business with a new idea or concept.	Intrapreneur refers to an employee of the organisation who is in charge of undertaking innovations in product, service, process etc.
Conduct	An entrepreneur may not necessarily operate from within the organisation.	An intrapreneur works within the organisation.
Risk	The entrepreneur is the ultimate risk bearer; being the owner of the enterprise.	Since an intrapreneur is ultimately an employee, he does not bear much risks involved.
Finance	The entrepreneur raises funds required to execute/run the enterprise.	An intrapreneur plays within an organisation. Thus, the company raises funds required to deploy an idea.
Dependency	He is independent in his operations. He does not work for others and his own boss.	An intrapreneur is dependent on the entrepreneur. He works for corporation under defined rules and regulations.

CHECK POINT 03

1. Who firstly used the word 'Intrapreneurship'?
2. What do you mean by intrapreneur?
3. Mention any one necessity of an intrapreneurship.
4. State any one consequence of not encouraging intrapreneurship.
5. Mention any one difference between entrepreneur and employee.

EXAM PATTERN EXERCISE

Objective Type Questions (1 Mark)

Multiple Choice Questions

1 .... entrepreneurs usually copy or adopt suitable innovations made by innovative entrepreneurs.

(a) Imitative (b) Fabian
(c) Drone (d) Go-getters

Ans (a) Imitative

2 .... entrepreneurs are also known as pure entrepreneurs.

(a) Spontaneous
(b) Induced
(c) Motivated
(d) None of the above

Ans (a) Spontaneous

3 Owners of coffee and tea plantations are examples of

(a) business entrepreneurs
(b) corporate entrepreneurs
(c) agricultural entrepreneurs
(d) None of the above

Ans (c) agricultural entrepreneurs

4 Mr. X become an entrepreneur because of government support provided in terms of financial assistance, incentives, concessions and other facilities. He is included in which category of entrepreneurs?

(a) Motivated entrepreneur
(b) Spontaneous entrepreneur
(c) Induced entrepreneur
(d) Technical entrepreneur

Ans (c) Induced entrepreneur

5 Basic competencies are acquired by an entrepreneur for efficient running of business. These competencies can be

(a) latent
(b) acquired
(c) Both (a) and (b)
(d) None of the above

Ans (c) Both (a) and (b)

6 Information helps an entrepreneur to be aware of the changes taking place in the environment. Entrepreneurs can get this information from

(a) personally conducting research
(b) using feedback from previous related experience
(c) Both (a) and (b)
(d) None of the above

Ans (c) Both (a) and (b)

7 According to ...., "Business ethics are the study of business situations, activities and decisions where issues of right and wrong are addressed."

(a) Andrew Crane (b) Johan Wempe
(c) Bill Wagner (d) C Danhof

Ans (a) Andrew Crane

8 In ethical entrepreneurship, entrepreneur follows the practice of

(a) judicious use of natural resources
(b) not to use child labour in production activities
(c) Both (a) and (b)
(d) None of the above

Ans (c) Both (a) and (b)

9 The factor(s) which influence entrepreneurial values is/are

(a) action factors
(b) environment factors
(c) personality factors
(d) All of the above

Ans (d) All of the above

10 'Care and Clean' manufactures shampoos and hair oils and they are packed in 200 ml and 500 ml bottles. Faced with fall in demand, they decided to pack them in sachets of 10 ml and 20 ml. This represents the core value of

(a) innovation and creativity
(b) respect for work
(c) quest for outstanding performance
(d) None of the above

Ans (a) innovation and creativity

11 Which amongst the following is/are the source(s) of attitude?
(a) Direct personal experience
(b) Group associations
(c) Influential others
(d) All of the above

Ans (d) All of the above

12 Sanjeev is 18 years old. He works as a courier boy to earn his living. He saves a part of his earning to provide for his education. Which need(s) is/are being fulfilled by him, according to Maslow's Theory?
(a) Physiological needs
(b) Safety needs
(c) Self-actualisation needs
(d) Both (a) and (b)

Ans (d) Both (a) and (b)

13 A young boy, Arjun got a job in MNC located in Gujarat. After getting a job, his two basic requirements are salary and safe working environment. Which need of Arjun is satisfied according to Maslow Need Hierarchy Theory?
(a) Safety needs
(b) Self-actualisation needs
(c) Social needs
(d) Ego and esteem needs

Ans (a) Safety needs

14 According to McClelland's Theory of Needs, ... are characterised by a drive to control and influence others.
(a) achievement needs
(b) affiliation needs
(c) power needs
(d) None of the above

Ans (c) power needs

15 Through the Google Intrapreneurship Programme, all the employees are empowered and encouraged to spend .... of their time on projects that interest them and that they think will benefit Google and their customers.
(a) 20%
(b) 15%
(c) 25%
(d) 30%

Ans (a) 20%

16 From the following, what an entrepreneur must not do to attain competency and take right decision at the right time?
(a) Proper resources should be searched in order to solve the problem
(b) He should understand the root cause of the problem
(c) He should work on the principle that says every problem has a solution
(d) He should understand that problem solving is not a part of each project/venture

Ans (d) He should understand that problem solving is not a part of each project/venture

17 **Assertion** (A) Walt Disney was an innovative entrepreneur.

Reason (R) Walt Disney started huge theme parks such as the Disney Land in America.

Alternatives
(a) Both Assertion (A) and Reason (R) are correct
(b) Assertion (A) is correct, but Reason (R) is incorrect
(c) Assertion (A) is incorrect, but Reason (R) is correct
(d) Both Assertion (A) and Reason (R) are incorrect

Ans (a) Both Assertion (A) and Reason (R) are correct

18 **Assertion** (A) Entrepreneurs share some of the qualities that guide and direct them.

Reason (R) These values are referred to as 'entrepreneurial values'.

Alternatives
(a) Both Assertion (A) and Reason (R) are correct
(b) Assertion (A) is correct, but Reason (R) is incorrect
(c) Assertion (A) is incorrect, but Reason (R) is correct
(d) Both Assertion (A) and Reason (R) are incorrect

Ans (a) Both Assertion (A) and Reason (R) are correct

19 Given below are types of entrepreneurs in Column I and their features in Column II. Match them correctly.

Column I	Column II
A. Innovative Entrepreneurs	(i) Very shy and lazy

Column I	Column II
B. Imitative Entrepreneurs	(ii) Aggressive in nature and exhibit cleverness
C. Fabian Entrepreneurs	(iii) Pure entrepreneurs by nature
D. Induced Entrepreneurs	(iv) Adaptive and more flexible

Codes

	A	B	C	D		A	B	C	D
(a)	(ii)	(iv)	(i)	(iii)	(b)	(ii)	(i)	(iii)	(iv)
(c)	(iii)	(iv)	(ii)	(i)	(d)	(ii)	(i)	(iv)	(iii)

Ans (a) (ii) (iv) (i) (iii)

20 Given below are entrepreneurial factors in Column I and their features in Column II. Match them correctly.

Column I	Column II
A. Action Factors	(i) Result of the influence of others on the entrepreneur
B. Environment Factors	(ii) Depend upon the personality of the entrepreneur
C. Personality Factors	(iii) Arise out of the environment in which an entrepreneur operates

Codes

	A	B	C		A	B	C
(a)	(ii)	(iii)	(i)	(b)	(i)	(iii)	(ii)
(c)	(iii)	(i)	(ii)	(d)	(ii)	(i)	(iii)

Ans (b) (i) (iii) (ii)

21 Competencies of a successful enterpereneur.

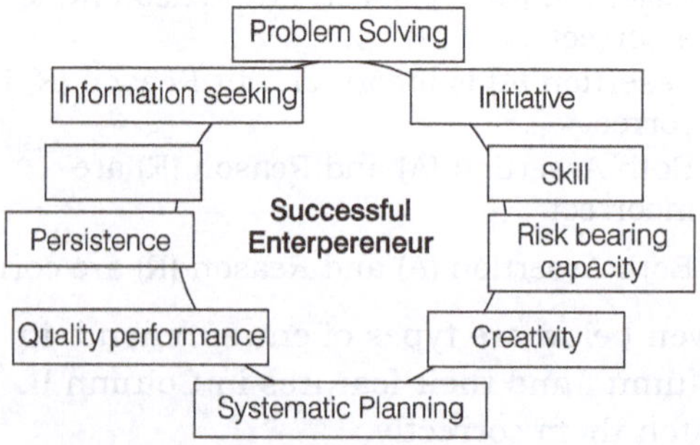

Identify the missing competency of an entrepreneur in the given figure.

(a) Leadership
(b) Clarity of voice
(c) Writing Skill
(d) None of these

Ans (a) Leadership

22 Shared traits between entrepreneurs and intrapreneurs

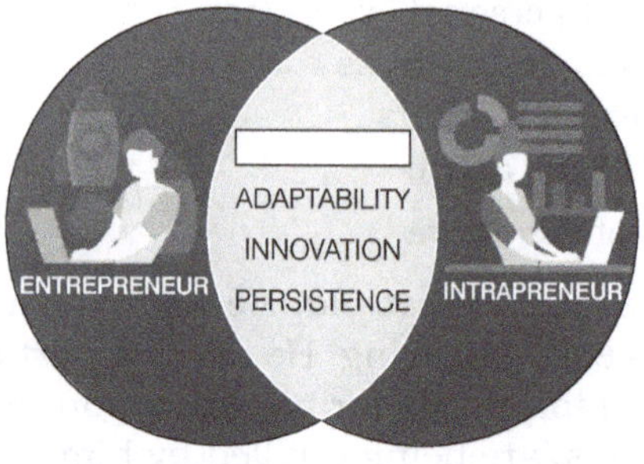

Identify the missing shared trait between entrepreneur and intrapreneur.

(a) Leadership
(b) Clarity of voice
(c) Invention
(d) None of these

Ans (a) Leadership

Fill in the Blanks

23 .... broadly classified entrepreneurs as innovative, imitative, fabian and drone.

Ans C Danhof

24 Kumar is a second generation member of a joint Hindu family business. He is rigid fundamental and cautious in his approach. He is a .... entrepreneur.

Ans fabian

25 .... concentrate more on production than on marketing.

Ans Technical entrepreneurs

26 XYZ is a local mobile company. It is using the same technology as big company uses to manufacture its products. This is an example of .... entrepreneur.

Ans imitative

27 .... basically refers to skills and inner strength that an individual possesses.

Ans Competencies

28 When faced with a cash crunch, Dhirubhai Ambani issued shares in 1977, when there was not much awareness regarding the share market. This shows that he had the competency of ....

Ans taking risk

29 Creating a demand in the market for the product/service requires .... on the part of the entrepreneur.

Ans persistence

30 .... refers to well-founded standards of right and wrong, that prescribes what an individual ought to do, usually in terms of rights, obligations, benefits to society, fairness or specific virtues.

Ans Ethics

31 According to ...... , "ethical entrepreneurship, in a nutshell, amounts to the achievement of ethical goals through entrepreneurship."

Ans Johan Wempe

32 .... can be defined as, "beliefs that guide actions and judgement across a variety of situation."

Ans Values

33 Attitude is basically a psychological phenomenon, hence it is ....

Ans invisible

34 Ranveer Singh appears in an ad, using 'Head and Shoulders' shampoo for dandruff problem. This advertisement tries to .... audience's attitude, so that they also use the same shampoo when faced with dandruff problem.

Ans influence

35 .... is an opportunity to learn.

Ans Failure

36 The process of motivation starts with a/an .... of an individual.

Ans unsatisfied need

37 'Intrapreneurship' word was first used by management consultant .... in the 1980s.

Ans Gifford Pinchot

State True or False

38 Mahesh is a farmer. He still uses traditional methods of cultivation and refuses to adopt the changes in modern technology related to farming. Mahesh is a drone entrepreneur.

Ans True

39 Reliance Industries was started by Dhirubhai Ambani and was then passed on to Mukesh and Anil Ambani. So, Mukesh and Anil are second generation entrepreneurs.

Ans True

40 Taking initiative is the most fundamental competency required in an entrepreneur.

Ans True

41 Ratan Tata shifted the manufacturing plant of Nano cars from Singur to Sanand due to unforeseen complexities. This shows that he was an innovator.

Ans False. This shows that he was a problem solver.

42 Entrepreneurs should have the competency of persuading and influencing others.

Ans True

43 Corporate Social Responsibility (CSR) exists with individuals or businesses who handle money or property for others.

Ans False. Fiduciary responsibility exists with them.

44 Core values are basic entrepreneurial values found in all the entrepreneurs. Research has shown that there are basically three core values.

Ans False. There are basically four core values.

45 In his quest for independence, Dhirubhai Ambani gave up his job in Yemen and returned back to India to start his own business. Core value discussed above is independence.

Ans True

46 Attitude is acquired and pervasive.

Ans True

47 In the absence of external intervention, attitude leads to intended behaviour.

Ans True

48 The process of motivation starts with a satisfied needs of an individual.

Ans False. The process of motivation starts with an unsatisfied need of an individual.

49 Maslow's Hierarchy of Needs Theory is based on the assumption that people are motivated by a series of six universal needs.

Ans False. It is based on the assumption that people are motivated by a series of five universal needs.

50 In Maslow's hierarchy of needs theory, safety needs are second in the pyramidical structure and emerge only after the physiological needs are fulfilled.

Ans True

Case Based Questions

51 Read the following article and answer the questions that follow

Label Cement Limited is cement manufacturing company that employees more than 100 employees. Vishnu, one of the employee came up with an idea of manufacturing grey cement from organic waste and plastic fillets. The management realised the feasibility of his idea and asked him to lead a team of 5 personnel and develop the product commercially.

Vishnu was very dedicated towards the production of the new product and worked hard for its success. He helped and motivated his team to work with their full potential and at last the product was manufactured. The product was tested for quality and the outcome was positive. The management was very impressed and offered Vishnu a higher position in the company and a share in profits of new project.

When asked by a senior manager how he managed to develop such a profitable product, Vishnu stated that he was firm on his idea and did not hesitated before suggesting it to the higher officials.

(i) Which competency of an entrepreneur is showcased by Vishnu?

(a) Creativity and innovation
(b) Risk taking and management
(c) Taking initiative
(d) All of the above

Ans (a) Creativity and innovation

(ii) Vishnu will be classified as a ....

(a) entrepreneur
(b) employee
(c) intrapreneur
(d) None of the above

Ans (c) intrapreneur

(iii) "Vishnu was very dedicated towards the production of the new product and worked hard for its success."

Which value of an entrepreneur is depicted by Vishnu?

(a) Self-reliance (b) Ownership
(c) Independence (d) Respect for work

Ans (d) Respect for work

(iv) What disadvantages would the company face if the management did not encouraged Vishnu's idea?

(a) Loss of innovative employee
(b) Loss of profit generating idea
(c) Both (a) and (b)
(d) None of the above

Ans (c) Both (a) and (b)

(v) "When asked by a senior manager how he managed to develop such a profitable idea, Vishnu stated that he was firm on his idea and did not hesitate before suggesting it to the higher officials."

Which of the following attitudes matches the above statement?

(a) Controlled ego
(b) Belief in oneself
(c) Timely decisions
(d) All of the above

Ans (b) Belief in oneself

52 Read the following article and answer the questions that follow

Sana and Rena are two sisters owning their own businesses. Rena wanted to take risks and opened her own nail salon. She was always fond of decorating nails, therefore, she studied nail art and started her own nail salon at a prime location in Mumbai.

Whereas, Sana did not wanted to take risks and was interested in her father's established business. Thus, Sana owns and operates her father's textile business.

Both sisters are different from each other and work according to their own capabilities. One day, both met and exchanged some words about their businesses. Sana stated that she has been in a loss since last six months.

Rena enquired about the processes and products and stated that Sana needs some innovation and creativity in her products to increase sales and profits.

Rena asked her sister what she wants to achieve and Sana replied that she wants to be stable and out of loss.

She wants the company to be safe from dissolution. So, Rena offered her some help by purchasing some sheets, textile bags and threads for her company. Rena also designed a plan for Sana and helped her innovate the business.

(i) "Sana owns and operates her father's textile business."

Sana is a .... entrepreneur.

(a) technical (b) motivated
(c) industrial (d) fabian

Ans (d) fabian

(ii) "Rena wanted to take risks and opened her own nail salon."

Rena is a .... entrepreneur.

(a) technical (b) motivated
(c) industrial (d) fabian

Ans (c) industrial

(iii) Which entrepreneurial competeny(ies) is/are not represented by Sana?

(a) Risk taking (b) Initiative
(c) Handwork (d) All of these

Ans (a) Risk taking

(iv) Which need of Maslow's theory is highlighted by Sana in the above case?

(a) Esteem needs
(b) Safety needs
(c) Self-actualisation needs
(d) All of the above

Ans (b) Safety needs

(v) Which characteristic of an entrepreneur is showcased by Rena in the above case?

(a) Effective risk taker
(b) Empathy
(c) Both (a) and (b)
(d) None of the above

Ans (c) Both (a) and (b)

Short Answer Type I Questions (2 Marks)

1 Entrepreneurs can be classified on a number of basis. State them.

Ans Entrepreneurs can be classified on the basis of their socio-cultural backgrounds, scale or potential of operations, generation of venture creation or personality characteristics exhibited by them.

2 Name the types of entrepreneurs according to Danhof. **CBSE TBQ**

Ans According to C Danhof, entrepreneurs are classified into following types

(i) Innovative Entrepreneurs
(ii) Imitative Entrepreneurs
(iii) Fabian Entrepreneurs
(iv) Drone Entrepreneurs

3 Explain in brief 'business entrepreneurs'.

Ans Business entrepreneurs are those who evolve an idea for a new product or service and then, set-up an enterprise and arrange resources to make an idea into reality. Most of the entrepreneurs belong to this category as majority of them is found in the field of small trading and manufacturing concerns.

4 The government launched a programme for pollution free zones and provides financial assistance to entrepreneurs. By including such assistance, Ms. A was induced to enter into entrepreneurship. This included in which category? Explain. **CBSE TBQ**

Ans Ms. A comes under the category of induced entrepreneurs. These entrepreneurs are not naturally inclined to start their own venture. They are generally induced to enter into business due to some personal compulsion. e.g. not being able to get a decent job or they enter into business to avail benefits of the schemes declared by the government.

5 Mr. Subhash Bhalla is the owner of 'Anupam Coffee Plantations' in Darjeeling. To which category of entrepreneurs does he belong to? He uses organic methods of agriculture.

Ans Mr. Subhash Bhalla is an agricultural entrepreneur. These entrepreneurs undertake agricultural and allied activities as an area of business.

They engage themselves in growing and marketing different crops, fertilisers and other inputs of agriculture by employing new and modern techniques, machines, good quality seeds and irrigation facilities.

6 What do you understand by 'basic competencies'? Are these competencies acquired or exist in an entrepreneur by birth?

Ans Basic competencies relate to the type of behaviour exhibited by the entrepreneur in performing various tasks related to the discharge of his functions as an entrepreneur. Some of these competencies already exist in an entrepreneur, which need to be identified and nurtured and some of these are acquired through training and practice.

7 An entrepreneur should have the competency of 'risk taking' and 'risk management'. Why?

Ans An entrepreneur generally ventures into new ideas and new services. There are several factors which will affect the success of his venture, *viz.* demand and supply in the market, resource availability, acceptability of the product design and service, etc.

All these factors are outside the control of the entrepreneur. Therefore, it can be said that an entrepreneur walks into the areas of uncertainty. So, an entrepreneur should have the competency of taking risks and when risk arises, he/she should be able to manage it.

8 Explain the term 'fiduciary responsibility' with the help of an example.

Ans Fiduciary responsibility exists with individuals or businesses who handle money or property for others.

The term 'fiduciary' refers to a relationship in which one person has a responsibility of care for the assets or rights of another person. e.g. this form of responsibility is generally witnessed in 'trusts' and 'companies'.

9 Define and explain 'business ethics'.

Ans Business ethics basically means to conduct business with a human touch in order to give welfare to the society. Business ethics are often guided by law.

Andrew Crane defines business ethics as, "Business ethics are the study of business situations, activities and decisions where issues of right and wrong are addressed".

10 What is meant by 'ethical standards'?

Ans Ethical standards include the virtues of honesty, compassion and loyalty. So, ethics also refers to the study and development of one's ethical standards. Also, it is necessary to constantly examine one's standards to ensure that they are reasonable and well-founded.

11 Explain following core values

(i) Respect for work

(ii) Innovation and creativity **CBSE TBQ**

Ans (i) **Respect for Work** The entrepreneurs have great respect for their work. Successful entrepreneurs believe that they can achieve anything through hard work and by respecting the work they do.

(ii) **Innovation and Creativity** Creativity is the ability to see new ways of doing things and innovativeness is the ability to make it work in practice.

12 Define entrepreneurial values.

Ans In relation to business, social values define the objective of the business, as well as, the manner in which business affairs should be conducted.

Entrepreneurs should possess certain qualities that guide and direct them and these are referred to as 'entrepreneurial values'.

13 Research studies have shown that there are certain core values which are found in entrepreneurs. State these values. Also state whether all entrepreneurs possess these values in same degree.

Ans Research studies have shown that there are basically four core values that are generally possessed by dynamic entrepreneurs.

These values are as follows

(i) Innovation and creativity

(ii) Independence or ownership

(iii) Respect for work

(iv) Quest for outstanding performance

No, these values are not present in all entrepreneurs in same degree, but rather in varying degrees.

14 Why attitude is called pervasive? **CBSE TBQ**

Ans Attitude has their presence felt in all aspects of society. It is formed in the process of socialisation and hence, may relate to anything in the world.

For instance, a person may have positive or negative attitude towards religion, politics, politicians or countries. So, because of these reasons, attitude is called pervasive.

15 There are certain attitudes present in an entrepreneur, which help him/her to achieve success. State any four such attitudes.

Ans Four attitudes present in an entrepreneur which help him/her to achieve success are as follows

(i) Have passion for business
(ii) Set an example of trustworthiness
(iii) Make timely decisions
(iv) Keep one's ego under control

16 Explain any two features of attitude. **CBSE TBQ**

Ans Attitude exhibits the following two features which are as follows

(i) **It is Invisible** Attitude is basically a psychological phenomenon which cannot be directly observed, but interpreted from the actions of an individual.
(ii) **It is Acquired** Attitude is generally learnt or acquired over a period of time.

17 Draw the model depicting the motivation process.

Ans

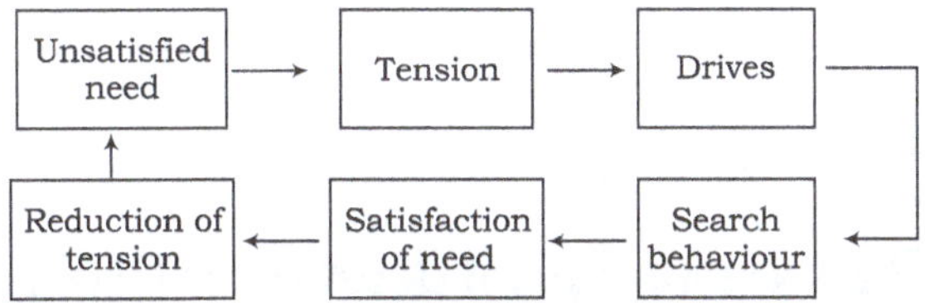

Motivation Process

18 What is the importance of an intrapreneur in an organisation? **CBSE TBQ**

Ans Intrapreneurs are the employees in a company, who usually have the resources and capabilities of the firm at their disposal. They turn special ideas or projects into a profitable venture. Intrapreneurs do well when the management empowers and supports them and hence, they show their interest in the organisation.

19 What is 'innovation time off' intrapreneurship program? **CBSE TBQ**

Ans This is a program initiated by Google. This program has a formal process for the selection of entrepreneurial projects, for the formal evaluation process and the monitoring of each Google approved entrepreneurial project.

For participating in this program, employees need to submit a project proposal with a timeline.

20 A company is bound to suffer if it does not promote 'intrapreneurship'. Give the consequences that a company can face if it does not encourage intrapreneurship.

Ans A company not encouraging intrapreneurship may face the following consequences

(i) Difficulty in retaining innovative employees.
(ii) Loss of profit generating ideas.

21 Differentiate between entrepreneur and employee on the basis of

(i) Status (ii) Risk Bearing

Ans Difference between entrepreneur and employee are as follows

Basis	Entrepreneur	Employee
Status	Entrepreneur is the owner of the enterprise.	Employee is the servant in the enterprise, owned by the entrepreneur.
Risk Bearing	Entrepreneur assumes all uncertainties and bears all risks.	Employee does not bear any risk.

22 Despite numerous research studies the theme of 'Why, when and how some people (entrepreneurs) and not others discover, evaluate and exploit entrepreneurial opportunities?' still needs intensive inquiry.

Entrepreneurial performance is influenced by both intrinsic individual and extrinsic environment factors. Earlier research indicates that a wide range of motives, personal traits, psychological characteristics and self-efficacy components influence the attitudes, intentions and behaviours of entrepreneurs.

However, despite existence of favourable factors, a potential entrepreneur might decide not to exploit entrepreneurial opportunity; certain people act differently from others in exactly the same situation. Earlier researchers, while using a variety of lenses, suggested a variety of frameworks and countless propositions.

Despite, the unified, comprehensive, and largely acceptable conceptualisations could not be evolved so far. In such a situation, more efforts in the direction of making an extensive review or meta-analysis and developing a more unified conceptualisation are required.

Here, a genuine attempt has been made to synthesize the outcomes of the surfeit of earlier researches so as to present the emerging hypothesized propositions and a simple framework of entrepreneurship and entrepreneurial competencies.

The outcomes of such an attempt provide a concrete base for more meaningful and useful further research as well as for setting up an agenda of entrepreneurial training for the future.

Source *Entrepreneurial Competencies: A Meta-analysis and Comprehensive Conceptualisation for Future Research*

(i) Identify the concept highlighted in the above paragraph.

(ii) State two factors influencing entrepreneurial performance.

Ans (i) Factors influencing entrepreneurial performance

(ii) Two factors influencing entrepreneurial performance are
(a) Action factors
(b) Environment factors

23 The characteristics of an entrepreneur are referred to as entrepreneurial competences, which enable the establishment, survival and development of a business enterprise. These elements of competence are subject to varying degrees of change.

The easiest ones are subject to modifications of knowledge resources, while the most difficult ones are personal features, which usually have an inborn character.

The interaction between the individual elements of an entrepreneur's competence and the actions undertaken by the entrepreneur takes place.

The effectiveness of the undertaken entrepreneurial activities depends on the competences, while competences are changed under the influence of feedback concerning the results of undertaken actions.

Therefore, the entrepreneur is constantly in an active interaction with the environment, which is a source of market opportunities and necessary resources for him.(Glinka & Gudkova, 2011, p. 122–123).

The results of many years of research carried out in the field of entrepreneurial personality features have so far not led to the creation of a consolidated concept, explaining the conditions for making decisions on setting up one's own company and achieving success on the market by entrepreneurs.

Source *own work based on (Glinka & Gudkova, 2011, p. 123) and (Urbaniec, 2016, p. 81-82)*

(i) Identify the concept highlighted in the above paragraph.

(ii) State any two competencies of an entrepreneur.

Ans (i) Entrepreneurial competency

(ii) Two competencies of an entrepreneur are
(a) Initiative
(b) Creativity and innovation

Short Answer Type II Questions (3 Marks)

1 "Entrepreneurs venture to take risks but some entrepreneurs are very shy and lazy by nature".

Mention the name of such entrepreneurs and explain. **CBSE TBQ**

Ans Such entrepreneurs are referred to as fabian entrepreneurs according to the classification given by Danhof.

These are usually second generation entrepreneurs in a family business. They follow the footsteps of their predecessors and are unwilling to take risks or start a new venture.

They initiate only when they are faced with a situation that will result in dwindling their relative share in the market.

2 Explain the types of entrepreneurs on the basis of 'use of technology'. **CBSE TBQ**

Ans On the basis of the use of technology, entrepreneurs can be, divided into two categories

(i) **Technical Entrepreneurs** They are the ones, who have the ability of developing new and improved quality of goods and services out of their own knowledge, skills and specialisation. They concentrate more on production than on marketing.

(ii) **Non-technical Entrepreneurs** They usually focuses on developing alternative ways of marketing the goods or services in order to promote their business. They concentrate more on marketing than on the technique of production.

3 'Systematic planning' is important for an entrepreneur. Why?

Or Why is systematic planning a must for an entrepreneur? **CBSE TBQ**

Ans Every entrepreneur has limited resources in terms of time, finance and manpower. They invest their life's savings and their total energy in creating entrepreneurial ventures and therefore, before putting the whole enterprise into operation, they should develop a detailed blueprint through systematic planning. Therefore, systematic planning is important for an entrepreneur.

4 Explain the following entrepreneurial competencies.

(i) Persistence (ii) Leadership
(iii) Systematic planning **CBSE TBQ**

Ans (i) **Persistence** Creating a demand in the market for the product/service is one of the main requirements for the success of the business venture and this calls for intense perseverance on the part of the entrepreneur. Road-blocks in his endeavour should not deter the entrepreneur.

(ii) **Leadership** An entrepreneur should also have leadership qualities, so that he/she is able to guide and motivate his/her team in times of distress. It is the will power and communication skills of a leader which oversees the success of a corporation, whenever a business faces any problem.

(iii) **Systematic Planning** Refer to text on page 32.

5 Explain the following competencies of an entrepreneur.

(i) Enterprise launching competencies
(ii) Enterprise management competencies

Ans (i) **Enterprise Launching Competencies** A lot of opportunities exists in the environment. Entrepreneurs respond to those opportunities and make efforts to ensure the best use of the resources which are available to all. Entrepreneurs should have the competency to identify opportunities and avail and facilitate the resources needed to launch their enterprise.

(ii) **Enterprise Management Competencies** An enterprise, whether big or small, demands management abilities. Various management functions such as production, marketing, finance, etc are crucial functions of an entrepreneur. These influence the result directly and therefore are necessary determinants for the sustenance of an enterprise. So, an entrepreneur should have management competency.

6 How competency in creativity and innovation helps an entrepreneur to meet the challenges of a situation? **CBSE TBQ**

Ans An entrepreneur might not have any new ideas, but he/she may use creative ideas and innovative products and services to meet the challenges of a situation and take advantage of the utility of an idea or a product to create wealth. e.g. packing shampoos in small sachets.

So, competency in creativity and innovation is basic trait required in an entrepreneur as it helps him/her to meet the challenges of a dynamic environment.

7 Mr. Vikram Singhal is a highly successful businessman, ranking among the top 10 industrialists of India. His company 'Singhal Group of Industries' operates in the fields of fertilisers, power generation and 3G network.

His son Virat Singhal, after completing his management degree from Oxford, decides to join the family business. Which type of entrepreneur is Virat? Explain other two types of entrepreneurs covered in this category.

Ans Virat is a second generation entrepreneur. These entrepreneurs do not start an enterprise on their own. Rather they join their family business which has already been started by their father.

Other two entrepreneurs covered in this category are

First Generation Entrepreneurs These entrepreneurs start their own business with their innovative skills and expertise. They usually combine different technologies to produce some goods or services. e.g. Infosys started by Narayan Murthy.

Third Generation Entrepreneurs These are those types of entrepreneurs wherein their grandparents have been original entrepreneurs (first generation), which has been passed onto their fathers (second generation) and then to themselves. e.g. Tata Industries.

8 Explain trading and industrial entrepreneurs.

Ans **Trading Entrepreneurs** They undertake trading activities either in domestic markets or in foreign markets. For this, they need to identify the potential of the market by looking at the market demand and hence, they put many ideas to promote their business. e.g. Big Bazaar.

Industrial Entrepreneurs They generally manufacture products and serve in the market which has a potential demand in the market. They are the one, who has the ability to transform economic resources and technology into a profitable avenue. e.g. Tata Industries.

9 "Innovation and creativity both are interrelated". Explain. **CBSE TBQ**

Ans Creativity is the ability to see new ways of doing things and innovativeness is the ability to make it work in practice.

So, creativity without innovativeness is of no use and both are interrelated, as one leads to the other. Entrepreneurs are guided by these values when they come out with creative ideas, new products, services, processes, etc to solve specific problems of the society.

e.g. people generally found it inconvenient to carry hair-oils in bottles while travelling. So companies came out with a creative idea of packing hair-oils in small sachets and then innovatively implemented this idea.

Thus, this helped them to generate additional profits with the help of implementing a creative problem.

Therefore, it can be concluded that creativity without innovation is of no use and that both are inter-related.

10 Define business ethics. Why is it important to an entrepreneur? **CBSE TBQ**

Ans **Definition of Business Ethics** Refer to Q. No. 9 of short answer type I questions (2 Marks).

Ethical behaviour can bring significant benefits to a business in the form of

(i) Attracting customers to the firm's products, which means boosting sales and profits.

(ii) Making employees wanting to stay with the business, thereby, reducing labour turnover and therefore, increasing productivity.

(iii) Attracting investors and keeping the share price high, thereby, protecting the business from takeover.

11 "An entrepreneur should not forget that for success to be long lasting, he will have to follow some ethical standards in their business practices". In the light of the given statement, state some ethical practices that can be followed by a business.

Ans Some ethical practices that can be followed by a business are as follows

(i) Providing good quality and correct quantity of goods to consumers.

(ii) Keeping in mind the environmental issues during production.

(iii) Paying the minimum and correct wages to the workers.

(iv) Not to use child labour in their factories.

(v) To make judicious use of natural resources.

12 What are the entrepreneurial values? Show by diagram. **CBSE TBQ**

Ans Entrepreneurs should possess certain qualities that guide and direct them and these qualities are referred to as 'entrepreneurial values'.

The various factors which influence entrepreneurial values are depicted in the diagram below

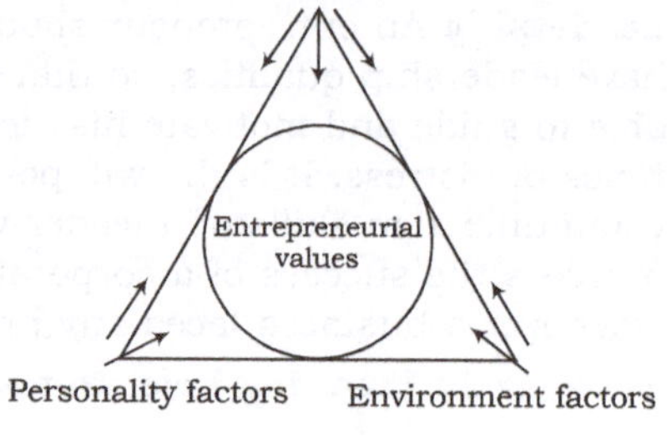

13 "The thoughts, feelings and tendencies to behave are acquired gradually". In the light of this statement, describe the sources of attitudes. **CBSE TBQ**

Or "Attitude is not by birth, it is acquired". Explain. **CBSE TBQ**

Or Briefly explain the various sources of attitude.

Ans Attitude is generally learnt or acquired over a period of time. The process of learning starts from childhood and continues throughout the life of an individual.

The thoughts, feelings and tendencies to behave are acquired or learned gradually from the following sources

(i) **Direct Personal Experience** The quality of a person's direct experience with the attitude object determines his/her attitude towards it.

(ii) **Group Associations** People are influenced to one degree or another by other members of the group to which they belong.

(iii) **Influential Others** A consumer's attitude can be formed and changed through personal contact with influential persons such as friends, relatives and experts.

14 Read the following story and answer the questions that follow

A young man was passing through a site of construction. He saw three labourers working at the site. He went to one of them and asked 'What are you doing here'? The worker answered, 'Don't you see? I am making out a living. I am working to earn'.

The young man moved towards the second man and asked him the same question. Pat came the reply 'Don't you see? I am constructing a wall'.

The young man moved towards the third man and repeated the question. The labourer replied 'Don't you see? I am building a beautiful mansion'.

(i) All three were doing the same work, then what differentiates them? **CBSE TBQ**

(ii) What is important to do a piece of work effectively and efficiently? **CBSE TBQ**

(iii) Whose answer reflected a positive attitude? **CBSE TBQ**

Ans (i) Their attitude towards work differentiates them.

(ii) Positive attitude towards work is important to do a piece of work effectively and efficiently.

(iii) The answer of the third labourer reflected a positive attitude.

15 'Human beings require respect in the society'. Explain the esteem needs in the Maslow's hierarchy of needs theory. **CBSE TBQ**

Ans 'Ego and esteem needs' rank fourth in the pyramidical structure and emerge after the social needs related to love and belongingness have been fulfilled.

These needs include the desire for self-respect, self-esteem and the esteem of others. When focused externally, these needs also include the desire for reputation, prestige, status, fame, glory, dominance, recognition, attention, importance and appreciation.

The distinct features of this need are

(i) This need arises only when the basic physiological needs, safety needs and social needs are fulfilled.

(ii) In general, employees at higher levels of the management chain experience this need.

(iii) This need is satisfied by greater autonomy in decision-making, appreciation from superiors, promotion to a coveted position, etc.

16 What are the basic differences between Maslow's and McClelland's theory of needs? **CBSE TBQ**

Ans Maslow's theory is based on the assumption that people are motivated by a series of five universal needs which he classified as

(i) Physiological needs

(ii) Safety needs

(iii) Belongingness and love needs

(iv) Esteem needs

(v) Self-actualisation needs

But, according to McClelland, people are driven by three motives, namely

(i) Achievement (ii) Affiliation (iii) Power

Also, according to Maslow's theory, one need emerges only if the previous one is satisfied.

But, according to McClelland's theory, the specified needs can appear collectively.

17 'We can appoint an employee but not an entrepreneur'. Describe difference between an employee and an entrepreneur in the light of this statement. **CBSE TBQ**

Ans Yes, the above statement is true that one can employ an employee but cannot employ an entrepreneur. An entrepreneur is the one who is innovative, capable, skillful, motivated, ready to take risk and works to earn profit.

They are the ones who start a new venture and introduce some new goods or services to the society. On the other hand, employees are the one who are hired by their entrepreneur to make their idea, a reality. An employee works to make the idea of an entrepreneur a reality, while entrepreneur is the one who initiates that idea. An entrepreneur hires an employee through the process of staffing.

18 Differentiate between an intrapreneur and an entrepreneur. **CBSE TBQ**

Ans Difference between an intrapreneur and an entrepreneur are as follows

Basis	Intrapreneur	Entrepreneur
Dependency	An intrapreneur is dependent on the entrepreneur.	An entrepreneur is independent in his operations.
Raising of Funds	Funds are not raised by the intrapreneur.	An entrepreneur himself raises the funds required by his business.
Risk	An intrapreneur does not fully bear the risk involved in the enterprise.	An entrepreneur bears the risk involved in the business.
Operation	An intrapreneur operates from within the organisation itself.	An entrepreneur operates from outside an organisation.

19 Intrapreneurship has become a necessity in today's corporate world. Why?

Ans Intrapreneurship has become a necessity because of the below mentioned reasons

(i) It helps organisations to grow.

(ii) It provides an environment conducive for innovation.

(iii) It helps organisations to effectively manage change.

(iv) It provides a platform to engage employees in work that is challenging and meaningful.

20 Do you think intrapreneur is necessary for an organisation? Support your answer with strong reasons. **CBSE TBQ**

Ans Yes, intrapreneurship is necessary for an organisation, as it is the best way of retaining talented and skilled staff, or otherwise these people may leave the organisation and develop their ideas on their own by starting their enterprise.

Keeping these talented staffs mean a win-win situation for both the enterprise as well as the talented employees.

We can take the example of Google, who has started the 'innovation time off, intrapreneurship program' to make use of those talented employees, who have the ability and idea to help the organisation earn huge profits.

21 Divij is a highly innovative person working in a cement company. He devised a new form of grey cement which is made from plastic fillets and organic waste.

His company immediately realised the potential of his idea and made him the head of the project to develop the above product commercially. He was also offered a share in profits of the above project. Is Divij an employee or an entrepreneur? Discuss. Also explain the difference between entrepreneur and employee.

Ans Divij is both an employee as well as an entrepreneur or more appropriately, he is an intrapreneur. Intrapreneurs are usually employees within a company, who are assigned a specific project, with instructions to develop it in the same manner as an entrepreneur. Intrapreneurs are capable individuals having the resources of the company at their disposal.

Their main job is to turn a specific project into a profitable venture for a company

Difference between Entrepreneur and Employee Refer to Q.No. 21 of short answer type I questions (2 Marks).

Long Answer Type Questions (5 Marks)

1 What do you mean by entrepreneurs? Mention the types of entrepreneurs. **CBSE TBQ**

Ans Entrepreneur is the person who starts an enterprise through the long process of entrepreneurship.

According to C Danhof, entrepreneurs are divided into following four types

(i) **Innovative Entrepreneurs** They introduce new products and methods of production. They are very aggressive in nature and exhibit cleverness to put the ideas into practice. e.g. Walt Disney.

(ii) **Imitative Entrepreneurs** They generally adopt or copy a suitable innovations and not innovate the same. They are very adaptive and flexible in nature. e.g. local mobile phone sellers.

(iii) **Fabian Entrepreneurs** They are the second generation entrepreneurs in a family business enterprise. They are generally risk-avoiders in nature, hence do not start a new venture. e.g. Joint Hindu Family business in India.

(iv) **Drone Entrepreneurs** They do not accept the opportunities coming to their way, they are not ready to make changes in their existing production methods. They are generally traditional in nature. e.g. farmers using traditional methods of cultivation.

2 Explain any four entrepreneurial competencies. **CBSE TBQ**

Or Briefly discuss the following competencies of an entrepreneur

(i) Quality performance (ii) Systematic planning
(iii) Leadership (iv) Persistence

Or 'Competencies is a set of defined behaviour'. State the type of competencies required by an entrepreneur and explain them. **CBSE TBQ**

Ans **Competencies of an Entrepreneur** Refer to text on page 31.

3 'Many problems are bound to come in the path of progress. Ratan Tata shifted the manufacturing plant of Nano cars from Singur to Sanand due to unforeseen complexities'. Which type of competency is shown here? Discuss. **CBSE TBQ**

Ans The competency discussed here is problem solving.

Once an entrepreneur is aware that he/she has ventured in a new business and has taken certain calculated risks, he/she should also be prepared for the problems that are bound to come in path of success of his/her venture. When faced with a problem, he/she should evaluate alternative strategies or resources that would help to solve the problem and in the process, generate new ideas, products or services.

So, an entrepreneur should possess the competency of 'problem solving', otherwise he/she would not be able to sustain his/her venture for long.

The following steps should be followed by an entrepreneur, when looking for solutions to a problem

(i) Identify the alternative solutions to the problem.

(ii) Arrange for the resources that would help to implement that particular alternative.

(iii) Identify any new idea, product or service that have evolved due to the above exercise.

In the example given above, in the light of unforeseen complexities in establishing a manufacturing unit at Singur, Ratan Tata came up with an alternative strategy to open that unit in Sanand.

So, he possesses the competency of 'problem-solving'.

4 Naman has just graduated from a college. His father wants him to take up a job, but Naman wants to be an entrepreneur.

He tries to convince his father by saying that he will venture into a business only if it is 'safe'.

Is Naman's argument valid? Which entrepreneurial competency is not possessed by Naman? Explain any three competencies of an entrepreneur.

Ans Naman's argument is not valid, as all businesses face uncertainty and the risk associated with it. Naman does not possess the entrepreneurial competency of risk taking and risk management.

For three competencies of an entrepreneur, refer to Q. No. 4 of short answer type II questions (3 Marks).

5 Explain the characteristics of an entrepreneur.

Ans Refer to text on page 33.

6 "Entrepreneurs cannot survive and grow without fulfilling the ethical responsibilities of the society". Explain. **CBSE TBQ**

Ans In today's world of increasing awareness among the consumers, the importance of ethics is greater than ever.

In order to survive and grow, entrepreneurs should work towards a model which is based on 3Ps, i.e. People, Planet and Profit.

Unethical behaviour such as adulteration, promoting misleading advertisements, cheating in weights and measures, black marketing, etc damage a firm's reputation and make it less appealing to stakeholders.

Also, it may lead to a fall in profits. Also, if a business does not give fair wages to its employees, or not provide them good working conditions, or exploit their employees, then it faces a large labour turnover rate which affects its productivity.

So, an entrepreneur should fulfill his/her ethical responsibilities and witness the long-term growth of his/her enterprise and also ensure cost and risk reduction.

7 "An entrepreneur who is fulfilling the ethics and moral responsibility towards society is an asset for society and should be allowed to survive and grow". Explain. **CBSE TBQ**

Ans An ethical entrepreneur follows the following practices

(i) He/She provides good quality products at reasonable prices to his/her customers.
(ii) He/She provides correct quantity of goods.
(iii) He/She keeps in mind environmental issues during production.
(iv) He/She pays reasonable wages to his/her workers and does not use child labour.
(v) He/She refrains from unethical trade practices such as adulteration, promoting misleading advertisements, cheating in weights and measures, black marketing, etc.
(vi) He/She makes judicious use of natural resources.

So, an entrepreneur providing the above valuable services is definitely an asset for the society and therefore, should be allowed to survive and grow.

8 Smita purchased a book from Sangam Book Stores. While reading the book, she found that 20 pages were missing. She informed about this discrepancy to the owner of the store, who assured Smita that he is willing to replace the book, if the publisher replaces the same.

After a week, the owner informed that the publisher has refused to replaces the book.

(i) Is the publisher's behaviour ethical?
(ii) Explain the meaning of ethical entrepreneurship.

Ans (i) No, the publisher's behaviour is not ethical as he has refused to replace a mutilated book.

(ii) Ethics refers to well-founded standards of right and wrong, that prescribe what an individual ought to do, usually in terms of rights, obligations, benefits to society, fairness or specific virtues.

Ethics means those standards that impose reasonable obligations on an individual to refrain from social and moral evils such as stealing, murder, assault and fraud. Ethics also mean the continuous efforts on the part of an individual for the betterment of his/her own moral beliefs and conduct.

Business ethics basically mean to conduct business with a human touch in order to give welfare to the society. Business ethics comprises of the study of proper business policies and practices regarding controvercial issues such as corporate governance, insider trading, bribery, discrimination, corporate social responsibilities and fiduciary responsibilities.

Business ethics are often guided by law or provide a basic framework that businesses may choose to follow in order to gain public acceptance.

According to **Andrew Crane**, "Business ethics are the study of business situations, activities and decisions where issues of right and wrong are addressed".

9 Explain in detail the various core values.

Ans Refer to text on page 35.

10 Explain features of attitude. **CBSE TBQ**

Ans Refer to text on page 36.

11 Briefly explain the following essential attitudes of an entrepreneur.
(i) Have passion for business
(ii) Set an example of trustworthiness
(iii) Make timely decisions
(iv) Be flexible, except with the core values

Or Explain any six essential attitudes of an entrepreneur. **CBSE TBQ**

Ans Refer to text on page 37.

12 Manish runs his own jewellery retail shop. He is well trusted by his customers. With changing times, he has also changed his way of business, by introducing light-weight jewellery, diversifying in diamond jewellery and introducing trendy designs in white gold jewellery.

He loves his business and is always the first to arrive and the last to leave. He had also ventured into the business of producing gold chains, but after sustaining a loss of ₹ 10 lakh, he closed that business. But, he did not dwell on that loss much, and was soon initiating certain other ventures. Quoting lines from the passage, identify the various attitudes possessed by Manish.

Ans The various attitudes possessed by Manish are as follows

(i) **Set an example of Trustworthiness** Lines from the passage which are indicative of this attitude is, 'He is well trusted by his customers'.

(ii) **Be Flexible** Lines from the passage bringing forth this attitude is, 'With changing times, he has also........... white gold jewellery'.

(iii) **Have Passion for Business** Lines from the passage indicative of this attitude are, 'He loves his business,....... last to leave.

(iv) **Rebound Quickly from Setbacks** Lines which bring forth this attitude are, 'He had also ventured into .... initiating certain other ventures'.

13 Motivation is a process, explain by a model. **CBSE TBQ**

Ans Motivation is essentially a process which starts with an unsatisfied need of an individual. Every individual possesses an urge or a need or a multitude of needs, desires or expectations.

These unsatisfied needs lead to tension within the individual and motivates him to search for ways to relieve his/her tension.

This leads to certain drives and searching alternatives to achieve one's goal which will eventually reduce tension.

For its model, refer to Q. No. 17 of short answer type I questions (2 Marks).

14 Explain in detail McClelland's theory of motivation. **CBSE TBQ**

Ans Refer to text on page 39.

15 Explain Maslow's theory of motivation. **CBSE TBQ**

Ans Refer to text on page 38 and 39.

16 Differentiate between an entrepreneur and an employee. **CBSE TBQ**

Ans The major difference between an entrepreneur and an employee are as follows (Any six)

Basis	Entrepreneur	Employee
Meaning	An entrepreneur is a person who works for himself.	An employee is a person who works for others.
Works for	An entrepreneur works for freedom.	An employee works for security.
Terms of Work	An entrepreneur himself decides his terms and conditions.	An employee works according to the terms and conditions laid down by his employer.
Degree of Freedom	Full freedom is enjoyed by the entrepreneur.	An employee does not enjoy any freedom.
Reward	Entrepreneurs are rewarded with profits.	Employee's reward is their salary.
Role Played by them	Entrepreneurs are solution finders.	Employees are problem solvers.
Perspective	Entrepreneurs look into the future.	Employees look into the past.

17 This study shed light on the impact of entrepreneurs' competencies on profitability and employee satisfaction. We used surveys conducted on 200 micro firms operating in Ghana.

We used both descriptive and regression to analyse the link between entrepreneur competencies, employee satisfaction and profitability.

The data from 150 participants suggest that entrepreneur competencies have a positive and significant effect on profitability. Additional, entrepreneur competencies have a positive and significant impact on employee satisfaction. Our findings clarify the role entrepreneur competencies play in enhancing profitability and employee satisfaction in the emerging market context.

Drawing on resource-based view, the paper addresses the 'human element' in entrepreneurship, thus enriching entrepreneurship debate, especially in Ghana.

Entrepreneurs have better understanding of the importance of competencies on their firm profitability and employee satisfaction. The authors concluded that entrepreneurs need robust competencies that can foster superior profitability and boost employee satisfaction level.

Source *International Journal of Management and Enterprise Development, 2021 Vol.20 No.1, pp.1 - 16*

(i) Identify the concept highlighted in the above paragraph.

(ii) Explain the entrepreneurial competencies of an entrepreneur.

Ans (i) Entrepreneurial competencies.

(ii) Refer to text on page 31.

18 The intrapreneurial behaviour of employees has become of strategic importance for the performance of organisations. However, the literature on intrapreneurship is dispersed and in need of an integrated overview of the characteristics and behaviours of intrapreneurial employees.

Based on a systematic literature review, we propose a new definition of intrapreneurship that emphasises its multilevel nature. Moreover, we propose a comprehensive model of intrapreneurship in which we integrate the new definition, dimensions, and determinants applicable to individual employees.

We find that innovativeness, proactiveness, risk-taking, opportunity recognition / exploitation and internal/external networking are important behavioural dimensions of intrapreneurship.

A certain skillset, a perception of their own capabilities, personal knowledge, past experience, the relation with the organisation, motivation, satisfaction and intention are the determinants of intrapreneurial behaviour that we derived from the literature review.

Based on our results and an integrated model of intrapreneurship, we suggest a number of future research directions

Source *Published online: 29th November, 2018 The Author(s) 2018*

(i) Identify the concept highlighted in the above paragraph.

(ii) Explain the importance of an intrapreneurship.

Ans (i) Intrapreneurial behaviour of an employee.

(ii) Refer to text on page 40 (Importance of intrapreneurship).

CASE STUDIES

Case 1

Carefully read the case study given below and answer the questions that follow

Steve Jobs and Apple

At 20, he and a friend (Steve Wozniak) started a company in a garage on 1st April, 1976. Later that year, the duo debuted the Apple I at the Homebrew Computer Club in Palo Alto, California. A local store offered to buy 50 machines and to finance the production, the duo had to sell their most expensive possessions. Jobs sold his Volkswagen van while Wozniak sold his Hewlett-Packard scientific calculator.

Jobs named their company - Apple in memory of a happy summer, he had spent as an orchard worker in Oregon.

By 1982 however, his company sales sagged in the face of competition from IBM's new PC. Jobs and Wozniak unveiled their new creation, Lisa to increase the company's bottom line, only to be another expensive failure.

Not wanting to dwell on these successive failures, they worked on a new machine called the Macintosh. Jobs was reported to commander the project, ruthlessly pushing its computer engineers and flying a pirate flag above the building where the team worked.

By 1986, the Mac, which Jobs promised to be 'insanely great' was a huge success. After 10 years, starting from 2 kids working in a garage, Apple computer had grown into a $2 billion dollar company with over 4,000 employees.

At 30, Jobs, however, was asked to leave the company he co-founded with Steve Wozniak. He left the company after losing a bitter battle over control with Apple's CEO, John Sculley (whom Jobs had recruited from Pepsi Cola).

After Apple

Apparently, both had different views of how the company should be handled and in one meeting, Sculley had told security analysts that Jobs would have no role in the operations of the company 'now or in the future'.

When Jobs heard of the message he said, 'You've probably had somebody punch you in the stomach and it knocks the wind out you and you cannot breathe. The harder you try to breathe, the more you cannot breathe. And you know that the only thing you can do is just relax, so you can start breathing again.'

Jobs sold over $20 million of his Apple stock, spent days bicycling along the beach, feeling sad and lost, toured Paris and journeyed on to Italy.

Recalling this publicly heart-breaking episode, Jobs said,

'I didn't see it then, but it turned out that getting fired from Apple was the best thing that could have ever happened to me.

The heaviness of being successful was replaced by the lightness of being a beginner again, less sure about everything. It freed me to enter one of the most creative periods of my life'.

During the next five years, he started two companies – NeXT Step and Pixar.

NeXT Step which produces NeXT, a $ 9,995 cube-shaped workstation, which aimed to create a workstation for research and higher studies, didn't do as well as Jobs had dreamed for. It did poorly and Jobs pulled the plug in 1993.

Pixar, however was a success story. The company produced the first computer-animated film, 'The Toy Story' and when Pixar's stock went public, Jobs became an instant billionaire.

Jobs, Back with a Vengeance

Meanwhile, his old company, Apple was under immense pressure from rival Microsoft and in 1996, posted billions of dollars in losses. In December 1996, Jobs convinced Apple to buy NeXT and make its software the foundation of the next generation Mac OS. The technology he developed at NeXT became the catalyst of Apple's comeback. Initially appointed as Apple's adviser, Steve Jobs was named Apple's interim CEO in 1997.

In 2004, he was diagnosed with cancer of the pancreas. Jobs was told that the cancer was incurable and he would only live for another three to six months.

Later, a biopsy showed that he actually had a very rare form of pancreatic cancer that is curable with surgery. He had the surgery and survived.

Under his leadership, Apple returned to profitability and introduced innovations such as the iPod.

Steve Jobs' Advice

'Sometimes life hits you in the head with a brick. Don't lose faith. I'm convinced that the only thing that kept me going was that I loved what I did. You've got to find what you love.

Your work is going to fill a large part of your life and the only way to be truly satisfied is to do, what you believe is great work. And the only way to do great work is to love what you do. If you haven't found it yet, keep looking. Don't settle. As with all matters of the heart, you'll know when you find it. And, like any great relationship, it just gets better and better as the years roll on.

So, keep looking until you find it. Don't settle. Your time is limited, so don't waste it living someone else's life. Don't be trapped by dogma which is living with the results of other people's thinking. Don't let the noise of others'opinions drawn out your own inner voice. And most important, have the courage to follow your heart and intuition. They somehow already know, what you truly want to become. Everything else is secondary'.

1 Danhof has classified entrepreneurs in four categories. To which category does Steve Jobs belong? Quote lines from the passage which indicate the same.

Ans According to the classification given by Danhof, Steve Jobs is an innovative entrepreneur. Lines which are indicative of this are "Not wanting to dwell on these successive failures, they worked on a new machine called the Macintosh".

2 Was Jobs a first generation entrepreneur or a second generation entrepreneur?

Ans Jobs was a first generation entrepreneur as he himself had started his company 'Apple' from a garage on 1st April, 1976.

3 An entrepreneur need not belong to only one category. He can belong to many. On the basis of the classification given in the chapter, into what different categories can Jobs be put? State giving reasons.

Ans Jobs can be put into different categories, as given below

(i) **Business Entrepreneurs** Because he developed an idea for a new product–Macintosh.

(ii) **Corporate Entrepreneurs** Because, he opened a company 'Apple' to carry on his business operations.

Case 2

Carefully read the case study given below and answer the questions that follow

Ethical Entrepreneurship

Read the following situations carefully

Three Character Types: Carly, Tonya and Jane

Entrepreneurship is increasingly studied as a fundamental and foundational economic phenomenon. Schumpeter (1950) and Kirzner (1978) were pioneers and their successors have generated a sizeable literature. Yet, entrepreneurship has received less attention as a moral phenomenon and correspondingly, less attention in the business ethics literature.

Consider the moral status of the entrepreneur in contrast to the two other types

(i) **Carly** As a student, Carly worked hard and received good grades. Upon graduation she took a job, but at the same time, saved money and worked on her business plan. When she was ready, she took the entrepreneurial plunge and started her own business, which she developed successfully and then, a few years later, sold it for $10 million.

She is now living the good life of travel, building her dream home, raising her family and managing her portfolio of investments.

(ii) **Tonya** She also worked hard in college and upon graduation, took a job in a financial institution. She discovered a flaw in its fund-routing procedures, which enabled her anonymously to divert $10 million to an offshore bank, from which it was quickly re-routed through several Caribbean and Swiss banks, ending up in account known only to Tonya.

One year later, Tonya resigned from her position at the financial institution and is now living in discreet luxury somewhere in Europe.

(iii) **Jane** While in college, Jane graduated with a good degree. Unfortunately, the summer after her graduation, Jane's parents died suddenly. Fortunately, they left her $10 million in their wills of which Jane immediately donated $9.9 million to charities devoted to the homeless, victims of floods and to the planting of trees in the Brazilian rainforest. Jane invested the remaining $100000 in a certificate of deposit earning 8% annually, the proceeds enabling her to live frugally and without too much discomfort.

Let us now ask the ethics question: Which of the three is the most moral? Whom should we uphold as the ideal? Should we teach our children and students to admire and strive to be like Carly, Tonya or Jane? All three require strength: It is not easy to build a successful business. It is not easy to figure out a con and get away with it. And it is not easy to give away all of one's money.

Tonya is representative of a predatory ethic, she harms others and uses the proceeds to benefit herself. She is representative of the zero-sum, gain at the expense of others practices widely condemned in the business ethics literature.

Jane is representative of an altruistic ethic: She is selfless and she places what she has at the disposal of others in society, keeping only the minimum for herself. She is representative of the 'social justice' practices widely praised in the business ethics literature.

Carly is the prototypical entrepreneur and is representative of a self-realisation, egoistic ethic. She creates value, trades with others and lives her dream life. Yet, she is not discussed in the business ethics literature. She is the invisible woman.

Yet, the character traits and value producing activities of entrepreneurs at least implicitly inform an ethic. To make this ethic explicit, let us begin with a standard description of the entrepreneur.

During the past few decades, there has been an explosion of new interest in entrepreneurs and their activities. Yet, only recently, serious research attention is known to have been devoted (in some developed countries) to the ethical problems encountered by entrepreneurs and their organisations. Entrepreneurs face uniquely complex moral problems related to basic fairness, personnel and relationships, distribution dilemmas and other challenges that need to be addressed by all concerned through appropriate legal framework, social order and perhaps also a 'Moral Re-armament Movement'.

In order to understand the role of ethics in entrepreneurship, we need to understand the concept of ethics in life. How should we live? Shall we aim at happiness or at knowledge, virtue or the creation of beautiful objects? If we choose happiness, will it be our own or the happiness of all? And what of the more particular questions that face us. Is it right to be dishonest in a good cause?

Can we justify living in opulence while elsewhere in the world people are starving? If conscripted to fight in a war we do not support, should we disobey the law? What are our obligations to the other creatures with whom we share this planet and to the generations of humans who will come after us?

Ethics deal with such questions at all levels. Its subject consists of the fundamental issues of practical decision-making and its major concerns include the nature of ultimate value and the standards by which human actions can be judged right or wrong.

1 Tonya is referred in the passage as 'representative of predatory ethics'. Why?

Ans Tonya is referred to as 'representative of predatory ethics' because she harms others and uses the proceeds to benefit herself.

She is representative of the zero-sum, gain at the expense of others practices widely condemned in the business ethics literature.

2 Who among the three, is representative of the 'social justice' practices widely praised in the business ethics literature?

Ans Jane is representative of an altruistic ethic. She is selfless and she places what she has at the disposal of others in the society, keeping only minimum for herself.

3 Who among the three is the prototypical entrepreneur?

Ans Carly is the prototypical entrepreneur and is representative of self-realisation, egoistic ethic. She creates value, trades with others and lives the dream life.

CHAPTER ASSESSMENT

Objective Type Questions (1 Mark)

1 C Donhof has broadly classified entrepreneurs into .... types.
(a) 5 (b) 6 (c) 4 (d) 3

2 Entrepreneurs that contribute to the development of underdeveloped economies are
(a) innovative entrepreneurs
(b) fabian entrepreneurs
(c) drone entrepreneurs
(d) imitative entrepreneurs

3 Competencies of an entrepreneur include
(a) initiative (b) creativity
(c) innovation (d) All of these

4 Entrepreneur acts as a ....

5 .... is a psychological phenomenon.

6 An entrepreneur who never prefer to go for a change is a drone entrepreneur. State true or false.

7 An entrepreneur is an employee who create innovative ideas. State true or false.

Short Answer Type I Questions (2 Marks)

8 State any two reasons of becoming an entrepreneur.

9 Define fabian entrepreneurs.

10 What do you mean by third generation entrepreneurs?

11 What is meant by ethical entrepreneurship?

12 Mention any two competencies of an entrepreneur.

Short Answer Type II Questions (3 Marks)

13 Explain in brief types of entrepreneurs based on the technology used in the business.

14 Differentiate between spontaneous entrepreurs and induced entrepreneurs.

15 Explain any three characteristics of an entrepreneur.

16 Which factors influence entrepreneurial values?

Long Answer Type Questions (5 Marks)

17 Explain the process of motivation.

18 Discuss in brief the importance of intrapreneurship.

19 Differentiate between entrepreneur and employee.

20 Discuss any five competencies of an entrepreneur.

For explanations scan the given QR Code

CHAPTER 03

Entrepreneurial Journey

In this Chapter...

- Idea generation
- Feasibility study
- Business plan
- Business plan execution

Idea Generation (Business Ideas)

Generating and evaluating business idea is an important step in the entrepreneurial process. Infact, it is the primary step in the process of foundation of a business. It involves spotting an idea, scanning of environment and finally selecting a product or service.

Selection of product or service is greatly influenced by the factors of environment. Thus, scanning of environment acts as an interface between idea spotting and selection of product or service.

Idea generation is the creative process or procedure that a person uses in order to figure out solutions to any number of difficult challenges. It involves coming up with many ideas in a group discussion, selecting the best idea or ideas, working to create a plan to implement the idea and then actually taking that idea and putting it into practice.

Misconceptions and Realities Related to Business Idea

The following misconceptions and realities related to business idea should be understood for a proper conception of a business idea

1. **Great Ideas Just Appear Out of Nowhere**
   This is the common misconception related to a business idea and assumes that business ideas appear out of nowhere.

   However, the reality is that, the best idea generators tend to develop a business idea in a structured and systematic way.

   They do not wait for the idea to appear itself. Instead, they approach idea generation as a top priority activity by devoting sufficient period of time to it.
2. **There are no Illogical Ideas**
   This is again a common misconception related to business idea and assumes that all business ideas are logical. But the reality is that, many business ideas may not be very good.

   However, to prevent idea generators from feeling that their contribution is not being valued, all ideas should be approached as worthy. Sometimes, a worthy idea can come from what earlier was thought to be an illogical idea.
3. **The Customer will Tell You What to Do, If You will only Listen**
   The best source of idea is undoubtedly the people, who will purchase an entrepreneur's products/services. But, the only problem with this belief is that, although customers can help identify unmet needs, more involvement with them is required in making a great idea workable. Simply listening to customers will lead to nowhere.

4. **We can Generate All the Ideas We will ever Need, If We Sit Down at a Meeting**
   Again, a very common misconception, that many ideas can be generated through a meeting.
   This can be true, but it should also be remembered that great ideas are best shaped through an ongoing dialogue, not restricted to a specific place and time. So, generating great ideas should not be restricted to a meeting.
5. **Great Ideas aren't the Problem, Implementing them Is**
   The reality is that, problems with implementation arise from not screening carefully enough, the ideas that are generated.
   If this were done, a lot of frustration could be minimised as ill-thought-out ideas could be screened out before even being implemented.

Process of Generating Ideas

Generating idea is an innovative and creative process. The process of generating ideas starts from where ideas come from, ways to generate ideas and the role of structured approach, analysis and intuition in the ways to generate ideas.

Where Ideas Come From?

All entrepreneurs need to have ideas to initiate their entrepreneurial ventures. The process of generating ideas is in itself an innovative process. The question is from where an entrepreneur can get the idea.

The different sources of idea are as under
- Individual interests or hobbies.
- Work experience, knowledge and skills.
- Existing products and current services surrounding the environment.
- Friends and families.

Ways to Generate Ideas

Ideas can be generated through structured approach or analysis and intuition. Structural approach is deliberately undertaken by an entrepreneur to generate ideas.

Various methods under this head are discussed ahead

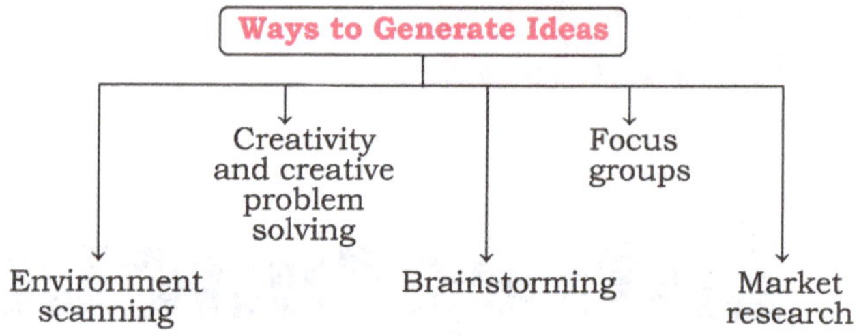

1. **Environment Scanning**
   One of the important techniques that can be used to generate ideas is environment scanning, i.e. the screening of large amount of information to detect emerging trends.
   A large amount of information is available from
   - Popular newspapers and magazines
   - Reviews
   - Government and consumer publications
   - Trade publications
   - Commercials, etc.

   An entrepreneur should scan this information to generate ideas. It requires a lot of effort, but the results are generally rewarding. The challenge in this method, however, is not having too little information to scan, it is having too much.
2. **Creativity and Creative Problem Solving**
   Creativity is the ability to combine ideas in a unique way or to make unusual associations between the ideas.
   It means cross thinking by seeing new angles, connections and approaches.
   For generating idea through this technique, a number of specific approaches can be used, which are as follows
   (i) **Attribute Listing** It is an approach, in which an entrepreneur develops a new idea by looking into positive and negative attributes of a product or service.
   (ii) **Free Association** It is an approach in which an entrepreneur develops a new idea through a chain of word associations, etc.

3. **Brainstorming**
   A group of persons sit together and generate a number of business ideas by innovating alternative ways of meeting the needs and solving problems. It is usually an unstructured discussion in which one idea leads to another. This is a very productive method for generating as many ideas as possible.
4. **Focus Groups**
   These groups of people provide information about projected products or services in a structured setting. In a focus group, a moderator focuses the group discussion on a number of issues. e.g. a focus group might look at a proposed product or service and answer specific questions asked by the moderator.

   Another method might be, that the focus group is given a moral general issue to discuss and the moderator simply leads the discussion based on interpretations made by the group. Thus, a focus group can provide outstanding techniques to generate innovative ideas and to screen proposed ideas and concepts.
5. **Market Research**
   This is a method of gathering information about products/services that already exist in the market. A systematic and in-depth study is undertaken to obtain useful data to determine demand and supply position for a particular product or service that is already available in the market. Such a research will help in getting new ideas for products and services.

Intuition as a Way to Generate Ideas

Intuition is a cognitive process, whereby, we subconsciously make decisions based on our cumulative knowledge and experiences. It is being called that 'Aha' feeling you get when your internal search engine hits its mark. You may have heard it called 'gut feeling'. Although, structured, methodical approaches to generate ideas are important, intuition can also play an important role. Intuition can be a powerful source of new ideas if you learn to use it.

Importance of Evaluating Ideas

Due to rapidly changing environment, it may seem that evaluating ideas is a waste of time and one should look for opportunity and grab it before the window of opportunity closes. However, there are good reasons that support evaluating ideas as an important step in researching the venture's feasibility.

These are as follows

Importance of Evaluating Ideas
- → To decide what is important
- → To identify strengths and weaknesses of the idea
- → To make the best use of limited resources
- → To minimise risks while maximising returns

1. **To Decide What is Important**
   Idea evaluation is important because it forces the entrepreneur to decide what is important to the entrepreneurial venture, which the entrepreneur is pursuing. Potential ideas should be evaluated against what is important for an entrepreneur.
2. **To Identify Strengths and Weaknesses of the Idea**
   Another reason for importance of idea evaluation is that all ideas are not created equally. Some ideas that an entrepreneur comes up with, will have better chances of success than others.

   By evaluating the strengths and weaknesses of each idea, the entrepreneur can identify and assess the strong and weak points, as it will help him/her in getting information which will help him/her to make a better decision.
3. **To make the Best Use of Limited Resources**
   Most entrepreneurs have limited amount of money, time, people or other resources that will be needed to pursue their entrepreneurial ideas. By evaluating their entrepreneurial ideas, they can make sure that their choices make the best use of those limited resources.
4. **To Minimise Risks while Maximising Returns**
   The final reason why idea evaluation is important is concerned with the desire to minimise risks while maximising returns.

Naturally, one does like to have the least uncertainty (risk) while getting the largest payback (return) from entrepreneurial ventures.

An entrepreneur puts in the effort to evaluate potential entrepreneurial ideas with a view to minimise the level of risk exposure while maximising the possible amount of payoff return.

CHECK POINT 01

1. Mention any one misconception related to business idea.
2. Define idea generation.
3. Mention any one source of idea.
4. Mention any one way to generate ideas.
5. What is market research?

Feasibility Study

Feasibility means whether the idea will be fruitful or not. This study relates to practical approach and viability of the proposed project.

This study analyses various risks involved in the project, potential aspects of the project like technical, financial, commercial and socio-economic, etc. This study helps the entrepreneur in implementing the project successfully.

Centre for Entrepreneurship at University of Rochester defines feasibility study as, "a controlled process for identifying problems and opportunities, determining objectives, describing situations, defining successful outcomes, and assessing the range of costs and benefits associated with several alternatives for solving a problem".

Importance of Feasibility Study for Entrepreneurs

Feasibility study is important for the entrepreneurs because it helps them to

- List in detail all the things they need to make the business work.
- Identify logistical and other business-related problems and solutions.
- Develop marketing strategies to convince a bank or investor that their business is worth considering as an investment.
- Serve as a solid foundation for developing their business plans.

Types of Feasibility Study

An entrepreneur may conduct the following types of feasibility studies

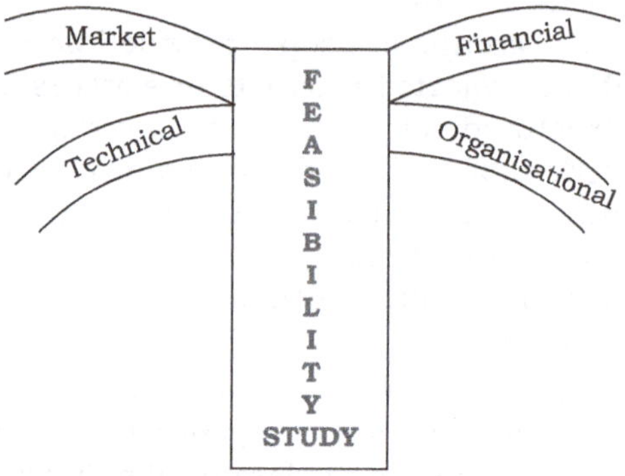

1. **Market Feasibility** This study includes a description of the industry, current market, anticipated future market potential, competition, sales projections, potential buyers, etc.
2. **Technical Feasibility** This study encompasses the details on how to deliver a product or service, i.e. materials, labour, transportation and where the business will be located, technology needed, etc.
3. **Financial Feasibility** This study projects how much start-up capital is needed, capital structure and sources of capital, returns on investment, etc.
4. **Organisational Feasibility** This study defines the legal and corporate structure of the business and may also include professional background information about the founders and what skills they can contribute to the business.

Features of Feasibility Study

The features possessed by a feasibility study are as follows

- A feasibility study is a process in which an idea is studied to see if it is 'feasible', that is, if and how it will work.

- A comprehensive feasibility study looks at the entire structure, needs and operations of a business.
- A limited or project feasibility study looks at one specific task, programme, idea or problem.
- A feasibility study looks at both sides considering advantages and disadvantages, and troubleshoots potential problems.
- A feasibility study is not a business plan, but serves as a foundation for developing a business plan.
- A market feasibility study is not a marketing plan, but studies markets and market potential, and can be used to support or develop a marketing plan.
- In addition to a business plan, an investor or lending institution may require the submission of a feasibility study before considering the request for capital.

A Good Outline of a Feasibility Study

A good outline of a feasibility study is given below

- Introduction
- Product or service
- Technology
- Market environment
- Competition
- Industry
- Business model
- Market and sales strategy
- Production operations requirements
- Management and personnel requirements
- Regulations and environmental issues
- Critical risk factors
- Financial predictions including balance sheet, income statement, cash flow statement, break-even analysis and capital requirements
- Conclusion

Opportunity Assessment

It is a more in-depth review of business opportunity including market research and due diligence that includes intellectual property analysis, opportunity development timing, legal liability issues, applications of the opportunity, barriers to entry, industry trends, growth potential, market positioning, competitive analysis, financial projections and pricing, resource requirement analysis and licensing, etc.

CHECK POINT 02

1. What do you mean by feasibility study?
2. Name any two types of feasibility study.
3. State any one reason that indicate importance of feasibility study for entrepreneurs.
4. Mention any one feature of feasibility study.
5. Mention any two points of a good outline of a feasibility study.

Business Plan

A business plan is a written summary of various elements involved in starting a new enterprise, of how the business will organise its resources to meet its goals and how it will measure its progress.

It describes the nature and context of the business opportunities and plans to exploit the opportunity. It is usually an integration of functional plans in finance, marketing, manufacturing and human resources.

Purposes Served by a Business Plan

A business plan serves the following purposes

- Provides a blueprint of actions to be taken in future.
- Guides the entrepreneur in raising the factors of production.
- Serves as a guide to organise and direct the activities of the business venture.
- Helps in measuring the progress of the venture at successive stages.
- Communicates to investors, lenders, suppliers, etc., about initiating the programmes of the business.

Elements of a Business Plan

Although, it is in the interest of a business of any size to prepare a business plan, yet the plan size may vary depending on the size of the business and complexity of operation.

e.g. the manufacturer of computer while entering a new market would definitely need a comprehensive business plan, but an entrepreneur who will be opening a small stationary shop will not require a detailed plan.

To be effective, an ideal business plan must define the following points

Elements of a Business Plan

- Objectives and strategies of the business
- Customer scenario
- Market segments
- Products and services to be offered
- Sales forecast
- Steps required to attain the objectives
- Description of the distribution system
- Promotional activities
- Pricing decisions

1. **Objectives and Strategies of the Business**
   The primary element to be defined by a business plan are the objectives and strategies of the proposed business. These objectives and strategies define the overall premises of the plan.

2. **Customer Scenario** The next element to be addressed by the business plan relates with the customer scenario.

   This part of the business plan identifies the potential customers of the business, choices available with them, their concerns and apprehensions and the solutions offered by the proposed business.

3. **Market Segments** This element of the business plan discusses the probable segments in which the market of the product/service offered by the business can be divided.

4. **Products and Services to be Offered** This segment of the business plan elaborately discusses the products/services offered by the business.

   It also campares it's products/services with the products/services offered by the competitors.

5. **Sales Forecast** This is an important element of the business plan, as it helps to assess the future viability of the business. It is also important because investors decision is influenced by this aspect.

6. **Steps required to Attain the Objectives** This is particularly an elaborative aspect, in which the various steps to be undertaken to achieve the objectives are specified.

7. **Description of the Distribution System** This element of the business plan describes the proposed distribution system for the product/services offered.

   The business can opt for direct or indirect channel of distribution, based on it's individual factors.

8. **Promotional Activities** This element addresses the problem of promoting the product/service and the various elements of promotion mix to be used in this regard.

9. **Pricing Decisions** This aspect of the business plan discusses the price of the product/service and the factors considered while arriving at this price.

General Format of a Business Plan

The general format of a proposed business plan is given below

1. **General Introduction**
   - Name and address of business.
   - Name and address of entrepreneur.
   - Stakeholders of business.
   - Nature of business and customers.
2. **Business Venture**
   - Product(s) to be offered.
   - Service(s) to be offered.
   - Scale of business operation.
   - Type of technology used.
   - Type of skilled personnel required.
3. **Organisational Plan**
   - Form of ownership, viz. sole proprietorship, partnership or joint stock company.
   - Identification of business, associated partners/members, etc.
   - Administrative structure.
   - Identification of management team.
4. **Production Plan**
   - Details of manufacturing process.
   - Physical infrastructure required.
   - Types of plant and machinery.
   - Raw materials to be used.
   - Requirement of power, water, etc.
5. **Human Resource Plan**
   - Categories of human resources or staff required.
   - Human resource already identified.
   - Human resource required to be procured.
   - Time frame for procurement of human resource.
6. **Marketing Plan**
   - Products and services offered.
   - Pricing policies.
   - Promotional strategies.
   - Logistics for distribution.
   - Channels of distribution.
7. **Financial Plan**
   - Break-even analysis.
   - Fixed capital requirements.
   - Working capital requirements.

- Sources of capital.
- Schedule of procurement of capital.
- Schedule of procurement of asset.
- Cash flow projection.

8. **Miscellaneous/Appendix**
   - Market research report.
   - Contract with vendors.
   - Contract with financial institutions.
   - Types of business risk.
   - Contingency plan.

Business Plan Execution

Execution of a business plan means putting a business plan into action. An efficient execution of the business plan is the key to success of a business, while inefficient execution might lead to its failure.

Key for a Successful Execution

An organisation should ensure proper execution of its business plan and this can be achieved through alignment. Strategies, people and work processes need to be effectively linked.

The strategic plan must be understood by the entire organisation. The right people need to be in the right jobs to allow for maximum work performance and action plans must be developed, implemented and reviewed. Communication channels should be effective, so that the whole organisation works in a sync.

To effectively align strategies, people and the tactical action plans that lead to a successful execution, a lot of hard work and diligent communication must happen.

Fundamentals for a Successful Execution of a Business Plan

Although, there is no singular process to manage the execution of business plan, there are basic processes and fundamentals to be followed

- After establishing the broad mission, vision and strategy for the organisation, core specific quantifiable goals to support the strategy must be formulated. These goals should be formulated, keeping in view the core competencies of the organisation.
- The organisation must be evaluated. Does the organisation has the right people with the right skills in the right job? Should human resources be reallocated? Does the organisation has the right number of employees in the appropriate departments? The answers to these questions will help an entrepreneur to correct deviations and ensure optimum performance.
- The key initiatives and broad actions that must be accomplished to achieve the strategy should be identified. The transitional issues or the gaps between where the organisation is today and where it plans to be, should be identified. The initiatives should be implemented throughout the organisation.

  They must be consistently understood in all functional departments. Every employee needs to understand his/her individual role in accomplishing some aspects of the plan.
- A budget should be developed to support the plan. This may be an iterative process until the right combination of strategies, tactics and financial prudence is achieved.
- Communication should be well effective. The message should be communicated to the entire organisation. Appropriate compensation and reward systems should be developed to support the future vision of the organisation.
- Decision filters should be created that help to guide the organisation through a thought process for those times, when the organisation faces a concept that opposes its strategy.
- A review process should be established. As the markets, customers, competitors, government regulations, economy etc. evolve; some priorities and possibly some goals, may change. Go back to the beginning, review each step and determine if further changes are necessary.

Causes of Failure of Business Plans

Many business plans fail because strategies are not executed well. The failure to execute the plan, not the plan itself, is most often cited as the reason why a strategic plan has underperformed.

Therefore, a business plan should be executed with utmost diligence. Due-diligence in execution of a plan is also important because failure of a business plan creates significant frustration and cynicism within an organisation and negatively impacts a business's reputation. So, to avoid a business plan from failing, care should be taken to effectively execute it.

Difference between Feasibility Study and Business Plan

Basis	Feasibility Study	Business Plan
Meaning	Feasibility means whether the idea is fruitful or not. This study relates to practical approach and viability of the proposed project. It helps to determine whether an idea or business is a viable option or not. It is completed prior to the formation of the business plan.	Business plan is a written summary of various elements involved in starting a new enterprise, of how the business will organise its resources to meet its goals and how it will measure its progress. The business plan is developed after the business opportunity is created and is found to be feasible.
Objective	Before investing anything in a new business, a feasibility study is carried to find out if the business venture is worth the time, effort and resources. This study is filled with calculations, analysis and estimated projections.	A business plan is mostly made up of tactics and strategies to be implemented in order to facilitate the growth of the business.
Linkage	A feasibility study can readily be converted to a business plan.	A business plan can be based on a feasibility study.
Benefit	Feasibility study helps an entrepreneur to assess the viability of his/her idea.	Business plan helps a business to sustain and grow.

CHECK POINT 03

1. Define business plan.
2. State any one purpose of a business plan.
3. Mention any one element of business plan.
4. Which is the first heading in the general format of a business plan?
5. Write one cause of failure of business plan.

EXAM PATTERN EXERCISE

Objective Type Questions (1 Mark)

Multiple Choice Questions

1 .... is an approach in which an entrepreneur develops a new idea by looking at the positive and negative attributes of a product or a service.

(a) Free association (b) Attribute listing
(c) Focus groups (d) Brainstorming

Ans (b) Attribute listing

2 Which of the following is/are the way(s) of generating ideas?

(a) Focus groups (b) Brainstorming
(c) Environment scanning
(d) All of the above

Ans (d) All of the above

3 Evaluating an idea is important because it helps to

(a) minimise risks (b) maximise returns
(c) Both (a) and (b) (d) None of these

Ans (c) Both (a) and (b)

4 A good outline for a feasibility study includes

(a) technology (b) business model
(c) industry (d) All of these

Ans (d) All of these

5 .... feasibility study includes a description of the industry, current market, anticipated future market, potential competition etc.

(a) Market
(b) Technical
(c) Financial
(d) Organisational

Ans (a) Market

6 Which one is not an element of business plan?

(a) Promotional activities
(b) Pricing decisions
(c) Environmental scanning
(d) None of the above

Ans (c) Environmental scanning

7 Vibhor wants to know the details related to products or services to be offered in the business in which he is planning to invest. Which part of business plan should he look into?

(a) General introduction (b) Business venture
(c) Organisational plan (d) Production plan

Ans (b) Business venture

8 Which amongst the following is/are the elements of a business plan?

(a) Customer scenario (b) Market segment
(c) Sales forecast (d) All of these

Ans (d) All of these

9 Marketing plan contains information related to

(a) products and services offered
(b) pricing policies
(c) physical infrastructure
(d) Both (a) and (b)

Ans (d) Both (a) and (b)

10 Megha wants to start her own business to supplement her family income. However, she does not have any business idea. Instead of actively searching for an idea, she believes that a great business idea will appear automatically.

Which misconception related to business idea is indicative here?

(a) Great ideas just appear out of nowhere
(b) There are no illogical ideas
(c) Implementing ideas is a problem
(d) None of the above

Ans (a) Great ideas just appear out of nowhere

11 Which of the following is not a purpose served by a business plan?

(a) It provides a blueprint of actions to be taken in future
(b) It serves as a guide to organise and directs the activities of the business venture
(c) It helps in measuring the progress of the venture at successive stages
(d) None of the above

Ans (d) None of the above

12 **Assertion** (A) Generation of ideas is not restricted to meetings.

Reason (R) Great ideas can be generated elsewhere also.

Alternatives

(a) Both Assertion (A) and Reason (R) are correct
(b) Assertion (A) is correct, but Reason (R) is incorrect
(c) Assertion (A) is incorrect, but Reason (R) is correct
(d) Both Assertion (A) and Reason (R) are incorrect

Ans (a) Both Assertion (A) and Reason (R) are correct

13 **Assertion** (A) Feasibility plan helps the entrepreneur by estimating the human and material resources required at various stages.

Reason (R) Feasibility plan does not act as guideline for implementation of the project.

Alternatives

(a) Both Assertion (A) and Reason (R) are correct
(b) Assertion (A) is correct, but Reason (R) is incorrect
(c) Assertion (A) is incorrect, but Reason (R) is correct
(d) Both Assertion (A) and Reason (R) are incorrect

Ans (b) A feasibility study looks at both sides considering advantages as well as disadvantages and troubleshoots potential problems.

14 Given below are types of feasibility plan in Column I and their features in Column II. Match them correctly.

Column I	Column II
A. Financial feasibility	(i) Helps the entrepreneur to maximise its production.
B. Market feasibility	(ii) A detailed investigation is done to find out how to import the technology etc.
C. Technical feasibility	(iii) Feasibility report must contain a detailed plan for marketing strategies.
D. Organisational feasibility	(iv) There should be holistic assessment of the enterprise.

Codes

	A	B	C	D		A	B	C	D
(a)	(iv)	(iii)	(ii)	(i)	(b)	(ii)	(i)	(iii)	(iv)
(c)	(iii)	(iv)	(ii)	(i)	(d)	(ii)	(i)	(iv)	(iii)

Ans (a) (iv) (iii) (ii) (i)

15 Given below are opportunity assessment factors in Column I and their features in Column II. Match them correctly.

Column I	Column II
A. Demographic	(i) It includes all the affairs related to government affairs.
B. Technological	(ii) It consists of GDP, National Income etc.
C. Economic	(iii) Refers to human population in terms of its size, density etc.
D. Political	(iv) Refers to changes that take place in the method of production.

Codes

	A	B	C	D		A	B	C	D
(a)	(iv)	(iii)	(ii)	(i)	(b)	(ii)	(i)	(iii)	(iv)
(c)	(iii)	(iv)	(ii)	(i)	(d)	(ii)	(i)	(iv)	(iii)

Ans (c) (iii) (iv) (ii) (i)

16 Which way of generating idea is highlighted in the given picture?

(a) Environment scanning
(b) Brainstorming
(c) Market research
(d) None of these

Ans (b) Brainstorming

17 Which concept is highlighted in the given picture?

(a) Idea generation
(b) Feasibility study
(c) Both (a) and (b)
(d) None of the above

Ans (b) This study analyses various risks involved in the project and potential aspects of the project like technical, financial etc.

Fill in the Blanks

18 .... is the first step in the process of finding a business.

Ans Business idea

19 A very common .... is that many ideas can be generated through a meeting.

Ans misconception

20 Evaluating idea is an important step in researching the venture's ....

Ans feasibility

21 .... study encompasses the details on how to deliver a product or service.

Ans Technical feasibility

22 A .... is a written summary of various elements involved in starting a new enterprise.

Ans business plan

23 .... of a business plan means putting a business plan into action.

Ans Execution

24 A business plan should be executed with ... .

Ans utmost diligence

25 Business plans generally fail because the entrepreneurs are not able to .... the plan properly.

Ans execute

26 Adhiraj is planning to venture into the business of manufacturing ventilators to cash on the demand generated due to the outbreak of corona pandemic. The plan size for his venture will be ....

Ans big

27 PQR Limited wants to diversify its operations. To generate idea related to the product in which to diversify, the CEO of the company, Mr Rajat Shekhar, called a meeting. In the meeting, an unstructured discussion took place where a number of business ideas were generated by innovating alternative ways of identifying the product and zeroing down to one such product. The idea here is being generated through ... .

Ans brainstorming

State True or False

28 A great business idea can just appear out of nowhere.

Ans False. Business idea is developed in a structured and systematic way.

29 Focus groups provide information about projected products or services in a structured setting.

Ans True

30 Evaluating ideas is important for the entrepreneurs as it helps them to identify logistical and other business related problems and solutions.

Ans False. The above is facilitated with the help of feasibility study.

31 Opportunity assessment is an indepth review of business opportunity including market research and due diligence.

Ans True

32 An entrepreneur who wants to open a small grocery shop in his colony will require a comprehensive and detailed plan.

Ans False. He will not require a comprehensive and detailed plan.

33 'Sales forecast' element of the business plan helps to assess the future viability of the business.

Ans True

34 Organisational plan contains the information related to products and services offered, scale of business operation, type of technology used etc.

Ans False. The above stated information is contained in 'business venture' plan.

35 For the successful execution of business plan, a budget should be prepared to support it. Preparing a budget is an iterative process.

Ans True

36 Feasibility study and business plan serve one and the same objective.

Ans False. A feasibility study is carried to find out if the business venture should be undertaken whereas a business plan is prepared to facilitate the growth of the business.

Case Base Questions

37 Read the following article and answer the questions that follow

Ritu and Pawan are married for more than 4 years and are now shifting to a new locality with better facilities. Both are very excited about the new phase of their lives. Ritu and Pawan are working professionals and leave their home in the morning till evening when they come back. One day, after shifting to their new home, Ritu and Pawan went for a walk but there was a short circuit in the house due to which a fire broke out.

When they saw this they tried to stop the fire using water, sand and various things before the fire service reached the location.

Nothing worked and most of their belongings were destroyed. They became hopeless. After that day, Pawan became curious of fires and started researching on everything that causes fire and that can immediately stop or reduce fire breakout. With intense research and experimenting in his free time, Pawan came out with a special fire bomb that can reduce fire for some time until the fire service arrives.

He developed a prototype with the help of his wife and took it to the fire station for testing. The fire fighters tested the product and it was a success.

Pawan and Ritu saw an opportunity in the product and after analysing various risks associated with the venture and getting enough information, left their jobs to invest their time and efforts on the product. They named the product 'FIREGO' and started a company to market and sell the product. They registered as a company and sold some of equity to investors in return of funds. Ritu and Pawan developed a plan containing the pricing, advertising and distribution strategies for the product and formed a team to take the product to the next level.

(i) Pawan used the process of .... to find solution for his problem.

(a) creativity (b) innovation
(c) research
(d) idea generation

Ans (d) idea generation

(ii) Which of the following is the source of Pawan's idea?

(a) Friends or family
(b) Work experience
(c) Problems or difficulties
(d) All of the above

Ans (c) Problems or difficulties

(iii) "After that day, Pawan became curious of fires and started researching on everything that causes fire and that can immediately stop or reduce fire breakout."

Pawan generated the idea of developing 'FIREGO' through the

(a) market research
(b) brainstorming
(c) focus group
(d) All of the above

Ans (a) market research

(iv) "Pawan and Ritu saw an opportunity in the product and after analysing various risks associated with the venture and getting enough information, left their jobs to invest their time and efforts on the product."

Which concept is highlighted above?

(a) Idea evaluation
(b) Idea generation
(c) Feasibility study
(d) None of the above

Ans (c) Feasibility study

(v) "Ritu and Pawan developed a plan containing the pricing, advertising and distribution strategies for the product and formed a team to take the product to the next level."

Which of the following types of business plan is highlighted in the above text?

(a) Organisational plan
(b) Financial plan
(c) Operational plan
(d) Marketing plan

Ans (d) Marketing plan

38 Read the following article and answer the questions that follow

'All Natural Cosmetics' is a popular cosmetics brand that produces and sell organic and herb based cosmetic products. The company has been in the market for more than 5 years and is now facing the issue of stable sales and profits where, the profits are not increasing by even a slight percentage. The general manager called a meeting of all the departmental managers and started an unstructured discussion to reap some innovative ideas for the brand.

In the discussion, the marketing manager suggested that the company should offer customised make-up and grooming kits to its customers. An online survey should be circulated to each customer asking for their priorities and then a customised kit with the customer's name engraved on it should be made. As it would be a customised product, higher prices will be accepted by the market. A team was formed and the idea was evaluated by the team.

After careful evaluation of the idea, the management showed a green signal to the idea. Another research and study was done by the management to extract the capital requirements, sources of capital and expected return for developing the kits. After all this, a detailed summary of all the elements was made that are required to go onboard with the new business idea. The summary focused on the production process and the distribution of the products to the customers.

It was decided that the orders will be taken from the website or the mobile application and the orders would be delivered to door. The company started taking customised orders and giving people what they want in their make-up kit rather than ordering the kit with same products. The customers can now order all different products of their choice.

The idea was a huge success and the business came out of stagnant profits due to the sales made after launching this new product idea.

(i) "The general manager called a meeting of all the departmental managers and started an unstructured discussion to reap some innovative ideas for the brand."

Which technique of idea generation is discussed in the above text?

(a) Market research
(b) Focus group
(c) Brainstorming
(d) Creative problem solving

Ans (c) Brainstorming

(ii) What advantages did 'All Natural Cosmetics' get for evaluating the business idea?

(a) Minimised risks
(b) Best use of limited resources
(c) Identify strengths and weaknesses of the idea
(d) All of the above

Ans (d) All of the above

(iii) "Another research and study was done by the management to extract the capital requirements, sources of capital and expected return for developing the kits."

Which of the following concepts is discussed above?

(a) Market study
(b) Financial feasibility
(c) Operational feasibility
(d) Organisation feasibility

Ans (b) Financial feasibility

(iv) "After all this, a detailed summary of all the elements was made that are required to go on board with the new business idea."

The detailed summary is called a ....

(a) business plan (b) mission
(c) vision (d) None of these

Ans (a) business plan

(v) Which of the following idea generation sources is depicted in the above case?

(a) Innovation and creativity
(b) Problem solving
(c) Both (a) and (b)
(d) None of the above

Ans (c) Both (a) and (b)

Short Answer Type I Questions (2 Marks)

1 Ideas can come from a number of sources. Name some sources.

Ans The different sources of ideas are as under

(i) Individual interests or hobbies.

(ii) Work experience, knowledge and skills.

(iii) Existing products and current services surrounding the environment.

(iv) Families and friends.

2 What do you mean by environment scanning? **CBSE TBQ**

Ans Environment scanning is one of the important techniques that can be used to generate ideas. In this method, a large amount of information is screened to detect emerging trends.

An entrepreneur scans the information to generate ideas.

This method required a lot of effort, but the results are generally rewarding.

3 What is brainstorming? **CBSE TBQ**

Ans Brainstorming is a method to generate ideas in which a group of people sit together and generate a number of business ideas by innovating alternative ways of meeting the needs and solving problems.

It is usually an unstructured discussion in which one idea leads to another. This is a very productive method for generating as many ideas as possible.

4 To scan the environment, a large amount of information is required. List some of the sources from where such information can be assessed.

Ans Information for environment scanning can be assessed from

(i) Popular newspapers and magazines

(ii) Reviews

(iii) Government and consumer publications

(iv) Trade publications

(v) Commercials, etc

5 What are focus groups? **CBSE TBQ**

Ans These groups of people provide information about projected products or services in a structured setting. In this group, a moderator focuses the group discussion on a number of issues.

Another method might be that the focus group is given a moral general issue to discuss and the moderator simply lead the discussion based on interpretations made by the group. Thus, a focus group can provide an outstanding technique to generate innovative ideas.

6 Akshay wants to start a business after completing his studies. However, he does not have any business idea.

He thinks that a great idea related to a business venture will appear out of nowhere. Is Akshay justified in his thinking? Discuss.

Ans No, Akshay is not justified in his thinking. He believes in a common misconception related to a business idea, that great business ideas appear out of nowhere.

However, the reality is that the idea generators develop a business idea in a structured and systematic way.

7 To check the feasibility of an idea, a number of feasibility studies are conducted. Explain the following feasibility studies

(i) Technical feasibility study

(ii) Financial feasibility study

Ans (i) **Technical Feasibility Study** This study encompasses the details on how to deliver a product or a service, i.e. materials, labour, transportation and where the business will be located, technology needed, etc.

(ii) **Financial Feasibility Study** This study projects how much start-up capital is needed, sources of capital, returns on investment, etc.

8 Explain feasibility study. **CBSE TBQ**

Ans Feasibility means whether the idea will be fruitful or not. This study relates to practical approach and viability of the proposed project.

This study analyses various aspects of the project like technical, financial, commercial and socio-economic.

9 Define a business plan.

Ans A business plan is a written summary of various elements involved in starting a new enterprise, of how the business will organise its resources to meet its goals and how it will measure its progress.

10 A business plan serves many purposes. State any two purposes.

Ans The purposes served by a business plan are

(i) It provides a blueprint of actions to be taken in future.

(ii) It guides the entrepreneur in arranging for the factors of production.

11 What do you think is the reason for failure of business plan? **CBSE TBQ**

Ans The reason for the failure of business plan is execution. Many business plans fail because strategies are not executed well.

The failure to execute the plan and not the plan itself, is most often cited as the reason, why a strategic plan has underperformed. So, an organisation should ensure proper execution of its business plan.

12 Failure of a business plan impacts an organisation in many ways. State any two of them.

Ans The impact of failure of a business plan is manifested in a business in the following ways

(i) It creates significant frustration and cynicism within an organisation.

(ii) It negatively affects a business's reputation.

13 Vardaan is planning to start a new business by opening a jewellery shop in an up-market mall. Which management tool will help him by providing him a blueprint of the operations to be performed while opening the jewellery shop.

Ans The management tool that will help Vardaan is business plan. A business plan is a written summary of various elements involved in starting a new enterprise.

14 Savar is planning to venture into the business of manufacturing steel utensils. What will be the plan size for his venture?

Ans Manufacturing steel utensils is a complex activity. Accordingly, a comprehensive and detailed plan is required. Therefore, plan size will be big.

15 Business plan is an important document for entrepreneurs to guide them managing their business. Business plan also assist the entrepreneur to make proper strategies for their business and manage future growth.

That is why Malaysian government has fostered all Higher Education Providers to set entrepreneurship education as compulsory course.

One of the entrepreneurship education learning outcome is that student can write effective business plan. This study focused on enhancing student's understanding in entrepreneurship through business plan simulation.

This study also considers which of the factors most facilitate the business simulation that helps the student to prepare effective business plan. The methodology of this study is using quantitative approach with pre-and post-research design.

114 students take part as respondent in the business simulation and answer quantitative survey pre-question and post question. The result has shown that the business plan simulation can enhance undergraduate student in understanding entrepreneurship by preparing effective business plan before opening new start-up.

Source *January 2018MATEC Web of Conferences 150(3):05091*

DOI:10.1051/matecconf/201815005091

(i) Which concept is highlighted in the given concept?

(ii) Mention its one purpose.

Ans (i) Business plan.

(ii) Business plan is made to grow and carry on the plan properly.

Short Answer Type II Questions (3 Marks)

1 There are many misconceptions related to a business idea. State any two such misconceptions and the realities behind such misconceptions.

Ans Two misconceptions and the realities behind these misconceptions are

(i) **Great Ideas just Appear out of Nowhere** This is the most common misconception related to a business idea and assumes that business ideas appear out of nowhere. The reality is that the best idea generators develop a business idea in a structured and systematic way.

(ii) **There are no Illogical Ideas** This is again a common misconception related to a business idea and assumes that all business ideas are logical. But the reality is that many business ideas might be totally illogical.

2 "Ideas can also be generated through intuition". Do you agree?

Ans Yes, I agree that the ideas can be generated through intuition. Intuition is a cognitive process, whereby, an individual makes decisions based on his cumulative knowledge and experiences.

It is being called that 'Aha' feeling when one's internal search engine hits its mark. Many people refer to it as their 'gut feeling'.

Although, structured and methodical approaches to generate ideas are important, but still intuition also plays an important role in idea generation if one learns how to use it.

3 Explain 'creativity and creative problem solving' as a method of generating ideas.

Ans Creativity is the ability to combine ideas in a unique way or to make unusual associations between the ideas.

It means cross thinking by seeing new angles, connections and approaches. For generating idea through this technique, a number of specific approaches can be used, which are as follows

(i) **Attribute Listing** It is an approach in which an entrepreneur develops a new idea by looking into the positive and negative attributes of a product or a service.

(ii) **Free Association** It is an approach in which an entrepreneur develops a new idea through a chain of word associations, etc.

4 Why are feasibility studies more important? **CBSE TBQ**

Ans Feasibility study is more important for an entrepreneur because it helps him to

(i) List in detail all things they need, to make the business work.

(ii) Identify logistical and other business related problems and solutions.

(iii) Develop marketing strategies.

(iv) Serve as a foundation for developing business plan.

5 What do you mean by opportunity assessment? **CBSE TBQ**

Ans Opportunity assessment is a more in-depth review of business opportunity, including market research and due diligence that includes intellectual property analysis, opportunity development, timing, legal liability issues, applications of the opportunity, barriers to entry, industry trends, growth potential, market positioning, competitive analysis, financial projections and pricing, resource requirement analysis, licensing, etc.

6 An ideal business plan must clearly define certain points. What are they?

Ans An ideal business plan must define

(i) Objectives and strategies of the business.

(ii) Customer scenario.

(iii) Market segments.

(iv) Products and services to be offered.

(v) Sales forecast.

(vi) Steps required to attain the objectives.

(vii) Description of the distribution system.

(viii) Promotional activities.

(ix) Pricing decisions.

7 A business plan is divided into many headings. Name them.

Ans The main headings of a business plan are as follows

(i) General introduction.

(ii) Business venture.

(iii) Organisational plan.

(iv) Production plan.

(v) Human resource plan.

(vi) Marketing plan.

(vii) Financial plan.

(viii) Miscellaneous/Appendix.

8 Alignment helps in effective execution of a business plan. How?

Ans Proper execution of a business plan can be achieved through alignment. Strategies, people and work processes need to be effectively linked. The strategic plan must be understood by the entire organisation.

The right people need to be in the right jobs to allow for maximum work performance and action plans must be developed, implemented and reviewed.

The communication channels should be effective. To effectively align strategies, people and the tactical action plans that lead to a successful execution, a lot of hardwork and diligent communication must happen.

9 Sarthak wants to know about the basic details of the business. Which part of the business plan should he look into? List the information contained in it.

Ans Sarthak should look into the 'general introduction' part of the business plan. The general introduction part contains the following information

(i) Name and address of business.
(ii) Name and address of entrepreneur.
(iii) Stakeholders of business.
(iv) Nature of business and customers.

Long Answer Type Questions (5 Marks)

1 Explain the various misconceptions and realities related to a business idea.

Ans Refer to text on page 63 and 64.

2 Explain the different methods through which ideas can be generated.

Ans Refer to text on page 64 and 65. (ways to generate ideas)

3 Evaluating idea is important. Why?

Ans Refer to text on page 65.

4 Explain the types of feasibility study. **CBSE TBQ**

Ans The different types of feasibility study are as follows

(i) **Market Feasibility** This study includes a description of the industry, current market, anticipated future market, potential competition, sales projections, potential buyers, etc.
(ii) **Organisational Feasibility** This study defines the legal and corporate structure of the business and may also include professional background information about the founders and what skills they can contribute to the business.
(iii) **Technical Feasibility** Refer to Q.No. 7 of short answer type I questions (2 Marks).
(iv) **Financial Feasibility** Refer to Q.No. 7 of short answer type I questions (2 Marks).

5 Give the distinct features of feasibility study.

Ans Refer to text on page 66 and 67.

6 Give the outline of a feasibility study.

Ans Refer to text on page 67.

7 Anupama loves gardening. Her garden is the envy of the whole neighbourhood. Her neighbours, relatives and friends are constantly asking her for shoots of various plants that she has in her collection.

She decides to turn her hobby into a profession and decides to open a nursery dealing in organic plants only. She also initiates a plantation drive in her locality.

(i) Identify the source of Anupama's business idea.
(ii) In addition to the above source, state any one more source of business idea.
(iii) Explain any one method of generating idea through structural approach.

Ans (i) The source of Anupama's business idea is 'individual interest and hobbies'.
(ii) One other source of business idea is 'work experience, knowledge and skills'.
(iii) **Environment Scanning** Refer to Q.No. 2 of short answer type I questions (2 Marks).

8 What purposes does a business plan serve? **CBSE TBQ**

Ans A business plan serves the following purposes

(i) Provides a blueprint of actions to be taken in future.
(ii) Guides the entrepreneur in raising the factors of production.
(iii) Serves as a guide to organise and direct the activities of the business venture.
(iv) Helps in measuring the progress of the venture at successive stages.
(v) Communicates to investors, lenders, suppliers, etc., about initiating the programmes of the business.

9 Explain in detail the elements of a business plan. **CBSE TBQ**

Ans Refer to text on page 67 and 68.

10 Give the general format of a proposed business plan.

Ans Refer to text on page 68 and 69.

11 Differentiate between feasibility study and business plan. **CBSE TBQ**

Ans Refer to text on page 70.

12 Although, there is no singular process to manage the execution of a business plan, there are basic processes and fundamentals to be followed. Enlist them. **CBSE TBQ**

Ans Refer to text on page 69.

13 Samir has decided to open a new business of supplying sports equipments to Sports Authority of India. He decided to charge least possible price for his products and to source them from small scale units. He tried to urge Sudhakar to join his business.

Before giving his final answer, Sudhakar wants to know about the business. Which part of business plan should Sudhakar look into?

Also, state any two parts other than the one identified in the given case.

Ans Sudhakar should look into the 'business venture' segment of the business plan, as it provides the following information

(i) Products to be offered.
(ii) Services to be offered.
(iii) Scale of business operation.
(iv) Type of technology used.
(v) Type of skilled personnel required.

Other two parts of the business plan are as follows

(i) **Human Resource Plan**
 (a) Categories of human resources or staff required.
 (b) Human resource already identified.
 (c) Human resource required to be procured.
 (d) Time frame for procurement of human resource.

(ii) **Marketing Plan**
 (a) Products and services offered.
 (b) Pricing policies.
 (c) Promotional strategies.
 (d) Logistics for distribution.
 (e) Channels of distribution.

14 Using a novel experimental paradigm, we explore how the experience of generating an idea and the possibility that another investor might adopt a rejected investment opportunity, bias the investment decisions of innovator and imitator entrepreneurs. We find that individuals who generate a business idea form biased evaluations of the economic potential of ideas, be it their own idea or somebody else's idea. On the one hand, they are over confident about the value of, and overly likely to invest in, their own idea.

On the other hand, when investing in another person's idea, even if it is not competing with their own idea, they are under confident about the value of, and insufficiently likely to invest in, the idea. Surprisingly, we find that entrepreneurial experience exacerbates this pattern of over and under confidence. In addition, we find that the threat that another investor can appropriate a declined investment opportunity increases willingness to invest.

We propose a theoretical account to explain the observed pattern of over and under confidence in imitative and innovative entrepreneurship. Our findings challenge the traditional account that lowering the cost of imitation has a disincentive effect on the investment decisions of pioneer entrepreneurs and provide evidence that a more lenient appropriability regime may, unexpectedly, have positive effect on entrepreneurship. Our findings also identify new psychological mechanisms that can play a role in important phenomena such as the emergence of spin-offs and rush to market entry.

Source *Published Online in Articles in Advance: 27th October, 2016 https://doi.org/10.1287/mnsc.2016.2566*

(i) Which concept is highlighted in the given concept?
(ii) Explain briefly the various ways of generating ideas.

Ans (i) Generation of ideas.
(ii) Refer to text on page 64 and 65.

CASE STUDIES

Nandita Bijur

'It's a dream come true'. People all around were saying, "There goes Malti's daughter, the successful business woman". Nandita was a brave child, a strong headed youngster, who had a dream which has reaped successful results. She is the owner of Uma Food Products, an enterprise worth several crores of rupees today.

How do you convert childhood pain and humiliation into ammunition for success? How do you take many small negatives and turn it into a huge positive?

Nandita Bijur is the best person to answer these questions because this is exactly what she did. Tall and attractive, Nandita exudes strength, determination and drive. She started her business with an investment of only ₹ 5,000 from her personal savings and through sheer grit and hard work, turned it into a huge success.

Nandita Never had a Childhood

Nandita's childhood was very traumatic and left many scars on her psyche. When she and her elder brother were only about six and eight, then their mother, Malti, fell ill. It was a long drawn illness. Since, their father was away at work most of the time and there was no one else to take care of her, Malti was moved to her father's house (Nandita's maternal grandfather's house). Malti needed a great deal of care and attention and she lived in her father's house for over fifteen years. While still a child, Nandita was thrust into the role of the 'woman of the house'. She never had much time to go out and play like the other little girls in the neighbourhood. She had to take care of her brother and father.

They seemed to lean on her for support. She shopped and cooked and went to school. She was always tired and often it was a struggle to stay awake to do homework. Sometimes, she was so tired in school that her eyes would automatically close and her head drop on her desk.

She remembers wanting pretty dresses to wear and colourful ribbons in her hair like the other girls. But, there was no one around to take her for shopping. Her father did the best he could, but he couldn't do very much. She had two aunts, who were kind and loving and she is eternally grateful to them.

The highlights of her life were those rare occasions when someone took her to visit her mother. She loved her mother dearly and her heart ached for her and she desperately wished she could wave a magic wand and make her well. But her mother's condition did not improve.

Nandita's Inner Strength and Determination Surfaces

Most relatives were not very kind and sometimes forgot she and her brother even existed. It hurts her deeply when they were not invited to their first cousin's wedding.

Relatives frequently referred to her as 'poor Nandita', which burned her up. Very early in her teens, Nandita decided that she was not a 'poor thing' and refused to be called that. She would show them. She decided that a day would come when the same people who now pointed to her and said, "There goes Malti's daughter, poor thing" would say instead, "There goes Malti's daughter, the successful businesswoman".

Nandita's Husband, a Good, Kind Man

Nandita married in her early 20's. Her husband was supportive. "He has a quiet strength that is very healing", she says. That was the beginning of her turnaround. Nandita was a school teacher and her husband, Pramod, a chemist. Neither had any entrepreneurs in their families. But they had a shared dream to start a small business of their own. However, there was one big problem. They didn't have the capital to invest in a business. Soon, they had two children and they needed both their incomes to live a comfortable life.

The Idea for an Ice-cream Mix

One evening, on his way back from work, Pramod felt like eating some ice-cream. He noticed an ice-cream mix in a store and bought it.

When he got home, he asked Nandita to make some ice-cream using the mix, which she did. When they finished their dinner, they had the ice-cream for dessert. Nandita was disappointed. It just didn't taste as good as the ice-cream she had earlier made at home. That night when everyone went to sleep, Nandita tossed and turned in bed, thinking about the perfect ingredients that would make a great ice-cream mix.

At about 4 am she woke up, tiptoed into the dining room and wrote down on a piece of paper the recipe for an ice-cream mix. Little did she know then that, this recipe that she penned down on a scrap of paper in the wee hours of the morning, would a few years later, make them rich.

When Pramod woke up in the morning, Nandita gave him the piece of paper with the recipe for the ice-cream mix and told him, I know what our business is going to be. We're going to make an excellent ice-cream mix that people are going to love.

When she made the ice-cream at home with her own recipe, her kids exclaimed, 'Mummy, this is yummy'! She decided to call it 'Yummy Ice- cream'. She took out ₹ 5,000 from her savings account and invested it in buying the ingredients and packaging materials.

The Start of a Business

At first, she made the ice-cream mix at home in her own kitchen. She packaged it and sold it to friends and neighbours. She continued with her teaching job and made the ice-cream mix in the evening. The demand for the ice-cream grew in leaps and bounds. Soon it grew so big that she had to work all night and even enlist the help of her children and husband to meet the demand. She realised that she would have to quit her job and do this full time as she couldn't do both. She recognised that she would need to rent a place to make her products. She couldn't continue to do it at home. So, she rented a small shed for her first factory in Jogeshwari. It covered an area of 550 square feet.

Malti's Daughter Becomes a Businesswoman

Nandita got a bank loan for ₹ 70,000 for the factory premises and pledged her jewellery to get an additional loan for ₹ 40,000. "I was such a novice that I didn't even know that I needed a current account to run a business", she says.

The first year was very tough. Since her business was new, nobody gave her any credit. All her suppliers wanted cash, yet she had to supply her retailers and customers on credit. At first, she couldn't afford to hire many staff, so her children helped at the factory after school. During this whole period, the one thing that kept her going was the determination, "Malti's daughter is not a poor thing".

She told me, "I wanted to prove to myself and others that I could succeed and make something out of my life. I wanted my children to be wealthy. I wanted them to give salaries to others and not work to get a salary. These thoughts kept me going even during the most difficult times".

As Nandita became more and more successful with her ice-cream mix, she introduced new products such as Gulabjamun mix and Basundi mix. She now has over 40 products. Soon her sales shot up and she hired more employees. Her husband still continued to work at his job.

A Crisis Hits and Almost Wipes her Out

Nandita hired a capable distributor for her products. Her sales quadrupled. She hired even more employees and moved to a bigger factory. The distributor suggested a major advertising blitz. So, she invested ₹ 6 lakhs on TV commercials, magazines and newspaper advertisements, displays, bill boards and so on.

Then one day, disaster struck. Nandita did not know that there was already a company by the name of 'Yummy Ice-creams' in Goa. Nandita had not bothered to find out if the name 'Yummy Ice-cream' was already registered and trademarked by someone else. The businessman from Goa arrived with CBI officers and stormed into her factory and her home. He threatened to sue her until she was ruined. The distributor intervened and mediated and she also took legal advice. They negotiated with the Goa businessman and settled out of court. This proved so expensive that she almost gave up.

Back to Square One

Now once again she had no money and nobody would give her any credit. Her accounts in the banks had been closed down. Once again she had to pay cash for everything she bought yet give credit to her retailers and customers.

This was a very trying period. Once again, her determination that "Malti's daughter will be a successful businesswoman", kept her going. She changed the name of her company to 'Uma Food Products' after her mother-in-law and grandmother, who were both called Uma. Her packaged mixes were renamed 'Eat me'.

Nandita and Her Husband Save the Business

At about this time, Nandita's husband quit his job and joined the business. He became the distributor of their products, thereby saving payments to the distributor. The first thing she did was to pay-off the bank loan because she needed to have a bank account in order to be able to write cheques. For this, she took a loan from a private lender at extortionate rate of 24%.

They worked day and night and paid off all their loans. Since that time, things have only looked up. She learned a great deal from her mistakes and felt confident to run a successful business venture. She has been successfully running her business now for the past 9 years.

Nandita's Advice to New Entrepreneurs

(i) Don't give up. Keep at it to succeed.
(ii) Pay the creditors, suppliers and vendors on time. It builds credibility.
(iii) Treat employees like family. If employees are happy, one's business will be successful.

1 Which factor was an hinderance in Nandita's dream to become an entrepreneur?

Ans The factor which was an hinderance in Nandita's dream to become an entrepreneur was 'finance'.

Nandita didn't have the capital to invest in a business.

2 Which business idea did Nandita had?

Ans Nandita had a business idea to make an ice-cream mix.

3 Was the business idea generated through structured methods or was it based on intuition?

Ans Nandita's business idea was based on intuition.

4 What advice does Nandita give to new entrepreneurs?

Ans Nandita's advices to new entrepreneurs are

(i) Don't give up. Keep at it to succeed.
(ii) Pay the creditors, suppliers and vendors on time. It builds credibility.
(iii) Treat employees like family. If employees are happy, one's business will be successful.

CHAPTER ASSESSMENT

Objective Type Questions (1 Mark)

1 A concept that can be used to make money is

(a) business idea (b) luck

(c) entrepreneur (d) Both (a) and (b)

2 The screening of large amount of information to detect emerging trends is called ....

(a) forecasting (b) environment scanning

(c) Both (a) and (b) (d) None of these

3 This study projects how much start-up capital is needed, sources of capital, returns on investment, etc?

(a) Market feasibility

(b) Technical feasibility

(c) Financial feasibility

(d) Organisational feasibility

4 .... is the ability to combine ideas in a unique way or to make unusual associations between the ideas.

5 .... describes the nature and context of the business opportunities and the plans to exploit the opportunity.

6 A business plan can be based on a feasibility study. State true or false.

7 Feasibility study is completed after the formation of the business plan. State true or false.

Short Answer Type I Questions (2 Marks)

8 Discuss any one misconception and realities related to business idea.

9 Explain briefly 'Intuition as a way of generating ideas'.

10 Explain environment scanning as one of the methods of idea generation.

Short Answer Type II Questions (3 Marks)

11 Explain any three points of importance of evaluating ideas.

12 How is feasibility study important for entrepreneurs?

13 Discuss briefly the purpose served by business plan.

Long Answer Type Questions (5 Marks)

14 Explain different types of feasibility study.

15 Write a short note on successful execution of a business plan.

16 How does feasibility study differ from business plan?

17 Describe all the elements of business plan.

18 Discuss the format of a business plan.

For explanations scan the given QR Code

CHAPTER 04

Entrepreneurship as Innovation & Problem Solving

In this Chapter...

- Entrepreneurs as problem solvers
- Innovation leading to entrepreneurial ventures
- Social entrepreneurship
- Role of technology and social media in creating new form of business

Entrepreneurs as Problem Solvers

An entrepreneur is a person, who undertakes risk and tries to resolve the problems faced by the society and earn profit in this process.

Entrepreneurial actions are efforts to solve problems for others. When one solves a problem, a new value is created, which leads to the creation of a new profitable enterprise. It can be represented as

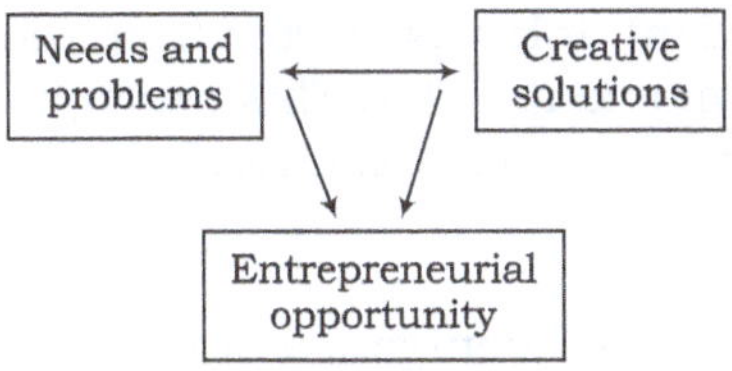

Therefore, entrepreneurs are referred to as 'problem solvers'. The more or larger problems an entrepreneurial organisation solves, the more profit it can generate, as it is clear from the **example** given below

The Story of Kellogg's

In 1894, Dr John Harvey Kellogg was a superintendent of a famous hospital and health spa in Battle Creek, Michigan. His younger brother, Will Keith Kellogg, was the business manager.

The hospital stressed healthful living and kept its patients on a diet that eliminated caffeine, meat, alcohol and tobacco.

The brothers invented many foods that were made from grains, including a coffee substitute and a type of granola, which they forced through rollers and rolled into long sheets of dough.

One day, after cooking some wheat, the men were called away. When they finally returned, the wheat had become stale. They decided to force the tempered grain through the rollers anyway.

Surprisingly, the grain did not come out in long sheets of dough. Instead, each wheat berry was flattened and came out as a thin flake. The brothers baked the flakes and were delighted with their new invention.

They realised that they have discovered a new and delicious cereal, but they had no way of knowing that they had accidentally invented a whole new industry.

Will Keith Kellogg eventually opened his own cereal business and its most famous product is still sold today. It wasn't until 1906 that Kellogg's corn flakes were made available to the general public.

So, it can be concluded that most entrepreneurial ventures have survived when they solved the problems of people, understanding their needs and accordingly changing the product to suit their needs.

Innovations Leading to Entrepreneurial Ventures

An entrepreneur is also known to be a person, who habitually creates and innovates to build something of recognised value around perceived opportunities. Creativity and innovation are the distinguishing marks of an entrepreneur.

Creativity is a continuous activity for the entrepreneur, who always sees new ways of doing things and **innovation** means to implement the idea in practice. It can be in the area of new technology, product or its production, etc. The innovation process involves imagination, intuition and risk.

After the accomplishment of a project, the entrepreneur seeks another 'mountain to climb' because for him or her, creativity and innovation are habitual, something that he or she has to keep on doing.

Given below are some innovations that led to successful ventures

1. Penicillin

Inventor Sir Alexander Fleming, a scientist.

What he was trying to make Ironically, Fleming was searching for a 'wonder drug' that could cure diseases. However, it wasn't until Fleming threw away his experiments that he found what he was looking for.

How it was created Fleming noticed that a contaminated Petri dish, he had discarded, contained a mould that was dissolving all the bacteria around it. When he grew the mold by itself, he learned that it contained a powerful antibiotic, penicillin.

2. Potato Chips

Inventor George Crum, a chef at the Carey Moon Lake House in Saratoga Springs.

What he was trying to make A plate of fried potato.

How it was created One day, a customer sent back his plate of potatoes many times and kept asking for them to be more fried and thinner. Crum lost his temper, sliced the potatoes insanely thin and fried them, until they were hard as a rock. To the chef 's surprise, the customer loved them and wanted more and this is how potato chips came into existence.

3. The Pacemaker

Inventor John Hopps, an electrical engineer.

What he was trying to make Hopps was conducting research on hypothermia and was trying to use radio frequency heating to restore body temperature.

How it was created During his experiment, he realised that if a heart stopped beating due to cooling, it could be started again by artificial stimulation. This realisation led to the invention of pacemaker.

4. Microwave Ovens

Inventor Percy Spencer, an engineer (with Raytheon Corporation).

What he was trying to make The engineer was conducting a radar-related research project with a new vacuum tube.

How it was created Spencer realised that the candy bar in his pocket began to melt during his experiment. He then put popcorn into the machine and when it started to pop, he knew he had a revolutionary device on his hands.

5. Inkjet Printers

Inventor A Canon engineer.

How it was created After resting his hot iron on his pen by accident, ink was ejected from the pens point a few moments later. This principle led to the creation of the inkjet printers.

6. X-Rays

Inventor Wilhem Roentgen, a physicist.

What he was trying to make He was interested in investigating the properties of cathode ray tubes.

How it was created When light passed through the tubes, he noted that sheets of fluorescent paper in his lab were illuminated even though his machine had an opaque cover.

It is clear from these examples, that people all over the world have tried, failed and succeeded sometimes by mistake in the course of their innovative process.

So, immediate results for one's actions should not be expected and one should keep on experimenting. It is also observed that ideas usually evolve through a creative process, whereby, imaginative people like the entrepreneurs, innovate the ideas so created.

It is also observed that most innovative ideas can be traced to an individual's interest in a specific problem or area of study.

CHECK POINT 01

1. What are entrepreneurs refer to?
2. Who invented Penicillin?
3. What is John Hopps' invention?
4. Who invented Microwave Ovens?
5. Who invented X-Rays?

Social Entrepreneurship

Social entrepreneurship is an attempt to draw upon business techniques to find solutions to social problems. In social entrepreneurship, the focus is not only on helping the poor and needy, but teaching them some competencies, some skills, using which, they can later improve their lives and economic conditions on a sustainable basis.

Social entrepreneurship can be considered as new and more effective way to serve the needs of the society.
It includes non-profit organisations which provide healthcare, education and other public services to masses, especially poor and underprivileged people. Donors are the source of funds for these organisations.

According to **J Gregory Dees**, "Social entrepreneurship is which combines the passion of a social mission with an image of business like discipline, innovation and determination".

Social Entrepreneurs

Social entrepreneurs are ambitious and persistent individuals, tackling major social issues and offering new ideas for wide scale change. Rather than leaving societal needs to the government, social entrepreneurs find what is not working and solve the problem by changing the system and spreading the solution.

They are visionaries and also realists and are ultimately concerned with the practical implementation of their vision.

Martin and Osberg define social entrepreneur as, "The social entrepreneur aims for value in the form of large scale transformational benefit that accrues either to a significant segment of society or to society at large".

A social entrepreneur targets his/her programmes at the undeserved, neglected or highly disadvantaged population that lack the financial means or political clout to achieve the transformative benefit on its own.

So, it can be influenced that a social entrepreneur can assess a social problem and find a solution to remove poverty among the masses and thus, improve their standard of living.

Characteristics of Social Entrepreneurs

Social entrepreneurs generally possess the following characteristics

Characteristics of Social Entrepreneurs

- Social catalysts
- Socially aware
- Opportunity seeking
- Innovative
- Resourceful
- Accountable

1. **Social Catalysts** Social entrepreneurs affect the whole society at large and are instrumental in bringing about fundamental changes by reforming social systems and creating sustainable improvements.

   According to **J Gregory Dees**, "Though they may act locally, their actions have the potential to stimulate global improvements in their chosen areas, whether that is education, health care, economic development, the environment, the arts, or any other social field".

2. **Socially Aware** These entrepreneurs are aware of the various problems facing society and work towards their removal. They aim at social improvement, as opposed to the creation of profit.

   The success of their venture is measured in terms of its impact and not by the amount of profits generated.

3. **Opportunity Seeking** These entrepreneurs are not disheartened by the obstacles in their path.

   They relentlessly pursue their goals, seeing every obstacle as an opportunity to develop and fine-tune their business models.

4. **Innovative** Social entrepreneurs are creative, willing to think outside the box and ready to apply ideas to new situations.

   They understand that not every innovation will be a success and they see failures as learning opportunities even as they strive for success.

5. **Resourceful** Their visions are not limited by the resources that they have. Besides optimising the use of existing resources, they actively expand their resource pool through collaboration with others.

6. **Accountable** Social entrepreneurs are accountable to their beneficiaries and they often ask themselves, "Am I creating value for the people I am serving? Do I understand their needs?"

   This is because social entrepreneurs want to know how they are actually making an impact.

   They are also accountable to investors who want to know whether their contributions are indeed stimulating social improvements as promised by the social entrepreneurs.

Need for Social Entrepreneurs

In the current economic crisis, financial pressures are further worsening the existing social problems of poverty and unemployment.

According to **J Gregory Dees**, Social entrepreneurship is necessary to mitigate the financial repercussions among vulnerable.

With pay cuts and job losses happening all over the world, the needs of the hour are ideas, innovations, creative solutions and fresh perspectives that can cater to the changing market demands, emerging economies and a new world economic order and social entrepreneurs fulfil these needs.

So, in the light of the above discussion, it can be concluded that social entrepreneurs are needed in a society because of the below mentioned reasons

Need for Social Entrepreneurs

- → Lead to employment development
- → Develop new goods and services
- → Provide social capital
- → Promote equity

1. **They lead to Employment Development** The first major advantage of a social entrepreneur is that he/she creates jobs and employment opportunities in a society.

2. **They Develop New Goods and Services** Social entrepreneurs develop an environment conducive for the growth of innovation, thereby, leading to the development of new goods and services.

   e.g. Brazilian social entrepreneur Veronica Khosa developed a new home based care model for AIDS patients which later changed the government's health policy.

3. **They provide Social Capital** Social entrepreneurs provide the much needed capital for the development of society by channelising the savings of the unorganised section of society.

4. **They promote Equity** Social entrepreneurs promote a equitable society by addressing social issues and trying to achieve ongoing sustainable impact through their social mission.

Examples of Some Social Entrepreneurs

1. **Muhammad Yunus** Founder of the Grameen Bank and winner of the 2006 Nobel Peace Prize. He found a solution to the plight of poor Bangladeshis, who were unable to acquire funds to start their own business in the form of microcredit.

   He lent $ 27 of his personal funds to a group of poor women, who quickly started a sewing business that was able to generate enough income to help them pay back the loan and more importantly, to rise above poverty. Thus, the idea of the Grameen Bank was born.

According to **Martin and Osberg**, "Grameen Bank sustained itself by charging interest on its loans and then recycling the capital to help other women".

Having thus, proven microcredit to be a sustainable method of combating global poverty, Yunus continues to inspire organisations worldwide to adopt the Grameen model to combat poverty in their own communities.

2. **Vinoba Bhave** Founder and leader of the Bhudaan Andolan (Land Gift Movement), he caused the redistribution of more than 70,00,000 acres of land to help India's untouchables and landless.
3. **Ela Bhatt** Founded in 1972, Self-Employed Women's Association (SEWA) is a rare trade union of poor, unorganised, self-employed women who work as vendors, hawkers and labourers.
4. **Dr Abraham M George** Founder of The George Foundation established in January 1995 in Bangalore, India. Their mission is to work towards poverty eradication, promote environmental health and strengthen democratic institutions and values in developing countries.
5. **Dr Verghese Kurien** Founder of the Amul Dairy Project.
6. **Bunker Roy** Founder of Barefoot College, which promotes rural development through innovative education programmes.
7. **Nand Kishore Chaudhary** Founder of Jaipur rugs, which promotes rural development through capacity building of rural people in carpet weaving.
8. **Harish Hande** Magsaysay Award Winner 2011. Founder of Selco India, a solar electric light company in 1995, which over the years has lit up over 1,20,000 households, to emerge as India's leading solar technology firm.

Differences between Entrepreneurship and Social Entrepreneurship

In entrepreneurship, the final objective is wealth creation. But, in social entrepreneurship the ultimate objective is upliftment of the poorer sections of the society.

The differences between entrepreneurship and social entrepreneurship would be more clear with the help of the following points

- The final objective of entrepreneurship is wealth creation, but for social entrepreneurship, wealth creation is simply a means to an end.
- In entrepreneurship, an entrepreneur participates in entrepreneurial venture with the aim of earning profit, but a social entrepreneur participates in business ventures only to use the profits generated to create valuable social programmes for the whole society.
- Entrepreneur works for self-development, but social entrepreneur works for societal development.

CHECK POINT 02

1. What do you mean by social entrepreneurship?
2. Mention any one characteristic of social entrepreneurs.
3. How is social entrepreneur useful? Mention any one point.
4. What is the full form of SEWA?

Role of Technology and Social Media in Creating New Form of Business

Over the past 25 years, digital revolution has changed the way a business works, by providing them with a cost effective technology to cope up with increasingly complex challenges.

However, the growing needs of the business demand for more complex and efficient technologies.

Satisfying these demands of business will lead to an explosive growth in data and analytics, new competition in almost every field, disruption and realignment of many industries.

Emerging markets will create plenty of opportunities related to smart technology, both in profit as well as non-profit enterprises.

e.g. in Kenya, mobile phones are being used to collect data and report on disease specific issues from more than 175 health centres serving over 1 million people.

This technology has reduced the cost of the country's health information system by 25 per cent and cut the time needed to report the information from four weeks to one week.

So, in today's dynamic world, it is very important for a business to embrace latest technology, as it helps in its growth and development. The role of technology and its importance for a business in generating new forms is being enumerated below

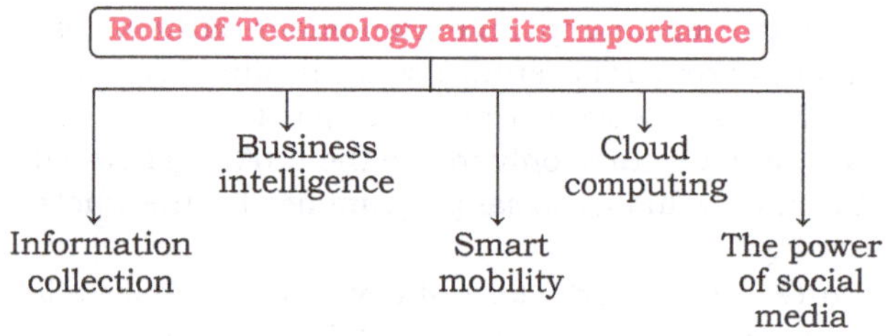

1. Information Collection

In this competitive world, in order to attract a customer, the entrepreneur needs to have the detailed information regarding customers.

Detailed information regarding customers like his age, regularity of visit to the shop, preferences of his purchases, etc., all these factors enable an entrepreneur to understand the taste and preference of the customers, so that he/she can serve them better and ensure their loyalty.

The growing number of embedded sensors collecting information about the world and the rise of social networks that store the data which people share, generate immense quantities of information.

This immense quantum of information will force the businesses to compete among themselves on analytics to differentiate themselves.

e.g. telemetric applications, similar to Global Positioning Systems (GPS) will allow organisations to send, receive and store information via telecommunication devices while controlling remote objects.

Although, commonly associated with the automotive industry, telemetric applications are also being developed for use in medical informatics, health care and other fields.

2. Business Intelligence

It is the ability of an organisation to collect, maintain and organise data. Business intelligence enables organisations to gather data on each related area of the business and analyse it in a way that yields information they can act on, thereby helping them to enhance their decision-making capabilities, improve their performance, mitigate risk and even create new business models.

The real benefit of business intelligence is that it enables a business to take a better strategic decisions.

Also, the large amount of information generated can help a business in identifying new opportunities and implementing an effective strategy which helps them to gain a competitive market advantage and long-term stability.

e.g. sales data during an off season may help a business in deciding the percentage of discount that can be offered.

3. Smart Mobility

The devices which are mobile, help in the growth of business. Smart mobility has changed the way people interact with each other. Increasingly, smart devices and portable tools that connect to the internet have become a part of our lives.

In the last quarter of 2010, sales of smart phones outpaced those of PCs for the first time, according to data from IDC. Since, 2014, more smart devices are used to access the internet than traditional computers. The move to an increasingly mobile world is creating new players and new opportunities for a variety of industries.

It is expected that new emerging market companies are significant competitors, growing rapidly in part because a lack of legacy systems has enabled them to earn profit more quickly from new technology as it becomes available.

4. Cloud Computing

It means storing and accessing data and programs over the internet instead of your computer's hard drive. The word 'cloud' is used as a metaphor for the internet, based on the standardised use of a cloud like shape to denote a network.

Earlier, when large-scale computer was available in academia and corporations, it was costly to buy a mainframe. However, as computers became more prevalent, scientists and technologists explored ways to make large-scale computing power available to more users through time sharing, etc.

Cloud computing helps an organisation to upload all its data on a cloud and then they can access it even from remote areas, when required. e.g. in case of a phone and a laptop of Apple Inc, whenever a photo is clicked on phone, it automatically gets updated on to the laptop through cloud computing.

When cloud computing becomes widespread, it will transform businesses and business models, potentially reducing both initial and recurring costs for IT buyers, increasing their flexibility and lowering their risks.

Despite concerns related to data security, privacy and business continuity, its value proposition makes the success of cloud computing inevitable.

Over time, cloud based services will grow increasingly and evolve into full-scale business process as a service.

5. The Power of Social Media

Google, Facebook, Twitter, smart phones, tablets and e-readers are technologies that originated in the consumer space, are now reshaping the way companies communicate and collaborate with employees, partners and customers.

Through the new possibilities for 'social listening', businesses are able to better understand what their customers and employees need and want.

More change can be expected when the generation that has grown up with new technologies and instant information gratification joins the workforce. These changes will definitely lead to the creation of new forms of business enterprises which will surely change the way business will be conducted in the future scenario.

CHECK POINT 03

1. Why is it important for a business to embrace latest technology? Mention any one reason.
2. What is the full form of GPS?
3. What do you mean by business intelligence?
4. Name some technologies that are originated in the consumer space.
5. Mention one importance of business intelligence.

EXAM PATTERN EXERCISE

Objective Type Questions (1 Mark)

Multiple Choice Questions

1 The distinguishing mark(s) of an entrepreneur is/are

(a) creativity (b) innovation
(c) Both (a) and (b) (d) None of these

Ans (c) Both (a) and (b)

2 Potato chips were invented by a chef who was trying to make a plate of fried potato. Name that chef.

(a) George Crum (b) Percy Spencer
(c) John Hops (d) Alexander Fleming

Ans (a) George Crum

3 Some qualities of social entrepreneurs include

(a) visionaries (b) realists
(c) Both (a) and (b) (d) None of these

Ans (c) Both (a) and (b)

4 The characteristic(s) of social entrepreneurs is/are

(a) they are social catalysts
(b) they are socially aware
(c) they are innovative
(d) All of the above

Ans (d) All of the above

5 Social entrepreneurs are needed in a society because

(a) they lead to economic development
(b) they develop new goods and services
(c) they promote equity
(d) All of the above

Ans (d) All of the above

6 'Social entrepreneurship is necessary to mitigate the financial repercussions among vulnerable'. Who said this?

(a) Martin and Osberg (b) Penicillin
(c) J Gregory Dees (d) None of these

Ans (c) J Gregory Dees

7 Founder and leader of Bhudaan movement was

(a) Vinoba Bhave (b) Bunker Roy
(c) Harish Hande (d) Era Bhatt

Ans (a) Vinoba Bhave

8 Nand Kishore Chaudhary is the

(a) founder of the George Foundation
(b) founder of Amul Dairy
(c) founder of Jaipur Rugs
(d) None of the above

Ans (c) founder of Jaipur Rugs

9 Lijjat papad was the brain child of .... Gujarati women from Mumbai.

(a) 5 (b) 6 (c) 7 (d) 10

Ans (c) 7

10 What is the final objective of entrepreneurship?

(a) Wealth creation (b) Compensation of loss
(c) Both (a) and (b) (d) None of these

Ans (a) Wealth creation

11 The word 'cloud' is used as a metaphor for

(a) internet (b) rain (c) web (d) site

Ans (a) internet

12 Google, Facebook and Twitter help the businesses to better understand what their customers need. These highlight the importance of

(a) business intelligence
(b) cloud computing
(c) artificial intelligence (d) social media

Ans (d) social media

13 Which of the following does not highlight the need of social entrepreneurs?

(a) They lead to employment development
(b) They develop new goods and services
(c) They provide social capital and promote equity
(d) None of the above

Ans (d) None of the above

14 **Assertion** (A) Entrepreneurs are referred to as 'problem solvers'.

Reason (R) Entrepreneurial actions are efforts to solve problems of others.

Alternatives

(a) Both Assertion (A) and Reason (R) are correct.
(b) Assertion (A) is correct, but Reason (R) is incorrect
(c) Assertion (A) is incorrect, but Reason (R) is correct
(d) Both Assertion (A) and Reason (R) are incorrect

Ans (a) Both Assertion (A) and Reason (R) are correct

15 **Assertion** (A) Creativity and innovation are the distinguishing marks of the entrepreneur.

Reason (R) In an entrepreneur, creativity is combined with the ability to innovate, to take the idea and make it work in practice.

Alternatives

(a) Both Assertion (A) and Reason (R) are correct
(b) Assertion (A) is correct, but Reason (R) is incorrect
(c) Assertion (A) is incorrect, but Reason (R) is correct
(d) Both Assertion (A) and Reason (R) are incorrect

Ans (a) Both Assertion (A) and Reason (R) are correct

16 Given below are the names of the inventors in Column I and their inventions in Column II. Match them correctly.

Column I	Column II
A. Wilhem Roentgen	(i) Penicillin
B. Percy Spencer	(ii) The pacemaker
C. John Hopps	(iii) Microwave ovens
D. Sir Alexander Fleming	(iv) X-Rays

Codes

	A	B	C	D		A	B	C	D
(a)	(iv)	(iii)	(ii)	(i)	(b)	(ii)	(i)	(iii)	(iv)
(c)	(iii)	(iv)	(ii)	(i)	(d)	(ii)	(i)	(iv)	(iii)

Ans (a) (iv) (iii) (ii) (i)

17 Which concept is highlighted in the given picture?

(a) Social entrepreneurship
(b) Entrepreneur as problem solver
(c) Both (a) and (b)
(d) None of the above

Ans (b) Entrepreneur as problem solver

18 Which concept is highlighted in the given picture?

(a) Social entrepreneurship
(b) Entrepreneur as innovators
(c) Both (a) and (b) (d) None of these

Ans (b) Entrepreneur as innovators. Entrepreneurs are gifted with the ability of identifying problems and providing their solutions in an innovative way.

Fill in the Blanks

19 .... are efforts to solve the problems of others.

Ans Entrepreneurial actions

20 .... is a continuous activity for the entrepreneur, who always sees new ways of doing things and .... means to implement the idea in practice.

Ans Creativity, innovation

21 .... was an engineer who was conducting a radar related research project with a new vacuum tube.

Ans Percy Spencer

22 Salman's family owned mango plantation. To help them pluck mangoes, Salman made pluching device attached with a net and a knife. Salman is playing the role of ....

Ans innovator

23 .... is an attempt to draw upon business techniques to find solutions to social problems.

Ans Social entrepreneurship

24 Muhammad Yunus lent $ 27 to a group of poor women to start a sewing business. The women paid back the loan and rose above poverty line. This led to the birth of ....

Ans Grameen Bank

25 Mamta Singh is working in her self established organisation, dedicated to offer education to the poor girls in India. Mamta Singh is an example of .... entrepreneur as she is working for a social cause.

Ans Social

26 .... means storing and accessing data and programs over the internet instead of computer's hard drive.

Ans Cloud computing

State True or False

27 Kellogg's corn flakes were made available to the general public in 1906.

Ans True

28 Ideas usually evolve through a creative process.

Ans True

29 Inkjet printers were invented by Percy Spencer.

Ans False. It was invented by a Canon engineer.

30 Social entrepreneurs assess a social problem and find a solution to remove poverty among the masses.

Ans True

31 The ultimate goal of social entrepreneurs is profit.

Ans False. The ultimate goal of social entrepreneur is social improvement.

32 Vinoba Bhave won the Magsaysay Award in 2011.

Ans False. Harish Hande won the Magsaysay Award in 2011.

33 Ela Bhatt founded SEWA in 1972.

Ans True

34 Social entrepreneur works for self-development.

Ans False. They work for societal development.

35 Smart mobility is the ability of an organisation to collect, maintain and organise data.

Ans False. Business intelligence is the ability of an organisation to collect, maintain and organise data.

36 Mr. Manish collected sales data related to an off season which will help him in deciding the percentage of the discount to be offered. This ability is called business intelligence.

Ans True

Case Based Questions

37 Read the following article and answer the questions that follow

Rupal was a fashion designer and owned her own boutique in Ahmadabad. Her boutique was popular in the surrounding areas but with the advancement in technology, she decided to venture into the field of e-commerce, trading the textile and fabric handicrafts of Gujarat.

Rupal started gathering data about the craftsmen working on the handicrafts and found out that despite being famous, these craftsmen do not have enough for their living. So, she decided to help them by appealing to people through social media marketing. She formed social media pages and website for the handicrafts and also registered the products on e-commerce. Rupal herself purchased the products and sold them at her boutique. Soon, she was able to provide a stable earning to the craftsmen of the nearby area. They also formed a co-operative society for the craftsmen of Gujarat which helped the people in gaining grants from the government.

(i) Which of the following technological advancements can Rupal use?

(a) Business intelligence
(b) Smart mobility
(c) Social media
(d) All of the above

Ans (d) All of the above

(ii) Rupal is a .... entrepreneur.

(a) social (b) commercial
(c) technical (d) None of these

Ans (a) social

(iii) "Rupal started gathering data about the craftsmen working on the handicrafts and found out that despite being famous, these craftsmen do not have enough for their living."

Which role of technology in entrepreneurship is highlighted in the above text?

(a) Smart mobility
(b) Business intelligence
(c) Information collection
(d) Power of social media

Ans (c) Information collection

(iv) What role is played by Rupal in the above case?

(a) Innovator
(b) Problem solver
(c) Both (a) and (b)
(d) None of the above

Ans (b) Problem solver

(v) What social problem did Rupal solved as a social entrepreneur?

(a) Poor exposure of craftsmen to markets
(b) Lack of market knowledge
(c) Low demand for handicrafts
(d) All of the above

Ans (a) Poor exposure of craftsmen to markets

38 Read the following article and answer the questions that follow

Arul was an engineering student and the son of a farmer. He completed his studies and came back to his village for some time. When he was at home, he noticed that his father and other farmers have to carry very heavy containers of fertilisers on their back at the time of spraying which was destroying their posture and created health issues.

Arul decided to work on a device that can lower this burden. He worked day and night and came up with an idea of a small cart that would carry the heavy cylinders and the farmers can easily push it through the crops. He made a prototype of the product and tried it with his father. The height and weight of the cart were perfect for a farm or field with crops and it helped his father a lot.

Arul then decided to use his invention as a road to the journey of entrepreneurship and he got funding from some venture capitalists to make more carts. He started working on his big venture that would help thousands of farmers across the world.

(i) Which of the following was the starting point for Arul to become an entrepreneur?
(a) Need and problem
(b) Change
(c) Creative efforts
(d) Entrepreneurial opportunity

Ans (a) Need and problem

(ii) "Arul decided to work on a device that can lower this burden." Which of the following led to the entrepreneurial idea of Arul?
(a) Creativity (b) Innovation
(c) Invention (d) All of these

Ans (d) All of these

(iii) Which of the following values is represented by Arul in the above case?
(a) Responsibility
(b) Accountable
(c) Empathy
(d) Honesty

Ans (c) Empathy

(iv) It is very obvious that Arul is a social entrepreneur. Which of the following characteristics will Arul possess?
(a) Resourceful (b) Socially aware
(c) Innovation (d) All of these

Ans (d) All of these

(v) "He started working on his big venture that would help thousands of farmers across the world."
What is the main aim of Arul's venture?
(a) Wealth creation
(b) Upliftment of poorer sections
(c) Both (a) and (b)
(d) None of the above

Ans (b) Upliftment of poorer sections

Short Answer Type I Questions (2 Marks)

1 Explain the role of entrepreneurs as innovators.

Ans An entrepreneur is known to be a person, who habitually creates and innovates to build something of value around perceived opportunities.

It has been observed that ideas usually evolve through a creative process, whereby, imaginative people like the entrepreneurs innovate the ideas so created.

2 Write about any two innovations which led to entrepreneurial ventures. **CBSE TBQ**

Ans The two innovations which led to entrepreneurial ventures are as follows

(i) **Potato Chips** Chef George Crum was trying to make a plate of fried potato. On a customer's complaint, he sliced the potatoes thinly and fried them until they were hard. This is how potato chips came into existence.

(ii) **Microwave Ovens** Percy Spencer, an engineer was conducting a radar-related research project with a new vacuum tube. He found that the candy bar in his pocket began to melt during his experiment. He then put popcorn into the machine and when it started to pop, he knew he had a revolutionary device on his hands.

3 Define 'social entrepreneur'.

Ans **Martin and Osberg** define social entrepreneur as, "The social entrepreneur aims for value in the form of large- scale transformational benefit that accrues either to a significant segment of society or to society at large".

4 State the different characteristics of social entrepreneurs.

Ans The different characteristics possessed by social entrepreneurs are as follows

(i) Social catalysts (ii) Socially aware
(iii) Opportunity seeking
(iv) Innovative (v) Resourceful
(vi) Accountable

5 "Though social entrepreneurs may act locally, their actions have the potential to stimulate global improvements in their chosen arenas, whether that is education, healthcare, economic development, the environment, the arts or any other social field." In the light of the above statement, discuss the characteristics of social entrepreneurs.

Ans Social entrepreneurs generally possess the following characteristics

(i) **Opportunity Seeking** These entrepreneurs are not disheartened by the obstacles in their path. They relentlessly pursue their goals, seeing every obstacle as an opportunity to develop and fine-tune their business models.

(ii) **Innovative** Social entrepreneurs are creative, willing to think outside the box and ready to apply ideas to new situations.

They understand that not every innovation will be a success and they see failures as learning opportunities even as they strive for success.

6 Give the contribution of the following social entrepreneurs
(i) Vinoba Bhave
(ii) Bunker Roy

Ans (i) **Vinoba Bhave** He is the founder and leader of the 'Bhudaan Andolan'. He caused the redistribution of more than 7,00,000 acres of land to help India's untouchables and landless.

(ii) **Bunker Roy** He is the founder of 'Barefoot College', which promotes rural development through innovative education programmes.

7 Differentiate between social entrepreneurship and entrepreneurship. **CBSE TBQ**

Ans In entrepreneurship, the final objective is wealth creation. But in social entrepreneurship, wealth creation is simply a means to an end. The social entrepreneur participates in profit making ventures only to use the profits generated to create valuable social programmes for the upliftment of the whole community.

8 Dr. Abraham M. George, is the founder of the George foundation. It was established in January, 1995 in Bangalore, India. Their mission is to work towards poverty eradication, promote environmental health and strengthen democratic institutions and values in developing countries. Dr. Abraham M George is totally different from Mr. Sanders, founder of KFC.

Mention two difference between two types of entrepreneurs discussed above.

Ans In the given case, Dr. George is social entrepreneur while Mr. Sanders is a normal entrepreneur. Following are the points of difference between the two

(i) In entrepreneurship, an entrepreneur participates in entrepreneurial venture with the aim of earning profit, but a social entrepreneur participates in business ventures only to use the profits generated to create valuable social programmes for the whole society.

(ii) Entrepreneur works for self-development, but social entrepreneur works for societal development.

9 Explain business intelligence. **CBSE TBQ**

Ans Business intelligence is the ability of an organisation to collect, maintain and organise data. Business intelligence enables organisations to gather quantifiable data on each related area of the organisation and analyse it in a way that yields information they can act on, thereby helping them to enhance their decision-making capabilities, improve their performance, mitigate risk and even create new business models.

10 Business intelligence is the ability of an organisation to collect, maintain and organise data. In the light of the above statement, give the benefits of business intelligence for an organisation.

Ans Benefits of business intelligence are as follows

(i) It helps business to gather data on each area of operation.

(ii) It enables a business to take a better strategic decision.

11 Entrepreneurship isn't an easy or simple profession, but as with any field, there are basic principles that govern success. The most fundamental truth in entrepreneurship is this: find a problem and be the solution.

If you want to become a successful entrepreneur, your business must fill a gap, solve an issue, or provide a product that didn't previously exist.

That's exactly what entrepreneurs Carl C. Schuessler, Jr. and Barry Murphy did. They understood that the healthcare crisis in America is ongoing and many employers are struggling to navigate it. They found that employer-provided health insurance can be a confusing road to navigate, and it is difficult for employers to provide quality benefits at a cost that respects the corporate bottom line.

With failed solutions from traditional health insurance carriers, many employers have given up on trying to find good, yet affordable, coverage for their staff.

Source *Forbes.com/ sites/ shamahyder/ 2021/ 08127.*

(i) Which concept is highlighted in the above paragraph?

(ii) Mention the reason for the concept so identified.

Ans (i) Entrepreneurs as problem solvers.
(ii) Entrepreneurs are considered as problem solvers because they offer effective solutions by using their creativity and innovation skills that exploit opportunities.

Short Answer Type II Questions (3 Marks)

1 Discuss the role of entrepreneurs as innovators and problem solvers.

Ans Refer to text on page 85.

2 Explain the role played by entrepreneur as that of a problem solver with the help of a diagram.

Ans An entrepreneur is a person who undertakes risk and tries to resolve the problems faced by the society and earn profit in this process. Entrepreneurial actions are efforts to solve problems of others.

When one solves a problem, a new value is created which leads to the creation of a new profitable enterprise.

It can be represented as

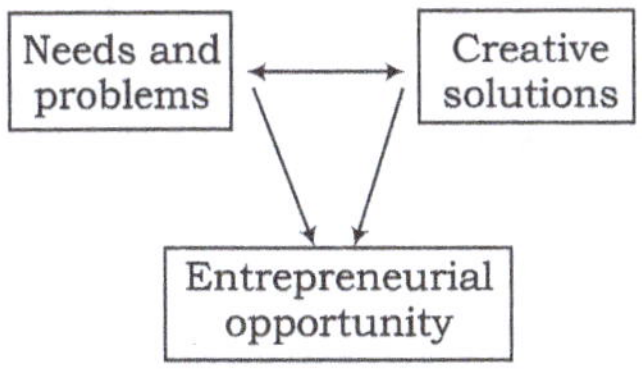

3 Sir Alexander Fleming, John Hopps and Percy Spencer are the names of prominent innovators and inventors. Discuss the innovations created by them and what were they originally trying to make?

Ans Refer to text on page 86.

4 Why there is a need for social entrepreneurs?

Ans In the current economic crisis, financial pressures are further worsening the existing social problems of poverty and unemployment.

According to **J Gregory Dees**, Social entrepreneurship is necessary to mitigate the financial repercussions among vulnerable. With pay cuts and job losses happening all over the world, the needs of the hour are ideas, innovations, creative solutions and fresh perspective that can cater to the changing market demands, emerging economies and a new world economic order and social entrepreneurs fulfil these needs.

5 Razaq is a native of the beautiful valley of Kashmir. His family owns an apple orchard. During his summer break, he decided to help his family at the orchard. He observed that a lot of time was lost in plucking and picking apples.

Being of an innovative mind, he worked on solving the above problem and made a simple plucking device attached with a net and a knife. This saved considerable time and money.

(i) Identify the role played by Razaq.
(ii) Discuss the inventions of any two entrepreneurs as innovators.

Ans (i) Razaq has played the role of innovator and problem solver.
(ii) Refer to text on page 86.

6 Discuss briefly the role of technology in today's business.

Ans Over the past 25 years, digital revolution has changed the way a business works, by providing them with a cost effective technology to cope up with increasingly complex challenges.

However, the growing needs of the business demand for more complex and efficient technologies.

Satisfying these demands of business will lead to an explosive growth in data and analytics, new competition in almost every field and disruption and realignment of many industries. Emerging market will create plenty of opportunities related to smart technology, both in profit and non-profit organisations.

7 What is cloud computing? **CBSE TBQ**

Ans Cloud computing means storing and accessing data and programs over the internet instead of through a computer's hard drive.

The word 'cloud' is used as a metaphor for the internet, based on the standardised use of a cloud like shape to denote a network.

Cloud computing helps an organisation to upload all its data on a cloud and then they can access it even from remote areas, when required.

e.g. in case of a phone and a laptop of Apple Inc, whenever a photo is clicked on phone, it automatically gets updated on to the laptop through cloud computing.

8 Explain smart mobility and information collection as new business forms. **CBSE TBQ**

Ans (i) **Smart Mobility** Those devices which are mobile help in the growth of business. Smart mobility will change the way people interact. Increasingly smart devices like portable tools that connect to the internet have become a part of our lives.

The move to an increasingly mobile world will create new players and new opportunities for a variety of industries.

(ii) **Information Collection** In this competitive world, in order to attract a customer, the entrepreneur needs to have the information regarding customers. Information related to a customer like his age, regularity of visit to the shop, preferences of his purchases, all these factors enable an entrepreneur to understand the taste and preference of the customer, so that they can serve him better and ensure his loyalty.

Long Answer Type Questions (5 Marks)

1 Kellogg's corn flakes have become a household name today, state the story regarding this invention.

Ans **Story regarding the Invention of Kellogg** Refer to text on page 85.

2 Discuss any five innovations, which led to successful ventures.

Ans Refer to text on page 86.

3 Who are social entrepreneurs? Give any three examples of social entrepreneurs.

Ans **Social Entrepreneurs** Refer to Q.No. 3 of short answer type I questions (2 Marks).

Examples of Social Entrepreneurs Refer to text on page 88 and 89.

4 Dinesh, after completing his studies, returned to his hometown, Jabalpur. Jabalpur is famous for its soft marble and many craftsmen make beautiful statues from this marble. Yet, he was surprised to learn that they made barely enough to fulfil their basic needs.

On researching about the probable reasons for their plight, he found that they were unorganised and lacked the financial strength to market their produce.

He decided to organise these craftsmen in the form of a cooperative society. The cooperative society provided finance to the craftsmen, and helped them to market their products through an e-portal. Within 2 years, the standard of living of the craftsmen improved considerably.

(i) To which category of entrepreneur does Dinesh belong to?

(ii) Explain its importance.

Ans (i) Dinesh is a social entrepreneur. Social entrepreneurs can assess a social problem and find a solution to the problem leading to eradication of poverty and improvement in the standard of living, as illustrated in the above case.

(ii) Refer to topic 'Need for social entrepreneurs' on page 88.

5 Enumerate the characteristics of social entrepreneurs. **CBSE TBQ**

or Discuss the various characteristics possessed by social entrepreneurs.

Ans Refer to text on page 87 and 88.

6 Briefly explain why social entrepreneurs are the need of hour?

Ans Social entrepreneurs are needed in a society because of the below mentioned reasons

(i) **They lead to Employment Development** The first major advantage of a social entrepreneur is that he/she creates jobs and employment opportunities in a society.

(ii) **They Develop New Goods and Services** Social entrepreneurs develop an environment conducive for the growth of innovation, thereby, leading to the development of new goods and services.

e.g. Brazilian social entrepreneur Veronica Khosa developed a new home based care model for AIDS patients which later changed the government's health policy.

(iii) **They provide Social Capital** Social entrepreneurs provide the much needed capital for the development of society by channelising the savings of the unorganised section of society.

(iv) **They promote Equity** Social entrepreneurs promote a equitable society by addressing social issues and trying to achieve ongoing sustainable impact through their social mission.

7 Discuss the contributions made by the following social entrepreneurs.
(i) Muhammad Yunus
(ii) Ela Bhatt
(iii) Dr Abraham M George
(iv) Nand Kishore Chaudhary
(v) Harish Hande

Ans Refer to text on page 88 and 89.

8 Swarna runs a high-end boutique. With growing competition from readymade clothes, she decided to venture into the field of e-commerce, trading in the handicrafts of our country. Suggest to her certain new technological advancements and also discuss any of two of them.

Ans The new technological advancements are as follows
(i) Information collection
(ii) Business intelligence
(iii) Smart mobility (iv) Cloud computing
(v) Power of social media

For explanation of any two technological advantages, refer to Q. No. 8 of short answer type II questions (3 Marks).

9 This article aims to understand the extent to which Social Entrepreneurship (SE) contributes to the construction of a collective dimension linked to Social Innovation (SI). We aim to propose new ideas that can deliver insights into the SE phenomenon.

This research is also distinct from entrepreneurial ecosystems as its development already requires some successful entrepreneurial action and to do it, the structuring and consolidation of an entrepreneurial ecosystem constitutes a real challenge for the development of SI.

This work has been based on a participant observation of eight major events dedicated to social entrepreneurship or the shared economy. In-depth interviews with Tunisian social entrepreneurs were also conducted in order to enrich our corpus.

The results show the necessary cooperation of social entrepreneurs for a sustainable and responsible social innovation.

Indeed, the analysis emphasizes that the viability and sustainability of a social innovation rests essentially on a collective construction, beyond common social values.

Source *Journal of Innovation and Entrepreneurship volume 10, Article number: 14 (2021)*

(i) Which concept is highlighted in the above paragraph?
(ii) Discuss some of its characteristics.

Ans (i) Social entrepreneurship.
(ii) Refer to text on page 87 and 88.

CASE STUDIES

Case 1

Japanese Like their Fish Fresh!

The Japanese have always loved fresh fish. But the waters close to Japan have not held many fish for decades. So, to feed the Japanese population, fishing boats got bigger and went farther than ever. The farther the fishermen went, the longer it took to bring in the fish. If the return trip took more than a few days, the fish were not fresh. The Japanese did not like the taste.

To solve this problem, fishing companies installed freezers on their boats. They would catch the fish and freeze them at sea. Freezers allowed the boats to go farther and stay longer. However, the Japanese could taste the difference between fresh and frozen and they did not like frozen fish. The frozen fish brought a lower price.

So, fishing companies installed fish tanks. They would catch the fish and store them in the tanks. After a little thrashing around, the fish stopped moving.

They were tired and dull, but alive. Unfortunately, the Japanese could still taste the difference because the fish did not move for days, they lost their fresh fish taste.

The Japanese preferred the lively taste of fresh fish, not sluggish fish. So how did Japanese fishing companies solve this problem?

How do they get fresh tasting fish to Japan? How do the Japanese manage to keep the fish fresh?

To keep the fish tasting fresh, the Japanese fishing companies still put the fish in the tanks. But now, they add a small shark to each tank.

The shark eats a few fish, but most of the fish arrive in a very lively state. The fish are challenged.

Have you realised that some of us are also living in a pond, but most of the time feel tired and dull, so we need a 'Shark' in our life to keep us awake and moving? Basically in our lives, sharks are new challenges to keep us active.

For an entrepreneur, the main motivating factor which urges them to continue in their entrepreneurial pursuit is challenge. The more intelligent, persistent and competent they are, the more they enjoy a challenge.

From this story, it is clear that, to be a successful entrepreneur, one has to be a problem solver.

The various problems involved in the story and the various solutions available to solve it are summarised below

	Problems	**Solutions**
(a)	Love for fish	Led to using of bigger boats
(b)	Need for fresh fish	Installation of freezers
(c)	Taste of fresh fish	Installation of fish tanks
(d)	To improve taste of the fresh fish	Added shark

1 Which entrepreneurial feature did the Japanese fishing companies exhibit?

Ans The Japanese fishing companies exhibited the feature that entrepreneurs are problem solvers.

2 List the innovative ideas they generated to keep the fish fresh.

Ans The innovative ideas generated by them are as follows

(i) Use of bigger boats for fishing.
(ii) Installation of freezers in the boats.
(iii) Installation of fish tanks in the boats.
(iv) Shark added to the fish tanks.

Case 2

Humble Beginning of KFC

In 1930, the then 40 years old Sanders was operating a service station in Corby, Kentucky, USA and he encountered a lot of hungry travellers who stopped for gas. He saw that the travellers wanted to eat something as there was nothing available in that area. He saw and understood the problem.

As a child, he used to cook for his siblings and so he knew how to cook, which instigated him to cook for the travellers. He did not even have a restaurant to serve food but his secret blend of 11 herbs and spices made his chicken recipe such a super hit among travellers that he started getting regular customers for his food, which prompted him to start a restaurant.

This is the humble beginning of the world famous fast food chain 'KFC-Kentucky Fried Chicken'.

1 Which problem did Sanders set to resolve?

Ans Sanders encountered a lot of hungry travellers, who stopped at his service station for gas. He saw that the travellers wanted to eat something and there was nothing available. So, this problem instigated him to cook for the travellers.

2 What is the reason behind the success of KFC?

Ans The reason behind the success of KFC is Sanders secret blend of 11 herbs and spices that make his chicken recipe a winner.

3 How did KFC begin its operations? **CBSE TBQ**

Ans In 1930, Sanders was operating a service station in Corby, Kentucky, USA. He observed that the travellers wanted to eat something and there was nothing available in that area. This instigated him to cook for the travellers. His chicken recipe with a secret blend of 11 herbs and spices was a hit and he started getting regular customers, which prompted him to start a restaurant.

Case 3

Operation Flood– The Man Behind Mr Verghese Kurien

This has been the story of a young engineer, who was born in Calicut and was later known as the Father of the White Revolution and was honoured with some of the most prestigious government awards like Padma Vibhushan, Ramon Magsaysay and Krushi Ratna.

He breathed his last on 9th December, 2012, but he will always be remembered for his immense contribution to the farmers, to the Amul brand and to the millions of consumers of dairy products.

The year was 1964 when our Prime Minister Mr Lal Bahadur Shastri was invited to Anand to inaugurate the new cattle-feed plant of Amul.

He was supposed to return back by end of the day but after reaching Anand, he insisted to stay there to learn about the success of the cooperatives.

He visited almost all the cooperatives with Dr Kurien and was impressed with the process with which Amul was sourcing the milk from farmers and at the same time helping them to improve their economic condition.

Later, he returned to Delhi and asked Dr Kurien to replicate the Amul pattern across the country. The combined effort resulted in creation of the National Dairy Development Board (NDDB) in the year 1965.

Dr Kurien took charge of NDDB and began the herculean task of replicating the overall pattern of the working at Anand to other parts of the country.

By this time, the demand for milk was growing at a faster rate than the supply. India could have easily become the largest importer of milk like Sri Lanka, if sufficient steps not been taken at that time by the Indian Government and NDDB.

Money was the biggest problem faced by NDDB during that period and was a critical resource needed to revolutionise the milk industry. To deal with it, NDDB tried to pursue the World Bank for loans and other grants with no conditions at all.

When the President of the World Bank came to India in 1969, Dr Kurien told him "Give me money and forget about it".

A few days later, World Bank approved the loan for NDDB without even a single condition. This help was part of an operation, later known as Operation Flood which was done to replicate the Anand working pattern across India.

Operation Flood was subsequently implemented in India in three phases, adding around 0.1 million cooperatives and 5 million milk producers.

Dr Kurien also took several other measures such as developing milk powder, developing several varieties of dairy products, emphasising on the health of cattle and development of vaccines, etc.

In 1973, he also set-up Gujarat Cooperative Milk Marketing Federation (GCMMF), an individual marketing unit of Amul to sell Amul as a brand in India as well as abroad.

He also founded Institute of Rural Management Anand (IRMA) in 1979, to pass on the gained knowledge to future generations and to place rural India on the map of India.

As a result of these combined efforts, Amul currently boasts of 15 million milk producers pouring their milk in 1,44,246 dairy cooperative societies across the country - a huge chain that has resulted in India's being the largest milk producing country today.

1 Who is known as the 'Father of White Revolution'?

Ans Dr Kurien is known as the 'Father of White Revolution'.

2 Which social problem was addressed by Dr Kurien in his role of a social entrepreneur?

Ans Dr Kurien addressed the problem of milk shortage in the country.

3 Which institutions were established by Dr Kurien?

Ans Dr Kurien established the following institutions

(i) National Dairy Development Board (NDDB)
(ii) Gujarat Co-operative Milk Marketing Federation (GCMMF)
(iii) Institute of Rural Management Anand (IRMA)

Case 4

Formation of SEWA

(Self-Employed Women's Association)

In 1971, a few women handcart pullers approached Ela Bhatt, head of the women's wing of the textile labour association in Ahmedabad, with problems like low and erratic wages, poor working conditions, etc.

Bhatt was aware that most of the women did petty jobs, working as garment makers, vegetable vendors, handcart pullers, milkmaids, hawkers, etc to supplement their family income. About 97% of the women lived in slums and 93% were illiterate. Bhatt soon realised that the women in the informal sector were unorganised, unprotected, economically weak and had no bargaining power.

In 1972, the garment workers formed their own cooperative. They were the first group to be organised under SEWA. By 1977, six other groups-used garment dealers, handcart pullers, vegetable vendors, junk-smiths, milk producers and miscellaneous workers formed their own cooperatives.

The cooperatives were formed with the share capital provided by the women. Each cooperative was run by a democratically elected executive committee of workers. Initially, SEWA provided the required capital to the cooperatives, but once they were established, they functioned on their own.

The members of the cooperatives shared their skills and expertise, developed new tools, designs and techniques and were engaged in joint marketing efforts.

The members of SEWA have increased from 320 in 1973 to 6,94, 551 in 2002. Any self-employed woman over the age of 15 was eligible to become a member of SEWA by paying a nominal annual fee of ₹ 3. In 1975, the annual membership fee was increased to ₹ 5.

Since, its inception in the early 1970s, SEWA has been working towards organising and empowering poor, self-employed women in rural and urban areas in India. SEWA has helped them to get regular employment, easy access to credit, childcare, healthcare facilities.

1 What problems were faced by the women working in the informal sector?

Ans The problems faced by the women working in the informal sector were

(i) Low and erratic wages
(ii) Poor working conditions.

2 In what ways has SEWA helped poor, self-employed women in the rural and urban areas of India?

Ans SEWA has helped them to get regular employment, easy access to credit, childcare and healthcare facilities.

3 SEWA is the brain child of which social entrepreneur?

Ans SEWA is the brain child of Ela Bhatt, head of the women's wing of the textile labour association in Ahmedabad.

Case 5

Lijjat Papad

Everyone enjoys 'rags to riches' stories and everyone likes tales of stupendous success achieved through sheer determination. The story of Shri Mahila Griha Udyog Lijjat Papad is all that and much more.

Shri Mahila Griha Udyog Lijjat Papad

Today, Lijjat is more than just a household name for 'papad'. Started with a modest loan of ₹ 80, the cooperative now has annual sales exceeding ₹ 301 crore. What's more stunning than its stupendous success is its striking simplicity.

Sticking to its core values for the past 40 years, Lijjat has ensured that every process runs smoothly, members earn a comfortable profit, agents get their due share, consumers get the assurance of quality at a good price and society benefits from its donations to various causes. How has all this been possible? Its story shows, how an organisation can infuse Gandhian simplicity in all its activities.

Lijjat was the brain child of seven Gujarati women from Bombay (now Mumbai). The women lived in Lohana Niwas, a group of five buildings in Girgaum.

They wanted to start a venture to create a sustainable livelihood using the only skill they had, i.e. cooking. Some of their names were Jaswantiben Jamnadas Popat, Parvatiben Ramdas Thodani, Ujamben Narandas Kundalia, Banuben N Tanna, Laguben Amritlar Gokani, Jayaben V Vithalani.

The women borrowed ₹ 80 from Chhaganlal Karamsi Parekh, a member of the Servants of India Society and a social worker.

They took over papad making venture, which was running in loss owned by Laxmidas bhai and bought the necessary ingredients and the basic infrastructure required to manufacture papads. On 15th March, 1959, they gathered on the terrace of their building and started with the production of 4 packets of papads. They started selling the papads to a known merchant in Bhuleshwar. From the beginning, the women had decided that they would not approach anyone for donations or help, even if the organisation incurred losses.

Chhaganlal Karamsi Parekh, popularly known as Chaganbapa, became their guide. Initially, the women were making two different qualities of papads, in order to sell the inferior one at a cheaper rate. Chaganbapa advised them to make a standard papad and asked them never to compromise on quality. He emphasised the importance of running it as a business enterprise and maintaining proper account.

Lijjat expanded as a cooperative system. Initially, even younger girls could join, but later eighteen was fixed as the minimum age of entry. Within three months, there were about 25 women making papads. Soon the women bought some equipment for the business, like utensils, cupboards, stoves, etc. In the first year, the organisation's annual sales were ₹ 6,196. The broken papads were distributed among neighbours.

During the first year, the women had to stop production for four months during the rainy season as the rains would prevent the drying of the papads. The next year, they solved the problem by buying a cot and a stove. The papads were kept on the cot and the stove below the cot so that the process of drying could take place inspite of the rains.

The group got considerable publicity through word of mouth and articles in vernacular newspapers. This publicity helped in increasing its membership. By the second year of its formation, 100 to 150 women had joined the group and by the end of the third year, it had more than 300 members.

The members were called as 'Ben/Sister'. By this time, the terrace of seven founders could no longer accommodate the members and the ingredients, so the kneaded flour was distributed among the members who would take it to their homes and make papads.

Every morning a group of women go to the Lijjat branch to knead dough, which is then collected by other women who roll it into papads. When these women come to collect the dough, they also hand in the previous day's production, which is tested for quality. If the quality is not maintained, then the woman would be served a warning and they might be removed from the organisation at a later stage.

They have accountants in every branch and every centre has to maintain daily accounts. Profit (or loss, if any) is shared among all the members of that branch. They have a committee of 21, that decides how the profits are to be distributed. We generally buy gold coins 5 gm or 10 gm, depending on the profit. Everyone gets an equal share of profit, irrespective of who does what work, irrespective of seniority or responsibility. Even a woman who has recently joined gets the same share as others who have been with the organisation longer. Each branch calculates its profit and divides it equally among all its members. Mumbai has 12,000 members, the rest of Maharashtra has 22,000 and Gujarat has between 5,000 to 7,000 members.

Exports

Exports alone account for ₹ 10 crores. They are not directly involved in exporting, but recognised professional merchant exporters (who also export other food products) place an export order.

Only on receiving the full advance through a cheque, they begin production. Because all exports are done from Mumbai, the supply also comes from there. Export production is of the same quality as daily production.

1 Which factors have contributed towards the stupendous success of Lijjat Papads?

Ans The factors which have contributed towards the success of Lijjat Papads are

(i) Ensuring that every process runs smoothly.
(ii) Members earn a comfortable profit.
(iii) Agents get their due share.
(iv) Consumers get the assurance of quality at a good price.
(v) Society benefits from its donations to various causes.

2 Which values of social entrepreneurship stand highlighted by this cooperative society?

Ans The values which stand highlighted are as follows

(i) Providing employment opportunities for the underprivileged.
(ii) Treating each and every worker as equal and giving them a share in profit.
(iii) Helping India earn foreign exchange and thus, contributing towards the economic development of the country.

3 Explain the success story of Lijjat Papad. **CBSE TBQ**

Ans Lijjat was the brain child of seven Gujarati women from Bombay (now Mumbai). They wanted to start a venture to create a sustainable livelihood using the only skill they had, i.e. cooking.

The women borrowed ₹ 80 from Chhaganlal Parekh, who was a social worker. They took over the papad making venture which was running in loss, owned by Laxmidas bhai and bought the necessary ingredients and the basic infrastructure required to make papads.

On 15th March, 1959, they gathered on the terrace of their building and started with the production of four packets of papad. They started selling the papads to a known merchant of Bhuleshwar. Chhaganlal became their guide. Initially, the women were making two different qualities of papads, in order to sell the inferior one at a cheaper rate. Chhaganlal advised them to make a standard papad and asked them to never compromise on quality.

He emphasised the importance of running it as a business enterprise and maintaining proper accounts. Lijjat expanded as a cooperative system. Within 3 months, there were about 25 women making papads. In the first year, the organisation's annual sales were ₹ 6,196.

The group got considerable publicity through word of mouth and articles in vernacular newspapers. This helped in increasing its membership. By the end of the third year, it had more than 300 members.

By this time, the terrace of the seven founders could no longer accommodate the members and the kneaded flour was distributed among the members who would take it to their homes and make papads. When these women came to collect the dough, they also handed in the previous day's production, which was tested for quality.

They have a committee of 21, that decides how the profits are to be distributed. Everyone gets an equal share of profit, irrespective of who does what work, irrespective of seniority or responsibility.

CHAPTER ASSESSMENT

Objective Type Questions (1 Mark)

1 Entrepreneurs are referred to as

(a) businessmen

(b) vendors

(c) Both (a) and (b)

(d) problem solvers

2 The more or larger problems an entrepreneurial organisation solves, the more .... it can generate.

(a) profit

(b) revenue

(c) Both (a) and (b) (d) None of these

3 .... are the distinguishing marks of an entrepreneur.

(a) Creativity

(b) Innovation

(c) Both (a) and (b) (d) None of these

4 Percy Spencer was an .... with Raytheon Corporation.

5 Fleming was searching for a .... that could cure diseases.

6 Inkjet printer was invented by Percy Spencer. State true or false.

7 The word 'cloud' is used as a metaphor for the internet. State true or false.

Short Answer Type I Questions (2 Marks)

8 What do you mean by 'Entrepreneurs as problem solvers'?

9 How was pacemaker created?

10 What was invented by Sir Alexander Fleming? What was he trying to make?

Short Answer Type II Questions (3 Marks)

11 Explain briefly the role of technology in today's business.

12 Discuss briefly business intelligence.

13 Write a short note on 'Smart mobility'.

14 Highlight the importance of social media in the present era.

Long Answer Type Questions (5 Marks)

15 Discuss briefly the terms 'Social entrepreneurship' and 'Social entrepreneur'.

16 Explain any four characteristics of social entrepreneurs.

17 Mention any two examples of social entrepreneurs. Also explain the importance of social entrepreneurs.

18 Differentiate between entrepreneurship and social entrepreneurship.

For explanations scan the given QR Code

CHAPTER 05

Concept of Market

In this Chapter...

- Market
- Analysing the market environment
- Market research
- Marketing mix

Market

The word 'market' is derived from the Latin word *'marcatus'* meaning merchandise, ware, traffic, trade or a place where business is conducted. In the most basic sense, market refers to a place where goods are purchased and sold.

However, the modern management thinkers define market as, "An arrangement of establishing effective relationship between buyers and sellers of the commodities. It consists of all the potential customers sharing a particular need or want, who might be willing and able to engage in exchange to satisfy that need or want".

Keeping the above definition in mind, it can be concluded that market includes mechanisms or means for

- Determining the price of the traded item with the help of market forces of demand and supply.
- Communicating the price information.
- Facilitating deals and transactions.
- Effecting distribution.

In a market, commodities and services flow from producers to consumers.

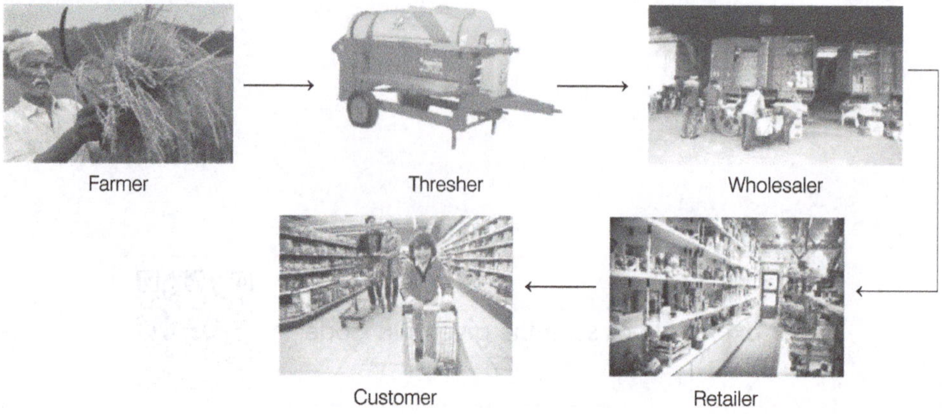

Concepts of Market

Markets which are responsible for making the economy strong and stable, have a very dynamic concept which is constantly evolving with the changing times.

The concepts pertaining to market can be classified as follows

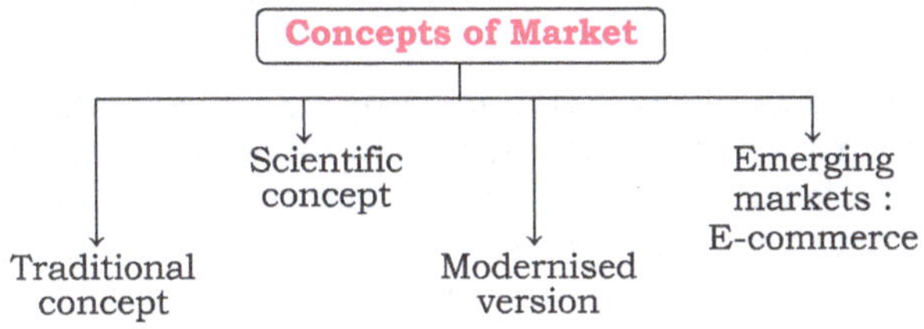

1. Traditional Concept of Market/Traditional Markets

The traditional market concept corresponds to the early production phase when there was a general scarcity of manufactured goods in the market.

This concept of market was prevalent in the 'pre-industrial revolution' era which was characterised by an agriculture-cum-handicraft economy, with no elaborate distribution system.

The agriculturist, whether he produced corn or cotton, meat or butter disposed of the surplus in his immediate neighbourhood. Because of this tendency, traditional concept focuses that market means 'a place' only, where actual buying and selling takes place.

As per **American Market Association**, the traditional concept of market is defined as, "At every point where a specific commodity is concentrated for sale, a market is found".

The definition gives the traditional meaning of market which lays emphasis on the following

(i) **Place** The goods available for sale are brought to a specific place and the buyers of those goods reach those places for buying them.

(ii) **Different Markets for Different Commodities** The traditional concept identifies different markets for different commodities. e.g. in a vegetable market, vegetables are bought and sold; in a foodgrain market, various foodgrains such as rice, wheat, lentils, etc., are bought and sold.

2. Scientific Concept of Market

According to **Cournot**, "The term 'market' is not any particular place in which things are bought and sold but the whole of any region where buyers and sellers are in such free intercourse with one another that the price of the same goods tends to equality easily and quickly".

This concept of market widens the area of market by advocating that

- Market is not restricted to a particular place, but to a region and the whole region is taken as a place of market.
- The buyers and sellers of the whole region have free access to one another.
- This accessibility enables the market forces of demand and supply to operate and helps in determining the market price.
- The whole region is taken as a place of market.

This concept of market was prevalent after the World War II, especially in the fifties and sixties, when the size and character of the markets changed due to the intensification of industrial activity in terms of

– Quantity
– Quality
– Variety of the products
– Competition
– Awareness on the part of consumers
– Emergence of laws and enactments to protect consumer's interest

3. Modernised Version

(Market of Seventies/Eighties)

Every business activity is consumer oriented. According to **Peter Drucker**, "The purpose of the business is to create customers and customers do not have geographical boundaries".

According to **Clark and Clark**, "In fact, for most commodities, the market must not be thought as a geographical meeting place, but as any getting together of buyers and sellers in person by mail, telephone, telegraph or by any other means of communication".

So, keeping the above two definitions in mind, this concept of market can be summarised as, "A market is the atmosphere of a region in which the forces of demand and supply operate directly or by means of any kind of communication that are sufficient to bring about transfer in the title of the goods and it does not necessarily mean only a place where actual buying and selling is conducted".

An analysis of the above definitions conveys that the market is not taken as a geographical place, but it is rather a meeting of

- Buyers and sellers of a given commodity.
- Buyers and sellers who remain in close contact with each other through any means, either personally or through mails, phones, etc.
- Buyers and sellers who are in competition with each other. Buyers want to pay the lowest price and sellers want to charge the highest price.
- The place of meeting can be regional, national or even international.

This concept of market was prevalent in the seventies and eighties when industrialisation was advanced and means of transport and communication had also developed, thus enabling buyers and sellers living anywhere to enter into a transaction.

4. Emerging Markets : E-commerce

The world today is changing fast and Indian economy has also undergone number of changes. The profile of the Indian market is vastly different from what it was ten years ago. Modern business is facing global competition due to globalisation and increased customer expectation due to changes in technology.

According to **DYDDY Concept,** "Markets are people with money to spend and desire to spend it".

This concept of market is prevalent now-a-days and the reason of its evolution could be traced to the changes in modern business in terms of

– Organisation
– Ways of working
– Use of technology
– Perspectives, scope and outlook

So, it can be safely concluded that this concept of market follows the adage 'market means people'.

This concept of market is also referred to as 'people oriented concept' as it totally ignores the place of activity. This concept of market advocates that

- People having money and desire to spend it are taken as market.
- A market cannot exist without people's willingness to buy and sell.

The major contributing factor towards this concept is the change in the advent of mass communication, which has helped in free flow of communication between the buyers and sellers.

The internet has evoked unparalleled and easier ways of conducting day-to-day transactions and business has been a major beneficiary of this boom.

E-business

E-business (i.e. electronic business) refers to carrying on business activities, both industrial and commercial through computer network, i.e. the internet.

E-business involves not only buying and selling, but through strategic use of electronic information, it enables an organisation to achieve objectives like creating new products and services, reaching new markets, enhancing organisational competitiveness, building new relationships between organisation and customers, etc.

Note *Students should keep in mind that business is a wider term and includes the following activities*
- *Industry, i.e. production and related activities.*
- *Commerce, i.e. trade and auxillaries to trade.*

Differences between e-business and e-commerce

Basis	E-business	E-commerce
Meaning	E-business can be defined as the conduct of industry, trade and commerce using the computer networks.	E-commerce involves the use of internet to place an order and pay for products and services.
Scope	E-business has a wider scope as it not only covers transactions relating to buying and selling, but also includes other business activities such as accounting, human resource management, etc.	E-commerce has a narrow scope as it only covers the interaction of the firm with its customers and suppliers over the internet. It basically revolves around buying and selling products and services over the internet. In fact, it can be said that e-commerce is a subset of e-business.

Role of E-business/E-commerce

E-business is offering great opportunities to entrepreneurs, especially in developing countries, by helping them to enter the prosperous global markets merely at the click of the mouse. E-business's growing popularity is because of the role it plays especially for the promotion of the business community.

The benefits that it provides to the entrepreneurs are discussed below

Benefits/Role of E-business

- Quick solution to doubts
- Updated information
- Extending markets
- Shortening of distribution channels
- Saving of time and cost
- Less risk in payments
- Easy to launch new products
- Lower personnel cost

(i) **Quick Solution to Doubts** E-business allows quick response to the queries and doubts of customers and other business houses, thus facilitating sales by increasing customer satisfaction.

(ii) **Updated Information** A company's website, which can be accessed from anywhere in the world, provides first hand latest information about the price of the product/service, discount offered, quality, features, range, etc., available to the consumers merely at the click of the mouse.

(iii) **Extending Markets** Because of e-business, the markets have become global. Sales can be made to customers spread all over the world. It has also made possible to make goods available in those areas where there are no physical markets present, like rural areas.

(iv) **Shortening of Distribution Channels** With the advent of e-business, producers have started having direct contact with the consumers, resulting in the reduction of middlemen and related costs.

This shortening of distribution channels has benefited both the consumers as well as the producers. Consumers get goods at relatively lower price directly from the producers and producers benefit in the form of increased sales revenues.

(v) **Saving of Time and Cost** Customers now do not have to physically visit the market to purchase goods.

They can now purchase the goods online because of e-commerce, thus saving time, cost and energy.

(vi) **Less Risk in Payments** Under e-business, payments can be made on the internet through the medium of credit cards and debit cards issued by the bank, thus reducing risks involved in the transfer of money.

(vii) **Easy to Launch New Products** Any company can launch its new products in the market through the medium of e-business much more easily. Mails, catalogues, photographs, etc., can help customers to understand the product better.

(viii) **Lower Personnel Cost** The number of personnel required decreases with the help of e-business because a single computer is good enough to do the job of many employees more quickly and correctly. This leads to help the entrepreneur in lowering the cost of production and raise sales.

Types of Market

Markets can be classified on the following basis

I. On the Basis of Geographical Area

1. **Local Market** In this type of market, buying and selling takes place in a limited area, in a town or a village.
2. **Regional Market** This is a market wherein buying and selling are restricted to a particular region or state.
3. **National Market** It is related to activities of buying and selling within boundaries of a country.
4. **International Market** It is a market where buyers and sellers of two or more nations are involved.

II. On the Basis of Position of Buyers and Sellers

1. **Primary Market** In this market, primary producers sell their agricultural output to wholesalers or their agents.
2. **Secondary Market** It is a market in which wholesalers sell their products to retailers.
3. **Terminal Market** It is a market where retailers sell their products to final consumers.

III. On the Basis of Nature of Transaction

1. **Spot Market** In this type of market, goods are transferred from sellers to buyers on the spot at the time of purchase.
2. **Future Market** In this type of market, buyers and sellers enter into a contract to buy/sell goods at a future date without the intention of actual delivery of goods. The purpose is to make profits through price fluctuations.

IV. On the Basis of Nature of Consumption

1. **Consumers' Market** When goods are produced for direct consumption of consumers, it is a consumers' market.
2. **Producers' Market** When goods are produced to be used further in the process of production, then it is a producers' market.

V. On the Basis of Subject of Exchange

1. **Commodity Market** Organised market for sale and purchase of commodities is referred to as commodities market. It is according to the prescribed rules and regulations.
2. **Money Market** Short-term finance market, which provides financing to business enterprises through a network of banking system is referred to as money market.
3. **Capital Market** Specialised market for providing long-term finance through a network of financial institutions, stock exchanges, investment trusts and insurance companies is known as 'capital market'.

VI. On the Basis of Competition

1. **Perfect Competitive Market** In this market, there are very large number of buyers and sellers of a commodity and homogeneous products are sold at a uniform price.
2. **Monoploy Market** In this market, there is a single seller and there are no close substitutes of the commodity sold by the monopolist.
3. **Monopolistic Competitive Market** In this market, there are many sellers of the product, but the product of each seller is somehow different from that of the others.
4. **Oligopoly Market** In this market, there are a few big sellers of a commodity and a large number of buyers.

CHECK POINT 01

1. What do you mean by market?
2. What is modern concept of market as per 'Peter Drucker'?
3. What does DYDDY Concept say?
4. What is meant by e-business?
5. Mention the names of types of market on the basis of position of buyers ad sellers.

Analysing the Market Environment

Market environment refers to the factors and forces that affect a firm's ability to build and maintain successful relationships with customers. A variety of environmental forces influence a company's marketing system.

Some of them are controllable while some others are uncontrollable. It is the responsibility of the marketing manager to change the company's policies along with the changing environment, or else be left behind in the market.

e.g. Google just appeared and captured, whereas solid companies like American Airlines and Avon are almost on the brink of winding up. Today, even the most established Indian brands are facing their biggest challenges in the changing environment and are drawing up plans to protect their market base.

Classification of Market Environment

The various factors and forces governing or exerting a pressure on the market can be categorised as

- Micro (Internal) Environment
- Macro (External) Environment

Micro Environment (Primary Forces)

This environment refers to the forces operating in the market that are close or within the organisation and affect its ability to serve its customers directly.

These factors are also termed as controllable factors because they can be controlled by the business. The goals, objectives, policies, strategies, etc, of the organisation are the foremost forces which govern a, firm's market strategy.

It comprises of the following forces

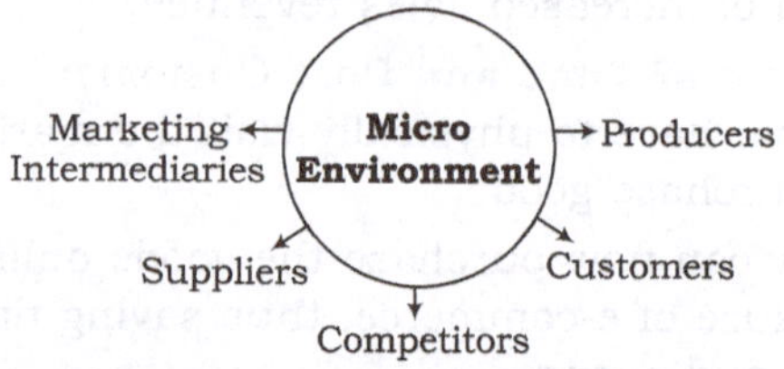

1. **Producers/Sellers** Producers/Sellers provide satisfaction to the consumers by making available the desired products or services to the customers with an objective of satisfying their needs and wants. e.g. Amul milk company tries to satisfy the customer's need for milk by providing them with good quality of milk.

If more is the number of producers, harder and healthier would be the competition. Ethics, values, principles, creativity, innovativeness of the seller help in setting trends for market.

It is the producer and his/her abilities that can create a market. Today we have markets for unconventional services like yoga, pranic healing, astrology, etc., and all credit goes to sellers.

Also, successful producers are those who can recognise and respond profitably to unmet needs and trends in the society. Unmet needs always exist in the society. Those producers who are able to satisfy these needs in a cost effective manner can be successful. Those producers rule the market, who are capable of

- Keeping themselves aware of market needs and trends.
- Giving market a solution for their unmet needs.
- Identifying opportunities and threats in the environment.

2. **Customers** According to **Charles G Mortimer**, "Instead of trying to market what is essential for us to make, we must find out much more about what the consumer is willing to buy .... we must apply our creativity more intelligently to people and their wants and needs, rather than products". What he actually wants to convey is that 'consumer is the king'.

   Consumer is the most influential force which rules the market. A business exists only because of its customers. Therefore, customer satisfaction is the foundation stone of a successful business. Business has to produce goods according to the needs of the customers.

   For creating, maintaining and retaining customers, a business should take into consideration the following factors

   - Traditions, customs, beliefs and values of society and customers.
   - Lifestyle, standard of living and consumption habits of the customers.
   - Propensity to consume and save.
   - Education level and thinking behaviour of the customers.
   - Income level of the customers.
   - Various other demographic characteristics of the customers, etc.

   Consumer demand is the most important factor of the micro environment as demand from consumers directly affects an enterprise's

   – Profitability – Reputation and goodwill
   – Expansion plans

3. **Competitors** They are such factors in the micro environment that provide similar goods and services. e.g. Coca-Cola is a competitor of Pepsi-Cola, while 'Sony' is a competitor of Matsushita.

   To remain competitive, an enterprise must consider who are their biggest competitors. With the introduction of the LPG (Liberalisation, Privatisation and Globalisation) policies, the level of competition has expanded to international level.

   For a business to be successful, it should make a correct assessment regarding

   - Who are our competitors?
   - Level/Size of competitors.
   - The areas of strengths/weaknesses of competitors.
   - The financial standing of competitors.
   - Overall image of competitors' products in the market.
   - Operational capacity of the competitors.

   Keeping the above factors in mind, an enterprise should develop a plan that gives them a strategic advantage over their competitors or else their business is bound to fail. As **Edmund Burke** very rightly said, "An opponent is our helper".

   For example, Eastman Kodak, in its film business, has been worrying about the growing competition from Fuji—the Japanese filmmaker. But in reality, Kodak faced a much greater threat from the recent invention of the 'filmless camera' sold by Canon and Sony, which takes video still pictures to be shown on a TV receiver. What greater threat is there to a film business than a filmless camera!

4. **Suppliers** A business is essentially a resource conversion machine that converts material, machines, labour and funds into useful products and these resources are obtained from the suppliers. Thus, suppliers are also the key component in the market system. The success of a business depends on how effectively a company manages its suppliers.

Lack of non-availability of suppliers can ruin the market for a product.

The following factors should be kept in mind for effective supplier management

- A business should always have multiple sources of suppliers.
- Cordial relationships should be built with the suppliers to ensure supply in times of shortage.
- Suppliers should be paid on time.

5. **Marketing Intermediaries** These are firms or individuals that facilitate the flow of goods and services between a business and its final consumers.

   These intermediaries aid a business in promoting, selling and distributing its goods to final buyers.

   They include re-sellers (i.e. wholesalers, retailers, agents and brokers), transporters, warehouses, banks and promoting agencies. All these institutions/individuals facilitate exchange in the market.

   The important factors to be kept in mind by an entrepreneur regarding this factor are as follows

   - Cost of distribution.
   - Retail margin of the intermediaries.
   - Nature of the product and the market.
   - Infrastructural facilities available.

Macro Environment (Secondary Forces)

It is also known as general and remote environment, and refers to factors which affect a business in general.

A business and the forces in its micro environment operate in a large macro environment that shapes opportunities and poses threats to the business. The macro forces are part of the larger society and are uncontrollable factors. Therefore, the success of a business depends on its adaptability to this environment with the help of micro environment forces.

e.g. if the cost of imported raw material increases substantially because of depreciation of domestic currency, then a company may adopt to this change by sourcing the material from domestic manufacturers.

The various forces operating in this environment are as follows

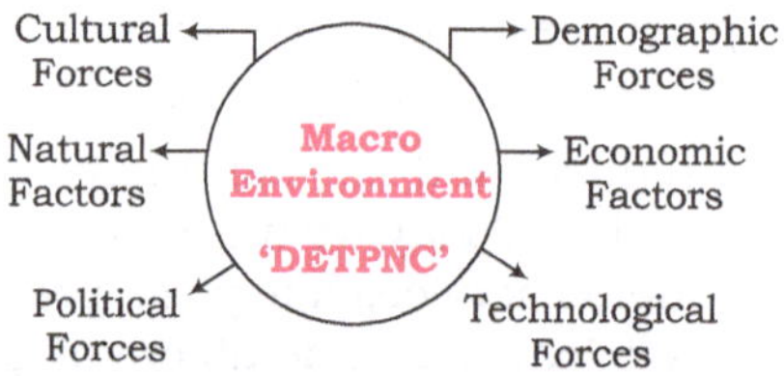

1. **Demographic Forces** These forces refer to human population in terms of size, density, location, age, gender, race and occupation. As we know that the demand of a product or a service depends on the people and their characteristics like their tastes and preferences, beliefs, income levels, etc, therefore, demographic forces are important factors of the macro environment.

   Important demographic bases of market segmentation include the following

   - Age structure, e.g. classifying groups of people according to the year they were born. These classifications can be referred to as 'baby boomers', who were born between 1946-1964; 'generation-X', who were born between 1965-1976; 'generation-Y', who were born between 1977-1994 and so on.
   - Gender
   - Income distribution
   - Family size
   - Family life cycle (e.g. young-single, young-married with no children, young-married with children, etc.)
   - Occupation
   - Education
   - Social class
   - Religion
   - Race
   - Nationality

   It should be remembered that the demographic environment differs from country-to-country and from place-to-place within the same country or region. Also, it changes significantly over time.

2. **Economic Factors** These factors include the structure and nature of economy, the stage of development of the economy, economic resources, the level of income, the distribution of income and assets, global economic linkages, economic policies of the government, etc.

   These factors are important as they affect the purchasing power of the customers and the way in which they spend their income. e.g. a buyer's behaviour will be different in boom than what it was in depression.

3. **Technological Forces** Technology is one of the important determinants of success of a firm as well as the factor affecting the economic and social development of a nation.

   Technology includes the tools, i.e. both machines (hard technology) and ways of thinking (soft technology) available to solve problems and promote progress between and among societies.

   The technological environment is perhaps one of the fastest changing factors in the macro environment.

   The following factors related to this environment are important for a business
   - Type of technology used.
   - Level of technological developments.
   - The speed with which new technologies are adopted and diffused.
   - The type of technology that is appropriate.
   - The technology policy, etc.

   This factor helps a business to gain a competitive edge over its competitors. As **Michael Porter** says, "Technological change is one of the principal drivers of competition. It plays a major role in an industry's structural change as well as in creating new industries. It is also a great equaliser, eroding the competitive advantage of even well-entrenched firms and propelling others to the forefront".

4. **Political Forces** The political environment includes all laws, government agencies and groups that influence or limit other organisations and individuals within a society. Market is regulated by these restrictions as they can be complex. It varies from place to place and time to time.

   As **Dimock** observes, "The two most powerful institutions in society today are business and government, where they meet on common ground amicably or otherwise, together they determine public policy, both foreign and domestic, for a nation".

   The important factors to be considered in this environment are as follows
   - Characteristics and policies of the political parties.
   - The nature of the Constitution.
   - The nature of the government system–whether democratic or dictatorial.
   - The government environment encompassing the economic and business policies and regulations.

   This factor is very important as the fate of businesses and markets depend to a large extent upon the political conditions of areas where they are situated. As laws and regulations change often, this is a very important aspect for a marketer to monitor.

5. **Natural Factors** These factors include the natural resources that a company uses as inputs and affects their marketing activities.

   As **Watrick and Wood** observe, "The natural environment ultimately is the source and support of everything used by businesses (and almost any other human activity), every raw material, every energy source, every life substaining factor, even every waste disposal site".

   The natural environment determines what can be got done in a society and how institutions can function.

   The major concerns in this area are as follows
   (i) **Increased Pollution** Pollutants emitted by an enterprise can negatively affect a firm's reputation if they are known for damaging the environment.
   (ii) **Shortage of Raw Material** As raw materials become increasingly scarce, the ability to create a company's product gets much harder.
   (iii) **Government Intervention** A firm may find it increasingly harder to achieve its goals if statutory requirements get more stringent.

6. **Cultural Forces** The cultural environment consists of institutions and basic values and beliefs of a group of people.

   The values can be further classified into core beliefs, which are passed on from generation-to- generation and are therefore difficult to change and secondary beliefs, which are acquired and therefore are easier to influence.

   Market reflects the values of a target audience, therefore a marketing manager must study the society in which he operates. e.g. in India, we have different cultural groups such as Assamese, Punjabis, Kashmiris, etc.

The marketing manager should take note of their cultural differences before finalising the marketing strategy.

Every organisation and industry is in a delicate balance with the forces in its environment. As the environment changes, it calls for a creative adaptation or response on the part of the entities interacting with it.

Nations (Assyria), species (dinosaurs) and industries (Kingfisher) have collapsed because they failed to meet environmental challenges with creative responses.

CHECK POINT 02

1. What is ment by market environment?
2. Which type of factors are referred to as controllable factors?
3. Mention any one point to be kept in mind for effective supplier management.
4. What is the other name of macro environment?
5. What does political environment include?

Market Research

According to **AGR Deiens**, "Market research is referred to as the systematic study and evaluation of all factors bearing on any business operations which involve the transfer of goods from a producer to a consumer".

Keeping the above definition in mind, it can be concluded that market research is a function which links the consumers and public to the marketer.

Marketing Research

Marketing research is versatile activity which is used by many different kinds of organisations to gather a variety of information needed to address different decisions.

According to **Philip Kotler**, "Marketing research is a systematic problem analysis, model building and fact finding for the purpose of improved decision-making and control in the marketing of goods and services."

Market research is the function which links the consumers and public to the marketer through information that is used to

- Identify and define marketing opportunities and problems.
- Generate, define and evaluate marketing actions.
- Monitor marketing performance.
- Improve understanding of marketing as a process.

It is a wide term and includes the following

1. **Market Research** Identification of a specific market and measurement of its size and other characteristics.
2. **Product Research** Identification of a need or want and the characteristics of the goods or services that will satisfy it.
3. **Consumer Research** Identification of the preferences, motivations and buying behaviour of the targeted customers.

How Marketing Research Helped Companies to become Market Leaders?

Amrutanjan was the market leader in the balm market when Vicks Vaporub was launched. The company had to decide whether to position their product directly against the leader or to carve out a separate niche. After much research work, it was finalised to position the brand 'Vicks Vaporub' exclusively as a rub for colds. Later, once again, based on research, it re-launched itself with a stronger formulation for faster relief. In the next few years, Vicks Vaporub became the largest selling brand for cold remedies.

Dabur Chyawanprash, after some research, went in for a change in packaging and advertising in 1993 witnessing a rise in its market share to 68.5%.

Similarly, **Rasna** on receiving poor response initially on its launch conducted detailed market research and thereafter incorporated the strategy of 'the influence – the child', the quality of ease in preparation, along with the economy did the magic. Advertisement campaigns reinforced all changes with a winning edge in the form of: 'Just one under-pack of Rasna makes 32 glasses of delicious soft-drinks'– now, Rasna dominates 85% of soft drinks concentrate market.

Procter and Gamble calls or visits over 1 million people in connection with about 1,000 research projects undertaken by its different product operating divisions.

Such rejuvenations by either new formulations or additional ingredients or improved aesthetic appeal, are normally the result of 'marketing research'.

Characteristics of a Good Marketing Information

Good marketing information is that which can be used for deriving meaningful decisions and which creates value. The value and usefulness of information depends on the extent to which it possesses the essential characteristics of good marketing infomation.

An infomation is characterised as 'good' if it has following characteristics

Basic Characteristics of Marketing Information

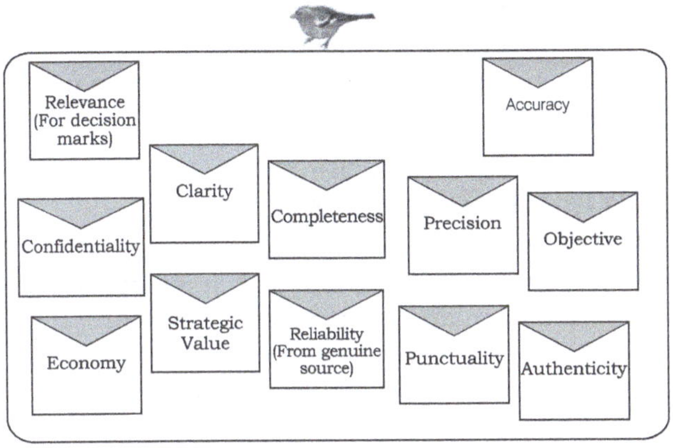

1. **Relevant** Information should be relevant for the purpose for which it is required. What is relevant for one user may not be relevant for another.

   The user will become frustrated, if information contains data irrelevant to the task in hand.
2. **Clarity** The information presented should be clear and precise. The presentation of information is important to the user. Information can be more easily assimilated, if it is aesthetically pleasing.
3. **Completeness** Information should contain all the details required by the user, otherwise it may not be useful as a basis for making a decision.
4. **Precision and Accuracy** Information need to be precise and accurate. However, to expect hundred per cent accuracy would be unrealistic, yet a reasonable degree of accuracy should be there, otherwise it would result in faulty decision-making.
5. **Objective** Information should be collected, keeping in mind a well-defined objective. Information collected without an objective is totally irrelevant.
6. **Confidentiality** As far as possible, efforts should be made to keep the information confidential, otherwise it could be used by competitors and the desired result could not be achieved.
7. **Strategic Value** The relative value of information for decision-making can increase or decrease its value to an organisation.
8. **Reliability and Authenticity** Reliability deals with the truth of the information. One can only use that information confidently, if one is sure that it has been collected from reliable sources and is authentic.
9. **Punctuality** Information must be available on time for the purpose for which it is required. Information received too late will be irrelevant.
10. **Economy** Information should be made available within set cost levels that may depend on individual situations. If costs are too high to obtain information, then an organisation should look for other sources for collecting the desired information. However, the accuracy and reliability of the information should not be compromised upon.

Important Role of Marketing Research

Marketing research is fast growing in its importance due to increasing competition, fast moving technological developments and changing consumer needs and expectations. The following points bring forward the importance of marketing research

1. **Planning and Execution of Marketing Plan** A business can plan and execute all activities right from manufacturing to marketing with reasonable accuracy due to the information made available through marketing research.
2. **Quick and Correct Decision-making** Marketing research facilitates quick and correct decision-making by providing marketing managers with accurate and relevant information about market.

3. **Effective Solutions of Marketing Problems** Marketing research provides effective solutions of marketing problems. It diagnoses the business ailments and suggests remedy to remove them. Marketing researcher acts like a business doctor and prescribes treatment for business ailments.
4. **Social Significance** Marketing research is of paramount importance from the social angle. It acts as a means by which the ultimate consumer literally becomes king of the market place.

Marketing Research Process

To help acquire valid, reliable and meaningful information, a series of steps are likely to be used which are defined collectively as 'marketing research process'.

Main steps involved in marketing research process are

Marketing Research Process

Steps

1. Identifying and defining a marketing problem
2. Specifying the information requirement
3. Developing the research design and research produce
4. Select the research instrument, sample type and size to be used
5. Analysing and interpreting the information
6. Summarise the findings
7. Preparing the research report

Step 1 Identifying and Defining a Marketing Problem

The first step in the marketing research procedure is to identify the marketing problem which needs to be solved. The problem may be related to product, price, market competition, sales promotion, etc.

The research process can start only when the researcher had identified and defined the problem clearly.

Step 2 Specifying the Information Requirement

In this stage, the researcher has to decide the type of information or data required for his/her study purpose. For collecting the information, the researcher can either use primary or secondary data or both.

Step 3 Developing the Research Design and Research Produce

Research design is the plan for the conduct of actual research investigation. This design provides guidelines for the researcher and helps him/her to know that he/she is moving in the right direction regarding data collection.

The research design contains answers to the following questions

- What is the nature and purpose of study?
- What type of data is required?
- How to collect required data?
- What is the technique of data collection?
- How much funds will be required?
- How much time will be needed for completion of research project?

Step 4 Select the Research Instrument, Sample Type and Size to be Used

In this stage, the researcher has to plan the sampling unit, procedure and size. It is not possible to interview each and every person. Therefore, the researcher must define the target population from which sample has to be drawn. A sample design should be adequately representative in character. It must represent the total population under study.

Step 5 Analysing and Interpreting the Information

The value of research is determined by its results. Thus, the data collected has to be analysed and interpreted.

For this purpose, the researcher tabulates the data and uses various statistical tools like averages and measures of dispersion to facilitate the analysis and interpretation of data.

Step 6 Summarise the Findings

After the process of analysing and interpretation is completed, the next step is to draw conclusions and summarise the findings in a compact and concise manner, so that more is conveyed through less.

Step 7 Preparing the Research Report

After drawing conclusions, the researcher can make appropriate suggestions/recommendations for solving the marketing problem in a satisfactory manner.

A researcher also prepares a document giving details of the research problem, data collected, conclusions drawn and the recommendations made.

Such document is called the research report which is the final outcome of the lengthy research process. The report is prepared in a suitable format and acts as a self-explanatory document.

Since, marketing research provides information which helps in taking strategic decisions, therefore this process should be carried as diligently as possible.

Research Instruments

Research instruments mean the instruments, tools, methods or techniques employed in research for gathering the information. There are many types of research instruments. Some of the primary instruments are listed below

- Aggregate data analysis
- Content analysis
- Observations
- Organisational analysis
- Market surveys, etc.
- Case studies
- Interviewing
- Experimental research

Of the above stated instruments, the most commonly used instrument by the entrepreneurs is 'market survery'.

CHECK POINT 03

1. Define market research.
2. .... provides effective solutions of marketing problems.
3. What is the first step in the marketing research process?
4. State any one characteristic of good marketing.
5. Which is the most commonly used research instrument by the entrepreneurs?

Marketing Mix

Marketing involves creating a market offering to match customer needs and wants. The combination of variables chosen by a firm to prepare its market offering is called **marketing mix.**

In other words, marketing mix represents the total marketing programme of an enterprise, as it refers to the tools or methods which a marketer uses in order to interact with a particular market.

According to **Albert W Emery**, "Marketing is merely a civilised form of warfare in which most battles are won with words, ideas and disciplined thinking."

In the words of **Philip Kotler**, "Marketing mix is a set of marketing tools that the firm uses to pursue its marketing objectives in the target market."

Market Offering

There are number of aspects involved in marketing a product or service. Some of them are controllable and others are uncontrollable.

Those which are uncontrollable, least could be done about them. But, some controllable aspects are

- The features of the product.
- It's price.
- It's selling system.
- It's advertisement mode selection, etc.

Since, a business cannot influence the uncontrollable aspects, therefore it plans its product on the basis of the controllable aspects and attempts to design a 'total offer or market offering' for its consumers in such a manner that

- The offer fulfills the needs of the consumer.
- The terms and attributes of the offer are acceptable and beneficial to the consumers.
- All the organisational goals, including profits, are achieved in the process.

As the foremost duty of the entrepreneur is to make this 'total offer', following step by step process of preparing a market offering is required to be performed by entrepreneur

- Firstly, choosing the 'product' that would actually meet the identified needs of the chosen consumer groups.
- Secondly, using the 'pricing' mechanism to determine the price of the product that is acceptable to the firm as well as to the consumers.
- Thirdly, performing various 'distribution' functions like transportation, warehousing, channel management, etc. so that the consumers conveniently get the desired product.
- Lastly, carrying out a number of 'promotional' measures like advertising, sales promotion, etc. with a view to communicate with the consumer and spread awareness about the product.

On the basis of the above discussion, it can be concluded that the 'Total offer' comprises of 4P's-Product, Price, Place and Promotion and these are commonly referred to as '4Ps of marketing' or 'variables of marketing mix'.

Benefits of Marketing Mix

The enterprise is benefitted by a marketing mix, as it helps to take suitable decisions regarding product, price, place and promotion. The benefits of marketing mix are summarised below

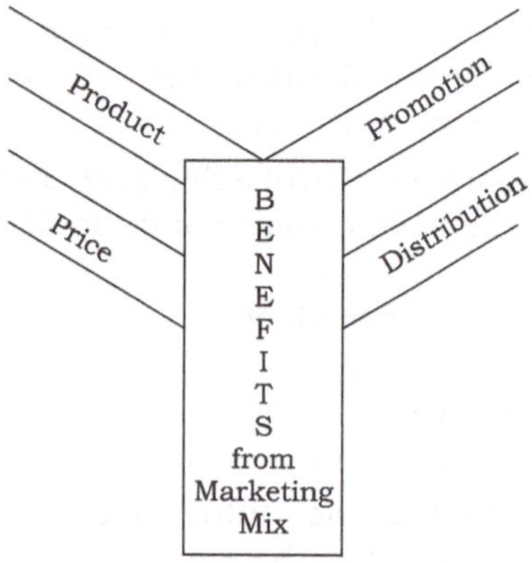

1. **Product Oriented Benefits**
   - Product is developed according to the needs of the customers.
   - Efforts are made to develop it to be of saleable quality.
   - Constant efforts in improving the quality of the product.
   - Due importance is given to attractive designing and packaging.
   - Provision of after sales services is also given due recognition.
2. **Price Oriented Benefits**
   - Determination of price according to the paying capacity of customers.
   - Fair pricing of the product to capture the market share.
   - Credit facility provided to make the product assessible.
   - Discount and allowances are offered, so that the demand of the product can be increased.
3. **Promotion Oriented Benefits**
   Creating awareness and increasing demand of the product with the help of the following tools of sales promotion
   - Advertising
   - Sales promotion
   - Personal selling
4. **Distribution Oriented Benefits**
   - Availability at the right place.
   - Availability through convenient outlets.

Marketing Mix Variables

Variables or elements of marketing mix are as follows

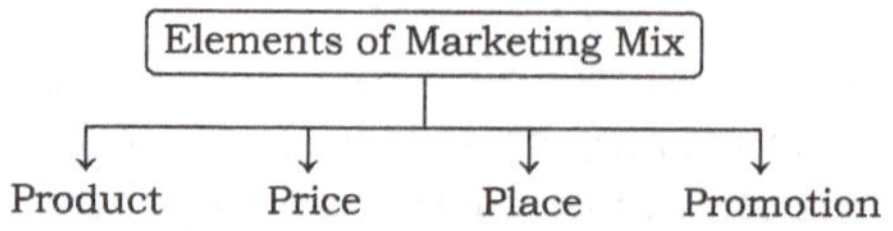

An entrepreneur needs to have best possible combination of the above variables in order to achieve optimum sales and optimum profits.

A brief discussion about each of these four variables will help us understand marketing mix better.

Product Mix

Product means anything of value, which is offered in the market to satisfy a want or need.

Product mix refers to all decisions related to product such as decisions related to features, packaging, labelling and branding of the products. Under product mix, the entrepreneur works out the set of all product lines and items which he would offer for sale to the buyers.

Marketing of a product requires on the part of the entrepreneur to carefully plan out the following dimensions of a product mix

- Volume of output, sales growth potential
- Shape, size, weight, colour and features of the product
- Quality and standard of the product
- Design and range of the product
- Brand name
- Packaging and labelling
- Product testing
- After sale service

The aim of preparing a product mix is to provide a product that offers variety of satisfaction to the consumers. It helps in easy acceptability of the product in the market and also helps it to fetch a good price.

Classification of Product

Product can be classified on the basis of

1. **Durability** Perishable, non-durable or durable product.
2. **Utility** Capital/Producer goods and consumer goods, intermediary goods.
3. **Weightwise** Heavy and bulky goods like iron and voluminous goods like cotton.

Components of Product Mix

Various components of product mix are as follows

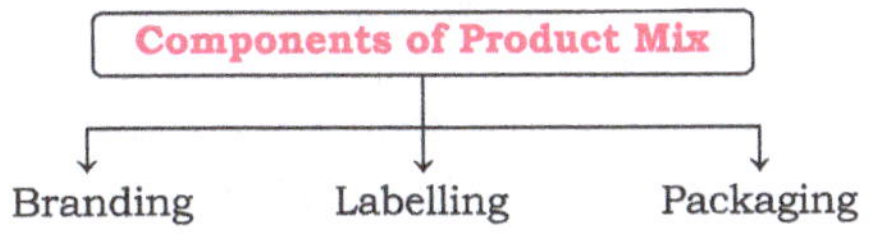

1. **Branding** It refers to the process of giving a name, sign, symbol or identification to a product by which it will be known and remembered. Branding is not only done to identify the seller or producer but also to make the product superior than competitor's product.

   It is a general term covering various activities, such as giving a brand name to a product, designing a brand mark and popularising it.

   Terms related to branding are as follows

   Brand A brand is a name, term, sign, symbol, design or some other combination of them for the identification of a product and to differentiate it from those of competitors e.g. Nike, Reebok, LG, etc.

   Brand Name The part of brand, which can be spoken is called brand name. It consists of words, numbers or combination thereof. e.g. Maggi, Lux, Ambuja Cement, etc.

   Brand Mark The part of brand, which cannot be spoken, but can be seen and recognised is known as brand mark. It consists of symbols, designs, sign, marks, etc. e.g. Maharaja sign of Air India, red and blue ball of Pepsi, etc.

   Trademark The part of brand, which is given legal protection is called trademark.

   A company which gets its brand registered gets the exclusive rights for its use. Thus, no other firm can use that name or sign, in the country, e.g. Maruti Suzuki sign on Maruti cars.

   The following points must be considered while deciding a brand name for a product

   - A brand name should be short, simple, easy to pronounce, spell, recognise and remember. e.g. Vim, Ponds, Lux, etc.
   - A brand should suggest the product's quality or benefit. e.g. Ujala, Fair and Lovely, etc.
   - A brand name should be distinct from the other brands present in the market. e.g. Liril, Sprite, Raymonds, etc.
   - A brand name should be adaptable to packing and labelling requirements in different media and languages.
   - A brand name should be versatile enough to include other products under it.
   - A brand name should be capable of being registered and legally protected.
   - A brand name should have long-lasting staying power and should not get out of date.

2. **Labelling** It means designing a label to be put on the package. A label may be a small slip attached or placed to the product to denote its nature, contents, ownership, destination, etc. A label describes the product, its usage and specifies its contents.

   A good label should provide the following information

   - Name and address of the manufacturer
   - Size, colour and appearance of the product
   - Weight and measurement of the product
   - Ingredients and contents used in the product
   - Directions for use or precautions to be taken while using the product
   - Date of manufacturing and date of expiry
   - Maximum retail price including local taxes
   - Statutory warning, if required

3. **Packaging** It refers to covering, wrapping, filling or compressing of goods to protect them from spoilage, pilferage, breakage, leakage, etc. Various kinds of goods are placed or packed into appropriate containers for protection and convenient handling.

   e.g., bulky materials like cotton and jute are compressed into bales, liquid materials like oil and wine are put into bottles, barrels and cans, etc.

   Thus, packing implies placing products in suitable packages for delivery of the product to customer or for the purpose of storage and transport.

   On the other hand, packaging refers to the act of designing and producing the container or wrapper of a product. A package is a container, wrapper or other receptacle used for packing products. It is more than simply the carrier of a product.

There can be three different **levels of packaging**. These are as follows

Primary Packaging It means the immediate container of a product. It may be kept till the customer is ready to use the product, or throughout the life of a product.

Secondary Packaging It means additional layer of protection.

Transportation Packaging It means packaging done to protect the product and help in the process of transportation and storage.

A good package should have the following **features**

- It should be secure and capable of protecting the product.
- It should be simple to handle and use. It must be simple to open and close.
- It should grab people's attention right away and provide aesthetic satisfaction in terms of design, beauty, and neatness. It should be pleasing and eye-catching.
- It should be cost-effective in respect to the product's value.
- It should give the product a distinct personality and status.
- It should build trust in customers by telling a true story about the product.

CHECK POINT 04

1. What is meant by marketing mix?
2. Mention any two elements of marketing mix.
3. Mention any one benefit of marketing mix.
4. Mention any one basis of classification of product.
5. Define labelling.

Price Mix

Price of a product is the amount of money paid by the buyer to own the product or service. To put it simply, 'price' is the exchange value of a product. Basically, price revolves around two major components

1. **Utility** It is the generic property of the product to satisfy the need or want of the consumer.
2. **Value** It is the quantitative worth the consumer attaches to the product, for which he is willing to part with a certain quantum of money.

Price mix is basically the value of the product as determined by the producers. It includes the decision as to the price level to be adopted, discount to be offered and terms of credit to be allowed to the customers. Pricing of a product is the most important decision of price mix.

Factors Influencing Pricing

The factors that influence the pricing decisions of any enterprise can be categorised into two factors

1. **Internal Factors** The pricing strategy of a business usually gets affected by the following internal factors
   - Corporate and marketing objectives of the firm.
   - The image sought by the firm through pricing.
   - Cost of manufacturing and marketing.
   - The uniqueness and utility of the product, i.e. the extent of distinctiveness of the product and the extent of product differentiation practiced by the firm.
   - Price elasticity of demand for the product.
   - Other elements of the marketing mix of the firm and their interaction with pricing.
   - Use pattern and turn around rate of the product.
   - Composition of the product line of the firm.
2. **External Factors** Business does not live in isolation. It is affected by several external factors such as legal, technological, political, economic, social and also by its consumers, competitors and suppliers. These factors affect the survival, growth and enterprise's functioning and also influence its pricing.

   External factors which exercise influence on pricing are
   - Market characteristics
   - Nature of economy
   - Nature of competition
   - Bargaining power of major consumers
   - Bargaining power of major suppliers
   - Competitors pricing policy
   - Government controls/regulations on pricing
   - Societal or social considerations

   From the marketer's point of view, an efficient price is a price that is very close to the maximum that customers are prepared to pay.

Therefore, before finalising the price of the product, the entrepreneur must work out in detail the following factors

- Cost of the product
- Demand of the product
- Competition in the market
- Government regulations related to pricing
- Consumer behaviour
- Objectives of the enterprise
- Terms of credit

Importance of Pricing

Price is the only element in the marketing mix that produces revenue. So, pricing is very important for a business as is conveyed through the following points

Importance of Pricing

- Key to revenue
- Attract customers
- Edge over competition
- Crucial to profit
- Platform for achieving other objectives

1. **Key to Revenue** Price and sales volume together decide the revenue of any business. As sales volume or quantity sold is dependent on price, so pricing becomes the key to the revenue of the business.
2. **Attract Customers** Pricing has the power to break customer's brand loyalty by offering a quality product at a lower price than that offered by a competitor.
3. **Edge Over Competition** Customers demand good quality at reasonable price. This gives rise to intense competition in the market and it is a firm's pricing decision which helps it to gain an edge over its competitors.
4. **Crucial to Profits** Pricing is crucial to profits. Mistakes in pricing decisions seriously affect the firm's profits, growth and future.
5. **Platform for Achieving other Objectives** The various other objectives that an enterprise seeks to achieve through its pricing policy are as follows
   - Profit maximisation in the short-term
   - Profit optimisation in the long-term
   - A minimum return on investment
   - A minimum return on sales turnover
   - Target sales volume
   - Target market share
   - Deeper penetration of the market
   - Entering new markets
   - Keeping competition out or keeping it under check
   - Keeping parity with competition
   - Fast turn around and early cash recovery
   - Providing commodities at price affordable by weaker sections.

Methods Used for Pricing

Some methods and policies, which are individually or collectively used in pricing decisions are as follows

Methods Used for Pricing

- Cost plus pricing
- Variable price
- Base price and discount
- Market rate
- Skimming price
- Penetrating pricing

1. **Cost Plus Pricing Method** In this method of pricing, price of a product is equal to its cost plus margin of profit.
2. **Variable Price Method** In this method, price of the product is decided by the order size or customer's bargaining power or on the ability of the consumer to pay.
3. **Base Price and Discount Method** Under this method, a list price of the product is fixed and then certain discounts are offered to various categories of consumers such as cash discount, trade discount, quantity discount, etc.
4. **Market Rate Method** Under this method, prices are decided keeping in view the prevailing rate in the market of similar product or service.
5. **Skimming Price Method** Under this method, at the beginning, business charges a very high price for its product and later on reduces the price.
6. **Penetrating Pricing Method** Under this method, prices are set very low, so as to capture maximum market share and later on the price is increased.

CHECK POINT 05

1. Mention two components of price.
2. State any one internal factor influencing pricing.
3. State any one external factor influencing pricing.
4. .... is the only element in the marketing mix that produces revenue.
5. In which method of pricing, price of a product is equal to its cost plus margin of profit.

Place or Physical Distribution Mix

Physical distribution is the task of moving the goods and services from the place of production to the place of their consumption. It creates both place and time utility as it makes a product convenient to be purchased when it is needed.

Place mix determines not only the place, where the product should be made available, but also whether the goods are to be marketed through wholesalers, retailers, retail outlets or any other channel. The entrepreneur generally decides upon

- Channels of distribution
- Modes of distribution

Channels of Distribution

Channels of distribution are like pipelines which take the right quantities of the right product to the right location, where the target consumers want them at the right time. These channels refer to the methods of marketing and most common ones are as follows

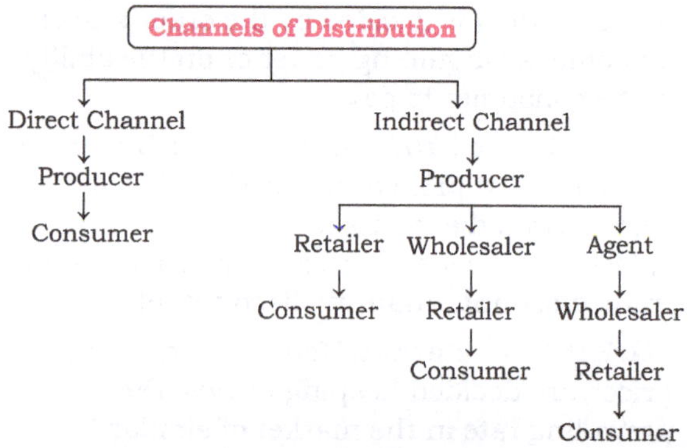

1. **Direct Channel/Zero-level** Through this channel, the producers supply the products directly to the consumers. The producer here either supplies directly to the consumer or through its retail outlets. Frontier Biscuits, Bata Shoe Company, etc. are the examples of this type of channel.
2. **Indirect Channels** In this type, the producers supply their products through one or more intermediaries. According to the number of intermediaries, the following are the types of indirect channels
   (i) **Producer-Retailer-Consumer** (One-level channel) Under this type, producer sells the product to retailer, who in turn sells to the consumer. The producers of refrigerators, washing machines, etc. sell their products to retailers, who then sell the same to the consumers.
   (ii) **Producer-Wholesaler-Retailer-Consumer** (Two-level channels) This is the most common channel of distribution. Under this channel, two intermediaries *viz.*, the wholesaler and retailer are involved between the producer and the consumer. Some popular products distributed through this channel are sugar, soaps, ghee, grains, etc.
   (iii) **Producer-Agent-Wholesaler-Retailer-Consumer** (Three-level channels) Under this type, the producers take the help of agents who, in turn, supply to wholesalers and then through the retailers, the goods ultimately reach the consumers.

   The channel is common where the producers have to distribute a limited product line to cover a wide market. The agents take the responsibility of covering a fixed area.

   e.g. Hindustan Levers appoints the agents or distributors, who sell both to the wholesalers and retailers for onward distribution to consumers.

Factors Affecting Channels of Distribution

The various factors affecting channels of distribution are as follows

1. **Product related Factors** Nature of product, unit value of product, perishability factors, complexity (technical product requires shorter channels) are considered while deciding the channels of distribution.
2. **Market related Factors** Market factors such as size of market, geographical concentration of potential buyers, quantity and frequency of orders, buying habits of consumers and credit facilities available influence the decision, while choosing the channels of distribution.
3. **Efficiency of Middlemen** Location of middlemen, financial strength, other services offered by middlemen (like warehousing, assorting, etc) is a deciding force in choice of an appropriate channel of distribution.
4. **Tendency of Producer** Producer's financial strength, degree of control desired over the channel, competency of managers, etc, also affect choice of channels of distribution.

Factors Determing the Choice of Channel

Nature of Product	Nature of Market	Middlemen	Tendency of Producer
• Unit value	• Location	• Availability	• Quantity of production
• Perishable	• Quantity and frequency of orders	• Customs of the trade	• Control over channels
• Products	• Number of buyers	• Competence of managers	• Competence of managers
• Size and weight	• Consumers of industrial products market	• Government control	• Financial position
• Standardised products	• Buying habits of consumer		• Distribution policy
• Technical products	• Credit facilities		
• Capital goods			
• Introduction of newly manufactured products			

Modes of Distribution

It includes all the activities relating to the physical movement of product from the seller to the buyer and includes decisions relating to

1. **Transportation** The common modes of transportation are classified as follows
   - Railways
   - Roadways
   - Waterways
   - Airways
   - Pipelines
2. **Warehousing** This function is related to holding and preserving goods till they are delivered to the buyers. The need for warehousing arises because there is a time gap between production and consumption of goods. Warehousing bridges this gap by providing storage facility. It creates time utility.
3. **Inventory Control of Products** It requires deciding about the level of inventory. Inventory means maintenance of stock of goods held for distribution.

Factors to be Considered while Selecting Mode of Distribution

An entrepreneur should study, compare and evaluate following variables before selecting any modes of transferring goods

- Cost
- Flexibility
- Availability
- Nature of commodity
- Requirement of customer
- Duration involved
- Speed and safety parameters

Promotion Mix

It refers to the combination of promotional tools used by an organisation with the twin objective of informing the potential customers about the product/service and persuading them to buy it. It is concerned with the activities which are undertaken to boost the sales through its sub-components/tools.

Role of Promotion Mix

The role of promotion mix is enumerated below

- Promotion mix helps to build the image of product.
- It creates product identity.
- It helps to educate the consumers.
- It helps to boost sale and profits.
- It ensures consumer's satisfaction.
- It helps to keep the memory alive for a product in consumer's mind.
- It encourages innovation.

Tools/Elements of Promotion Mix

The various elements of promotion mix are as follows

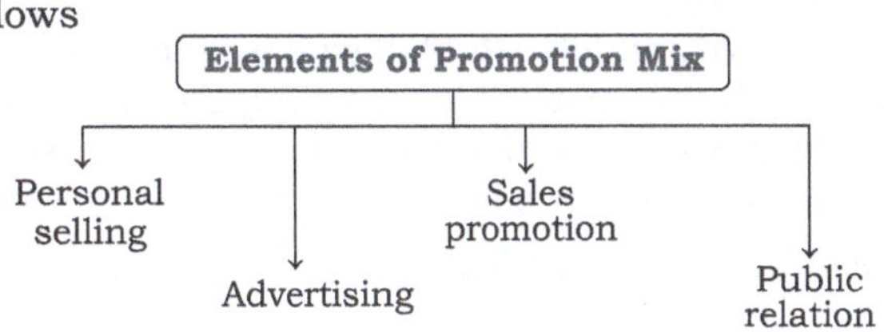

1. **Personal Selling**

It is an art to induce people to buy the product. It is an effort to win the everlasting confidence of the consumers through directy interacting with them.

Main **features of personal selling** are as follows

- There is a personal or face-to-face contact between the buyer and the salesman.
- Harmonious relationship can be established between the sales person and the possible buyer.
- Features of the product can be explained orally by the salesperson.
- The prospective buyers can get solution to their queries regarding the product.

Following points explain the **importance or benefits of personal selling**

- It is a two way communication process. Salesman can provide essential information about the offered products to the customer and get adequate feedback about the product from the customer.
- It is an effective method of solving personal problems of the customers.
- Salesman can provide a demonstration about the use of a product which makes possible the ease in the use of the product by the customer.
- It removes the drawbacks of advertising and sales promotion.
- It is flexible in nature as sales talks and presentation can be adjusted as per the situation.

A person possessing the following **qualities** can prove to be successful salesman

– A good salesman should always has a smile on his face.
– A good salesman should possess the sufficient degree of patience.
– He should try to find out his limitations and make constant efforts to overcome them.
– A good salesman should possess good health, attractive appearance and impressive voice.
– A good combination of mental qualities like imagination, sound judgement etc. should be possessed by a good salesman.
– He should be polite and courteous towards his customers.

2. **Advertising**

It is an activity which establishes non-personal contact with the customers regarding the product, idea and service. It is an effort to create and sustain the demand for the product.

Some of the important **features of advertising** are as follows

- The main goal of advertising is to promote idea about the products and services of a business.
- It is a paid form of communication.
- In advertisement, there is no face-to-face contact with the customers.

Important **benefits of avertising** are as follows

– It enables the manufacturer to expand his market.
– It helps in the introduction of a new product in the market.
– It helps in the introduction of a manufacturer and his product to the people with enhanced goodwill.
– It greatly facilitates the work of a salesman.
– It provides and creates more employment opportunities for many talented people.

3. **Sales Promotion**

It is an effort to stimulate customers to buy more and more of particular commodities with the help of schemes such as buy one get one free, discount coupons, etc.

Some of the important **features of sales promotion** are as follows

- Sales promotion is costly.
- It consists of offering wide variety of tools/incentives.
- It includes impersonal incentives. They are offered openly to all.
- It involves all the promotional efforts other than advertising, personal selling and publicity.
- It supports personal selling and advertising efforts.

Following are the **benefits of sales promotion**

– It provides an opportunity to the customers to enjoy hands on contact with a new product.
– It encourage consumers, dealers and salesmen at the sametime.
– It is flexible in nature and can be used at any stage of a new product introduction.
– It helps the salesman and makes his effort more productive and meaningful.
– It helps to increase the demand of a product.

Important **techniques of sales promotion** are as follows

Rebate In the situation of excess stock, products are offered at some reduced price.

Contests To increase the popularity of the product, different producers organise contests.

Samples The producer of the product distributes free samples among the consumers.

Coupons Its objective is to maximise the redemption rate. This is the proportion of customers actually using the coupon.

Free Gifts Distribution In this technique, the customer gets something in addition to the main purchase of a product.

Money Refunds In this technique, a customer receives a money refund after submitting a proof of pruchase to the manufacturer.

4. **Public Relation**

The enterprise may start public contact programmes to introduce the product in the market.

Following are the main **features of public relations**

- As every organisation wants to run successfully. So to get support from public, public relation is very important.
- It helps in developing better relations with public.
- It is like an effort to satisfy different groups like consumers, employees etc.
- It is an ongoing activity.
- It is reconginsed in the form of a specialised activity.

Some of the **benefits of public relations** are

- It is one of the most credible and trusted form of promotion and can be persuasive.
- It is an economical and cheap method.
- It helps in the maintenance of goodwill of the company.

Factors Affecting Choice of Element of Promotion Mix

Each promotional tool has its own unique characteristics and costs. The entrepreneur should carefully evaluate each alternative medium, considering

- Cost
- Objective
- Market trend
- Nature of the product
- Consumer targeted
- Effectiveness
- Coverage
- Competitors tool

Factors Affecting Marketing Mix

While determining suitable marketing mix, following factors must be taken into consideration regarding consumers, dealers, competitors and government behaviour.

These behaviours are enumerated herewith

1. **Consumers' Buying Behaviour**
   Consumer's behaviour is studied with regards to
   - Buying habits
   - Living habits
   - Purchasing power
   - Attitude and preferences
   - Local environment and situations
   - Number of consumers of the product
2. **Dealers' Behaviour**
   The behaviour of wholesalers and retailers is studied with regards to
   - Factors that could motivate them
   - Structure, practice and attitude of dealers
   - Financial strength of dealers
   - Expected change in their behaviour with change in incentives offered
3. **Competitors' Behaviour**
   The following factors are considered while studying competitor's behaviour
   - Size and strength of competing units
   - Number of competitors
   - Practices and attitudes of the competitors
   - Motives
   - Trends in demand and supply
4. **Government Behaviour**
   It implies government controls regarding
   - Products
   - Prices
   - Competitive practices
   - Restrictive trade practices
   - Advertising and promotion

Constant Juggling

Blending the marketing mix elements into a winning combination is a continouous task as it may require constatn changes due to

- Changing environmental variables.
- Internal changes happening, within the enterprise.
- Ever changing preferences, liking trends of customers.

Thus, there is no marketing mix like a strait jacket to fit in every enterprise due to

- Different in the nature of busines undertaken
- Difference in sixe of operation
- Difference in type and nature of product
- Legal requirements
- Technological specifications

CHECK POINT 06

1. What is meant by direct channel?
2. Mention any one market related factor affecting channels of distribution.
3. State any one mode of transportation of goods.
4. Mention any one element of promotion mix.
5. .... is the paid form of communication.
6. Mention any one factor affecting marketing mix.

EXAM PATTERN EXERCISE

Objective Type Questions (1 Mark)

Multiple Choice Questions

1 The word 'market' is derived from the Latin word 'Marcatus' meaning.
(a) Merchandise
(b) Wake
(c) Place where business is conducted
(d) All of the above

Ans (d) All of the above

2 The traditional concept of market lays emphasis on
(a) place
(b) different markets for different commodities
(c) Both (a) and (b)
(d) None of the above

Ans (c) Both (a) and (b)

3 .... concept of market was prevalent after the World War II, especially in the 50s and 60s when the markets changed due to intensification of industrial activity.
(a) Traditional (b) Scientific
(c) Modern (d) Emerging

Ans (b) Scientific

4 "E-business is offering great opportunities to entrepreneurs in developing countries by helping them to enter the prosperous global markets merely at the click of the mouse."

In the light of this statement, identify the benefit(s) that it provides to the entrepreneurs.
(a) Updated information
(b) Easy to launch new products
(c) Higher personnel cost
(d) Both (a) and (b)

Ans (d) Both (a) and (b)

5 In which market, the demand for the goods is limited to one specific country?
(a) National market (b) International market
(c) Monopoly (d) Oligopoly

Ans (a) National market

6 .... is also known as general and remote environment, comprising of uncontrollable factors.
(a) Internal environment
(b) Micro environment
(c) Macro environment (d) None of these

Ans (c) Macro environment

7 Marketing research includes
(a) market research (b) product research
(c) consumer research (d) All of these

Ans (d) All of these

8 Piyush wanted to launch a ready-to-make range of mocktails. However, he was not sure about the market demand for such drinks in India. He decided to conduct marketing research to check the viability of his idea. The research instrument(s) which can be used by him is/are
(a) aggregate data analysis
(b) interviewing
(c) experimental research
(d) All of the above

Ans (d) All of the above

9 Availability of required materials is an/a .... aspect of marketing.
(a) controllable (b) uncontrollable
(c) Both (a) and (b) (d) None of these

Ans (b) uncontrollable

10 Controllable aspects of marketing are
(a) features of the product
(b) price of the product
(c) Both (a) and (b) (d) None of these

Ans (c) Both (a) and (b)

11 'Determination of price according to the paying capacity of customers', can be classified under which benefit of marketing?
(a) Product oriented benefit
(b) Promotion oriented benefit
(c) Price oriented benefit
(d) Distribution oriented benefit

Ans (c) Price oriented benefit

12 The 4P's of marketing mix include
(a) product (b) price
(c) place (d) All of these

Ans (d) All of these

13 To which tool of marketing mix does 'Brand name' pertain? **CBSE TBQ (M)**
(a) Product mix (b) Place mix
(c) Price mix (d) Promotion mix

Ans (a) Product mix

14 Anything of value, which is offered in the market to satisfy a want or need is called
(a) product (b) promotion
(c) price (d) All of these

Ans (a) product

15 Price revolves around
(a) utility (b) value
(c) Both (a) and (b) (d) None of these

Ans (c) Both (a) and (b)

16 In which method of pricing, prices are decided keeping in view the prevailing rate in the market of similar product or service?
(a) Market rate method
(b) Penetrating price method
(c) Variable price method (d) None of these

Ans (a) Market rate method

17 Under .... method of pricing, at the beginning, business charges a very high price for its product and later on reduces the price.
(a) cost plus pricing (b) market rate
(c) skimming price (d) penetrating price

Ans (c) skimming price

18 Under which channel, the producers supply the products directly to the consumers?
(a) Direct channel (b) Indirect channel
(c) Both (a) and (b) (d) None of these

Ans (a) Direct channel

19 Hindustan Lever, the FMCG giant, appoints agents or distributors who sell the products to wholesalers and retailers for onward distribution to consumers. The indirect channel of distribution followed by it is
(a) one-level channel (b) two-level channel
(c) three-level channel (d) four-level channel

Ans (c) three-level channel

20 Modes of distribution includes decisions related to
(a) transportation (b) warehousing
(c) inventory control of products
(d) All of the above

Ans (d) All of the above

21 Transportation can be initiated through
(a) railways (b) waterways
(c) roadways (d) All of these

Ans (d) All of these

22 ....means maintenance of stock of goods held for distribution.
(a) Rebate (b) Transportation
(c) Inventory (d) Warehousing

Ans (c) Inventory

23 Factors to be considered while selecting modes of distribution include
(a) cost (b) flexibility
(c) availability (d) All of these

Ans (d) All of these

24 'Buy one get one free' is an example of which technique of promotion mix?
(a) Quantity gift (b) Samples
(c) Coupons (d) Rebate

Ans (a) Quantity gift

25 Marketing manager has been defined as a 'Mixer of ingredients', by
(a) James Culliton (b) Philip Kotler
(c) Stanton (d) Behham

Ans (a) James Culliton

26 Mr. Raj wants to buy a LCD for his family. When he visited Anand Electronics to make the purchase, he got confused. Which promotional tool brought him to the shop and which promotional tool is required now to remove his confusion?
(a) Advertising, personal selling
(b) Personal selling, advertising
(c) Sales promotion, personal selling
(d) Public relation, advertising

Ans (a) In this question, at first, his decision to buy a LCD was influenced by advertising. Later, his decision was influenced by personal selling in which he would be convinced to buy LCD.

27 "Personal selling creates effective demand which results in increase in income, with increase in income, there will be more products and services, which in turn brings economic growth".

This statement signifies the importance of personal selling to

(a) businessman
(b) customers
(c) society
(d) None of the above

Ans (c) Personal selling plays an important role in marketing goods by serving businessman, customers and society. It serves society by converting latest demand into effective demand.

28 When Sarita opened the door on hearing the doorbell, a person was standing who was selling Britannica world 'encyclopedia'. Here, Britannica is using which element of promotion mix?

(a) Public relation
(b) Sales promotion
(c) Advertising
(d) Personal selling

Ans (c) Advertising

29 Which of the following is not a feature of good package?

(a) It should be secure and capable of protecting the product
(b) It should be complex to handle and use
(c) It should be cost-effective in respect to the product's value
(d) It should give the product a distinct personality and status

Ans (b) It should be complex to handle and use

30 **Assertion** (A) Macro environment factors too have bearing on the market.

Reason (R) Macro environment factors are the uncontrollable factors.

Alternatives

(a) Both Assertion (A) and Reason (R) are correct
(b) Assertion (A) is correct, but Reason (R) is incorrect
(c) Assertion (A) is incorrect, but Reason (R) is correct
(d) Both Assertion (A) and Reason (R) are incorrect

Ans (a) Both Assertion (A) and Reason (R) are correct

31 **Assertion** (A) Technological advancement in the transportation industry has helped in bringing markets closer.

Reason (R) With the advancement in technology, manufacturers can deliver their products to retailers and wholesalers more quickly and in cost effective manner.

Alternatives

(a) Both Assertion (A) and Reason (R) are correct
(b) Assertion (A) is correct, but Reason (R) is incorrect
(c) Assertion (A) is incorrect, but Reason (R) is correct
(d) Both Assertion (A) and Reason (R) are incorrect

Ans (a) Both Assertion (A) and Reason (R) are correct

32 Given below are macro environment factors in Column I and their features in Column II. Match them correctly.

Column I	Column II
A. Demographic forces	(i) includes all laws, government agencies and groups
B. Economic factors	(ii) fastest changing factors in the macro environment
C. Technological forces	(iii) purchasing power of potential customers
D. Political forces	(iv) human population in terms of size, density etc

Codes

	A	B	C	D
(a)	(iv)	(iii)	(ii)	(i)
(b)	(ii)	(i)	(iii)	(iv)
(c)	(iii)	(iv)	(ii)	(i)
(d)	(ii)	(i)	(iv)	(iii)

Ans (a) (iv) (iii) (ii) (i)

33 Match the following

Column I	Column II
A. Social process	(i) Market
B. Set of potential customers	(ii) Marketing
C. Controllable variables	(iii) Function of marketing
D. Marketing activities	(iv) Marketing mix

Codes

	A	B	C	D		A	B	C	D
(a)	(i)	(iii)	(iv)	(ii)	(b)	(ii)	(i)	(iv)	(iii)
(c)	(iv)	(iii)	(ii)	(i)	(d)	(iii)	(ii)	(iv)	(i)

Ans (b) (ii) (i) (iv) (iii)

34 Which concept is highlighted by A and B in the given picture?

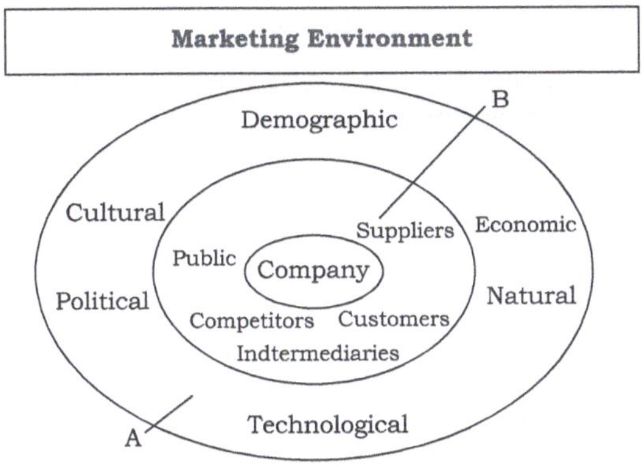

(a) A – Micro environment ; B – Macro environment
(b) A – Macro environment ; B – Micro environment
(c) Components of marketing mix
(d) None of the above

Ans (b) A – Macro environment ; B – Micro environment

35 Which concept is highlighted in the given picture?

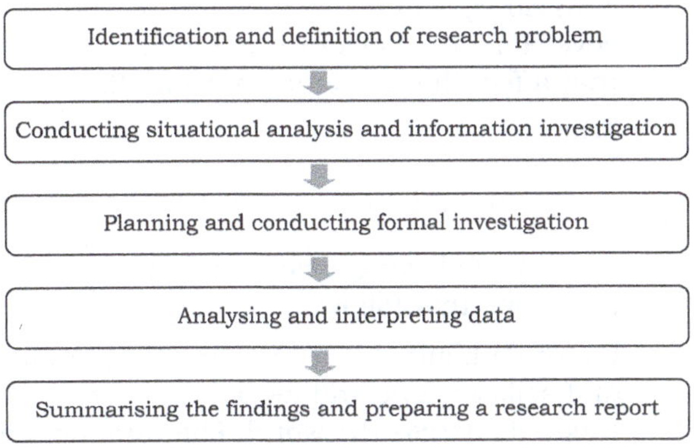

(a) Market research process
(b) Marketing mix (c) Both (a) and (b)
(d) None of the above

Ans (a) Market research process

Fill in the Blanks

36 .... is defined as an arrangement of establishing effective relationship between buyers and sellers of the commodities.

Ans Market

37 The .... concept of market was prevalent in the pre-industrial revolution era.

Ans traditional

38 According to ...., "markets are people with money to spend and desire to spend it."

Ans DYDDY Concept

39 .... refers to the factors and forces that affect a firm's ability to build and maintain successful relationships with customers.

Ans Market environment

40 .... are firms or individuals that facilitate the flow of goods and services between a business and its final consumers.

Ans Marketing intermediaries

41 .... is referred to as the systematic study and evaluation of all factors bearing on any business operations which involve the transfer of goods from a producer to a consumer.

Ans Market research

42 .... is the plan for the conduct of actual research investigation.

Ans Research design

43 XY Limited requires information related to their competitor YZ Limited and this information is critical to their own decision on whether to invest in new machinery or not. This information is of ....

Ans strategic value

44 .... is a process of discovering and translating consumer needs and wants into products and services, creating demand for these products and services and then increasing this demand.

Ans Marketing

45 In .... method, price of the product is decided by the order size or customer's bargaining power or on the ability of the consumer to pay.

Ans variable price

46 Arvind, the manufacturer of footwear sells the same to different retailers, who then sell to the consumers. The channel of distribution involved here is............ .

Ans one-level channel

47 Size of market, concentration of potential buyers, buying habits of consumers, etc. are all .... factors which should be kept in mind while deciding on the channel of distribution.

Ans market related

48 A juice manufacturing company is spending some amount of money to persuade the target customer to buy juice packets through advertising, personal selling and sales promotion techniques. .... element of marketing mix is referred here.

Ans Promotion mix

State True or False

49 Modern concept of market was prevalent in the 70s and 80s, when industralisation was advanced.

Ans True

50 Scientific concept of market is also referred to as 'people oriented concept' and follows the adage that market means people.

Ans False. The above features are of 'emerging concept of market'.

51 The technological environment is the fastest changing factor in the macro environment.

Ans True

52 In India, we have different cultural groups such as Assamese, Punjabis etc. Mr. Mohan is a marketing manager who takes care of their cultural differences before finalising the marketing strategy.

Component of macro environment referred here is cultural forces.

Ans True

53 'Identifying and defining a marketing problem' is the first step in the marketing research process.

Ans True

54 Market research is a narrow concept in comparison to market survey.

Ans False. Market research is a broad term and market survey is a part of it.

55 XYZ company is offering a number of consumer goods like packaged foods, beverages etc.
'Product mix' element of marketing mix is referred here.

Ans True

56 'Summarising the findings' is the last step of the marketing research process.

Ans False. 'Preparing research report' is the last step of the marketing research process.

57 Reliance fresh is gaining popularity by providing good quality products at reasonable prices.

Ans True

58 Promotion mix helps to build the image of the product.

Ans True

59 Consumers' buying behaviour, dealer's behaviour, competitor's behaviour and government behaviour are the factors that affect the marketing mix of a firm.

Ans True

Case Based Questions

60 Read the following article and answer the questions that follow

Phantom Limited is a company that produces and sells organic and herbal hair care products across the world. Phantom Limited was created with a view to create customers and serve as many customers as possible at every possible place.

Phantom has various close competitors, but the company's quality products and esteem customer service has differentiated it from all the other market players in the same product line.

The success of Phantom Limited is the result of structured and detailed strategies and clear goals. The company now wants to enter into the line of skin care in addition to hair care products and the management has asked the marketing department to analyse the market environment because the management wants to have a positive impact on its existing as well as potential customers.

The marketing department analysed the market and decides that the price of the products should be kept low because of the financial impact of the post-pandemic era. The products were manufactured with the same motto of selling organic herbal products that are natural and have no side effects or harmful ingredients.

The customer base of the company was strong and there were early adopters who purchased the products as well as promoted them with a positive word of mouth.

The company decided to give 30% discounts to the first 100 customers on their next purchase and the sales were up with a margin of 40%. The management was happy with the successful launch of the new product line.

(i) "Phantom Limited was created with a view to create customers and serve as many customers as possible at every possible place."

Which market concept is highlighted in the above text?

(a) Traditional
(b) Modernised
(c) Scientific
(d) All of the above

Ans (b) Modernised

(ii) How can you describe Phantom Limited's market on the basis of competition?

(a) Oligopoly (b) Monopoly
(c) Duopoly (d) Monopolistic

Ans (d) Monopolistic

(iii) Which of the following macro-environment factors should the company analyse?

(a) Legal (b) Political
(c) Technological (d) All of these

Ans (d) All of these

(iv) "The marketing department analysed the market and decides that the price of the products should be kept low because of the financial impact of the post-pandemic era."

Which of the following factors influenced the pricing of Phantom's products?

(a) Laws and regulations
(b) Market economy
(c) Technological advancements
(d) All of the above

Ans (b) Market economy

(v) "The company decided to give 30% discounts to the first 100 customers on their next purchase and the sales were up with a margin of 40%."

Which of the following promotional techniques is used in the given lines?

(a) Personal selling (b) Direct marketing
(c) Sales promotion (d) Rebate

Ans (c) Sales promotion

61 Read the following article and answer the questions that follow

Seema is a veterinarian in a private hospital and is very fond of animals. She has been working as a vet for almost 8 years and is now seeking funds to establish her own pet care brand 'Pretty Paws'. Pretty Paws will produce and sell high quality fur care, grooming, accessories, and medicinal products for cats and dogs.

Seema has been researching her clients and their pets for so many years and has managed to develop a thorough study of their needs and wants. Therefore, she is confident that "Pretty Paws" will satisfy these needs and wants. Seema has used this market research for developing a perfect marketing plan for the production and selling of the products.

The production utility will be set in the outskirts of her town and she has reached out to many qualified people who can be employed in the process. The raw material will be acquired from known suppliers. Seema has designed an attractive jute packet for the products depicting different breeds of cats and dogs for different products and items.

It can be stated that Seema has drafted a very structured and clear marketing plan after a lot of research and study about the markets, products and customers. The products can attract many customers due to Seema's professional reputation and the company can grow in the coming years.

(i) "Seema has been researching her clients and their pets for so many years and has managed to develop a thorough study of their needs and wants."

Which type of research has been highlighted in the above text?

(a) Market research (b) Customer research
(c) Product research (d) None of these

Ans (c) Product research

(ii) "Seema has used this market research for developing a perfect marketing plan for the production and selling of the products."

What role of marketing research is highlighted in the above case?

(a) Planning and executing market plan
(b) Social significance
(c) Solution to marketing problems
(d) All of the above

Ans (a) Planning and executing market plan

(iii) "Pretty Paws" is a ....

(a) logo (b) brand
(c) brand name (d) brand mark

Ans (c) brand name

(iv) "Seema has designed an attractive jute packet for the products depicting different breeds of cats and dogs for different products and items." Which component of product mix is discussed above?

(a) Branding (b) Labelling
(c) Packaging (d) None of these

Ans (c) Packaging

(v) According to you, which technique of promotion is most suitable for a brand like 'Pretty Paws'?

(a) Sales promotion
(b) Personal selling
(c) Direct marketing (d) All of these

Ans (a) Sales promotion

Short Answer Type I Questions (2 Marks)

1 Define market. **CBSE TBQ**

Ans The modern management thinkers define market as, "An arrangement of establishing effective relationship between buyers and sellers of the commodities. It consists of all the potential customers sharing a particular need or want, who might be willing and able to engage in exchange to satisfy that need or want".

2 Define traditional market. **CBSE TBQ**

Ans American Market Association defines the traditional concept of market as, "At every point where a specific commodity is concentrated for sale, a market is found". According to this concept, market means 'a place' only, where actual buying and selling takes place.

3 The traditional concept of market lays emphasis on two conditions. What are they?

Ans The traditional concept of market lays emphasis on the following

(i) **Place** The goods available for sale are brought to a specific place.

(ii) **Different Markets for Different Commodities** there are different markets for different commodities. e.g. vegetable market, fruit market, etc.

4 In what terms, with the passage of time, did industrial activity intensified? **CBSE TBQ**

Ans In the fifties and sixties, industrial activity intensified in the terms of

(i) Quantity (ii) Quality
(iii) Variety of the products
(iv) Competition
(v) Awareness on the part of consumers
(vi) Emergence of laws and enactments to protect consumer's interest

5 "Markets have a very dynamic concept which is constantly evolving with the changing times". In the light of the above statement, state the different concepts of market.

Ans The concepts pertaining to market can be classified as follows

(i) Traditional concept of market
(ii) Scientific concept of market
(iii) Modern concept of market
(iv) Emerging concept of market

6 Which concept of market is not restricted by boundaries? Identify it and explain it briefly.

Ans The modern concept of market is not restricted by geographical boundaries. Clark and Clark defines the modern concept of market as, "In fact, for most commodities, the market must not be thought as a geographical meeting place, but as any getting together of buyers and sellers in person by mail, telephone, telegraph or by any other means of communication".

7 Modern management thinkers define market as, "An arrangement of establishing effective relationship between buyers and sellers of the commodities.

It consists of all the potential customers sharing a particular need or want, who might be willing and able to engage in exchange to satisfy that need or want".

Keeping the above definition in mind, what can be concluded about market mechanisms?

Ans Keeping the above definition in mind, it can be concluded that market includes mechanisms for

(i) Determining the price of the traded item with the help of market forces of demand and supply.
(ii) Communicating the price information.
(iii) Facilitating deals and transactions.
(iv) Effecting distribution.

8 Megha has just launched an e-portal to sell the handicrafts of the tribal people of Bastar.

(i) Which form of business has Megha launched?
(ii) Explain its meaning.

Ans (i) Megha has just ventured into e-business.
(ii) E-business refers to carrying on business activities, both industrial and commercial through computer network, i.e. the internet.

9 Define market environment. **CBSE TBQ**

Ans Market environment refers to factors and forces that affect a firm's ability to build and maintain successful relationships with customers.

A variety of environmental forces influence a company's marketing system, forcing it to change its policies along with the changing environment or be left behind.

10 Define customers. **CBSE TBQ**

Ans A customer, also referred to as buyer or purchaser is the recipient of a good or a service obtained from a seller, vendor or supplier for a monetary or other valuable consideration. The customer is the end goal of the business, since it is the customer who pays for supply and creates demand.

So, it can be concluded that customer is a party that receives or consumes products (goods or services) and has the ability to choose between different products and suppliers.

11 Define macro environment. **CBSE TBQ**

Ans Macro environment also known as 'general and remote environment' refers to factors which affect a business in general. These are the factors on which the company has no control. Hence, company has to frame its policies within the limits set by these forces. Important macro environment factors include demographic, political, economic, socio/cultural and regulatory factors.

12 Release of the Bollywood movie 'Billu Barber' was opposed by certain segments of society, as they thought that the name aims to derogate a specific community.

(i) Which aspect of business environment is being discussed above?
(ii) Why is it important for a business to systematically analyse and diagnose this environment?

Ans (i) Cultural environment.
(ii) It is necessary for a business to analyse cultural environment as it helps to determine the products, services and standards of conduct that are acceptable to society.

13 Due to the enforcement of Euro-IV emission norms, Maruti Limited had to phase out the production of 'Esteem' model of cars. Identify and state the dimension of environment highlighted in the given statement.

Ans 'Legal environment' is highlighted in the given statement. This environment refers to the framework of laws and various legislations within which business transactions take place.

14 To be characterised as good market information, enlist any four essential characteristics to be possessed by it. **CBSE TBQ**

Ans The four basic characteristics to be possessed by good market information are as follows

(i) Relevance (ii) Clarity
(iii) Reliability (iv) Punctuality

15 Explain the last step of the marketing research process.

Ans The last step of the marketing research process is preparing research report. After drawing conclusions, the researcher can make appropriate suggestions/recommendations for solving the marketing problem in a satisfactory manner.

A researcher also prepares a document giving details of the research problem, data collected, conclusions drawn and recommendations made. Such document is called the 'research report which is the final outcome of the lengthy research process. The report is prepared in a suitable format and acts as a self-explanatory document.

16 Define research instruments. **CBSE TBQ**

Ans Research instruments means the instruments, tools, methods or techniques employed in research for gathering the information. There are many types of research instruments such as data analysis, interviewing, market surveys, etc. Among these instruments, market survey is the most commonly used instrument.

17 'Market' and 'marketing' are different concepts. Do you agree? Give reason in support of your answer.

Ans Yes, I agree. Market is defined as an arrangement of establishing effective relationship between buyers and sellers of the commodities and marketing refers to all activities which facilitate this buying and selling.

18 Define the term 'marketing mix'. **CBSE TBQ**

Ans Marketing involves creating a market offering to satisfy customer needs and wants and the combination of variables chosen by a firm to prepare its market offering is called 'marketing mix'. Philip Kotler defines marketing mix as, "Marketing mix is a set of marketing tools that a firm uses to pursue its marketing objectives in the target market".

19 Enlist any four product oriented benefits from marketing mix. **CBSE TBQ**

Ans Four product oriented benefits of marketing mix are as follows

(i) Product is made keeping in mind the needs of the customers.
(ii) The product is of saleable quality.
(iii) Efforts are made to improve the quality of the product.
(iv) Proper attention is given towards attractive designing and packaging of the product.

20 Products can be classified on a number of basis. Give their classification.

Ans Product can be classified on the basis of

(i) **Durability** Perishable, non-durable or durable product.
(ii) **Utility** Producer goods and consumer goods.
(iii) **Weightwise** Heavy and bulky goods and voluminous goods.

21 List any four factors which influence the pricing decisions. **CBSE TBQ**

Ans Internal factors influencing pricing decisions

(i) Corporate and marketing objectives of the firm.
(ii) The uniqueness and utility of the product.

External factors influencing pricing decisions

(i) Market characteristics.
(ii) Nature of economy.

22 'Advertising' and 'publicity' are two important elements of promotion mix.

Explain them.

Ans **Advertising** It is an activity which establishes non-personal contact with the customers regarding the product, idea or the service.

It is an effort to create and sustain the demand for the product by informing the consumers about the product.

Publicity It means mention of the enterprise, its product and brand by the news media in newspaper, journals, radio or television. It is an unpaid and uncontrolled form.

23 While deciding on the marketing mix, a number of factors relating to dealer's behaviour are required to be kept in mind. State those factors.

Ans The behaviour of dealers is required to be studied with respect to

(i) Factors that could motivate them.

(ii) Structure, practice and attitude of dealers.

(iii) Their financial strength.

(iv) Expected change in behaviour with change in the incentives offered.

24 "Marketing manager plays an important role in the organisation". In the light of the above statement, explain his role.

Ans James Culliton described the marketing manager as 'mixer of ingredients'. In the words of James, "The marketing man is a decider and an artist-a mixer of ingredients who sometimes follows a recipe prepared by others, sometimes prepares his own recipe as he goes along; sometimes adopts a recipe to the ingredients immediately available, sometimes invests some new ingredients and sometimes experiments with ingredients as no one else has tried before."

So, by performing the above function, he helps to increase the demand for an organisation's products.

25 To be successful, companies must adapt to ongoing trends and developments in their macro and micro environments. Therefore, it is in the interest of organisations to scan their marketing environment to deal with any possible threats from the market and to capitalise on any available opportunities. The external environmental factors include political, economic, social and technological influences while internal environmental factors include capital structures, resources, capabilities and marketing intermediaries.

Sources *September, 2017*
DOI:10.1007/ 978-3-319-49849-2_3
Mark Anthony Camilleri; University of Malta

(i) Which concept is highlighted in the above paragraph?

(ii) Mention any two components of macro environment.

Ans (i) Micro and macro environment.

(ii) (a) Demographic forces. (b) Cultural forces.

Short Answer Type II Questions (3 Marks)

1 The scientific concept of market widens the area of market. How?

Ans The scientific concept of market widens the area of market by advocating that

(i) Market is not restricted to a particular place, but to a region and the whole region is taken as a place of market.

(ii) The buyers and sellers of the whole region have free access to one another.

(iii) This accessibility enables the market forces of demand and supply to operate and helps in determining the market price.

2 Discuss the role of e-business in promoting the business community. **CBSE TBQ**

Ans E-business helps in promoting the business community in the following ways

(i) **Quick Solution to Doubts** E-business allows quick response to the queries and doubts of customers.

(ii) **Updated Information** Latest information about the product can be displayed on company's website.

(iii) **Extending Markets** E-business helps the markets to become global.

(iv) **Shortening of Distribution Channels** Because of direct contact with customers, distribution channels are shortened.

(v) **Easy to Launch New Products** A company can launch its new products in the market through e-business easily.

(vi) **Lower Personnel** Cost A single computer can perform the jobs of many employees. This helps a business to lower its cost of production and raise sales.

3 Modern concept of market has been defined by Peter Drucker as, "The purpose of the business is to create customers and customers do not have geographical boundaries".

What features of this concept of market can be inferred on the basis of the above definition?

Ans An analysis of the above definition conveys that the market is not taken as a geographical place, but it is rather a meeting of

(i) Buyers and sellers of a given commodity.

(ii) Buyers and sellers who remain in close contact with each other, either personally or through mails, phones, etc.

(iii) Buyers and sellers who are in competition with each other.

(iv) The place of meeting can be regional, national or even international.

4 Give three points of difference between the traditional market and modern market. **CBSE TBQ**

Ans Differences between traditional market and modern market are as follows

Basis	Traditional Market	Modern Market
Meaning	Traditional market means 'a place' only where actual buying and selling takes place.	Modern market is not taken as a geographical area, but it is rather a meeting of buyers and sellers of a commodity who remain in close contact with each other.
Prevalent	This concept of market was prevalent in the 'pre-industrial revolution' era.	This concept of market was prevalent in the seventies and eighties when industrialisation and means of transport and communication has developed significantly.
Emphasis	This market lays emphasis on place and different markets for different commodities.	This concept emphasises on interaction between buyers and sellers.

5 Differentiate between e-commerce and e-business. **CBSE TBQ**

Ans Refer to text on page 108.

6 Performing sellers sustain and succeed in the market. How? **CBSE TBQ**

Ans In today's dynamic and ever changing scenario of market environment, only performing sellers can sustain and succeed in the market.

Performing sellers mean entrepreneurs, who can recognise and respond profitably to unmet needs and trends in the society. These sellers keep an eye on changing environment to detect early signs of threats or an unexploited opportunity.

These sellers are capable of

(i) Keeping themselves aware of the market needs and trends.

(ii) Giving market a solution for their unmet needs.

(iii) Identifying opportunities and threats in the environment.

By performing the above functions, they are able to sustain and succeed in the market.

7 What do you understand by market environment? State the elements of market environment.

Ans Market environment refers to factors and forces that affect a firm's ability to build and maintain successful relationships with customers.

The various factors and forces governing or exerting a pressure on the market can be categorised as follows

(i) **Micro Environment** This environment is made up of factors that are close to the firm and affect it on a day-to-day basis. Usually, these factors interact with the firm or are involved in the same industry.

(ii) **Macro Environment** This environment comprises of factors that are outside the control of a business and affect business in general.

The various forces operating in this environment are cultural, demographic, economic, technological, political and natural forces.

8 Which major concerns are being faced by the business in the natural environment?

Ans The major concerns being faced by the business in the natural environment are as follows

(i) **Increased Pollution** Pollutants emitted by a business can negatively affect its goodwill if they are known for damaging environment.

(ii) **Shortage of Raw Material** As raw materials become increasingly scarce, the ability to create a company's product gets much harder.

(iii) **Government Intervention** A firm may find it increasingly harder to achieve its goals if statutory requirements related to environment sustenance get more stringent.

9 Marketing research is a function which links the consumers, customers and public to the marketer. How?

Ans Marketing research is a function which links the consumers, customers and public to the marketer through information that is used to

(i) Identify and define marketing opportunities and problems.

(ii) Generate, define and evaluate marketing actions.

(iii) Monitor marketing performance.

(iv) Improve understanding of marketing as a process.

10 Does marketing research has a wider scope than market research? Discuss.

Ans Yes, marketing research has a wider scope than market research and includes

(i) **Market Research** Identification of a specific market and measurement of its size and other characteristics.

(ii) **Product Research** Identification of a need or want and the characteristics of the good or service that will satisfy it.

(iii) **Consumer Research** Identification of the preferences, motivations and buying behaviour of the targeted customer.

11 Explain in brief the research report.

Ans Preparing research report is the last step in the marketing process. Through this report, the researcher gives details of the research problem, data collected, conclusions drawn and recommendations or suggestions made for solving problem in a satisfactory manner.

This is the final outcome of the lengthy research process. The research report is prepared in a suitable format and acts as a self-explanatory document.

12 'Developing the research design and research produce' is an important step in the marketing research process. Explain this step and also state the questions to which this step provides the answers.

Ans This step plans for the conduct of actual research investigation. This step provides guidelines for the researcher and helps him/her to know that he/she is moving in the right direction regarding data collection. This step provides answers to the following questions

(i) What is the nature and purpose of study?

(ii) What type of data is required?

(iii) How to collect required data?

(iv) What is the technique of data collection?

(v) How much funds will be required?

(vi) How much time will be needed for completion of research project?

13 A firm attempts to make a 'market offering' keeping some fundamental objectives in view. What are those objectives?

Ans The objectives to be kept in mind are as follows

(i) The offer should be such that it fulfills the needs of the consumers.

(ii) The terms and attributes of the market offering should be acceptable and beneficial to the consumers.

(iii) All the organisational goals, including profits, should be achieved through this offering.

14 'Market offering' can be prepared by following a step-by-step process. Explain the steps involved in the process of preparing a 'market offering '.

Ans The steps involved in the process of preparing a 'market offering' are explained below

First Step Choose the product that will meet the unsatisfied needs of the chosen consumer group.

Second Step Determine the price of the product that is acceptable to the consumers and achieves the objectives of the firm.

Third Step By performing various distribution functions, ensure that the consumers conveniently receive or have assess to the desired product.

Fourth Step Through various promotional measures spread the awareness about the product.

15 'Pack and Go' is a leading bag manufacturer company of India. It recently launched a new range of bags for school going children with a bottle holder and a detachable compass. Which element of marketing mix are they laying stress on? State and explain that element alongwith other two elements.

Ans 'Pack and Go' are laying stress on 'product mix'. Product mix refers to all decisions related to product, such as decisions related to features, packaging, labelling and branding of the products. For other two elements of marketing mix, refer to text on page 118 to 120.

16 Define product mix. What dimensions of the product are to be considered by the entrepreneur herein? **CBSE TBQ**

Ans **Product Mix** Refer to text on page 118.

The dimensions of the product to be considered by the entrepreneur are as follows

(i) Volume of output and sales growth potential.
(ii) Shape, size, weight, colour and features of the product.
(iii) Quality and standard of the product.
(iv) Design and range of the product.
(v) Brand name.
(vi) Packaging and labelling.
(vii) Product testing.
(viii) After sale service.

17 What is pricing? What are the factors influencing pricing?

Or What is pricing? Discuss the various factors that determine the price of a product. **CBSE TBQ**

Ans Pricing is the process of determining what a business will receive in exchange for its products or services.

The factors influencing pricing are as follows

(i) **Internal Factors** These factors accrue from within a business and comprise of the objectives of the firm, cost of manufacturing, etc.
(ii) **External Factors** Business does not operate in isolation. It is affected by several external factors such as legal, technological, political, etc. These factors influence the pricing decision of a firm.

18 You are the marketing manager of a company manufacturing toy car. Explain briefly, the factors to be considered by you before finalising the price of the toy car. **CBSE TBQ**

Ans The following factors will be considered by me before deciding the price of the toy car

(i) Internal factors to be considered as follows
(a) Cost of manufacturing and marketing the toy car.
(b) The uniqueness of the product.
(c) Price elasticity of the product, which in this particular instance will be high.
(d) Image sought to be conveyed through pricing.

(ii) External factors to be considered as follows
(a) Competitor's pricing policy.
(b) Bargaining power of consumers and suppliers.
(c) Societal or social considerations.

19 State the different methods used for pricing. Explain any two.

Ans Some methods and policies which are individually and collectively used in pricing decisions are as follows

(i) Cost plus pricing method.
(ii) Variable pricing method.
(iii) Base pricing and discount method.
(iv) Market pricing method.
(v) Skimming pricing method.
(vi) Penetrating pricing method.

For explanation, refer to text on page 121.

20 Promotion mix plays an important role in marketing mix. Elaborate.

Ans Refer to text on page 123.

Long Answer Type Questions (5 Marks)

1 Briefly discuss the role of e-business in today's market.

Ans Refer to text on page 108.

2 Explain briefly the various concepts of market.

Ans Refer to text on page 107 and 108.

3 Briefly classify the market on the basis of position of buyers and sellers as well as nature of consumption.

Ans Refer to text on page 109 and 110.

4 Discuss the primary forces that comprise the internal environment of the market. **CBSE TBQ**

Ans Refer to text on page 110 to 112.

5 Differentiate between competitors and suppliers as primary forces of market. **CBSE TBQ**

Ans Differences between competitors and suppliers are as follows

Basis	Competitors	Suppliers
Meaning	Competitors are such factors in the primary environment that provide similar offerings for goods and services.	Suppliers are such factors in the primary environment that provide an enterprise the necessary resources for producing the final product.

Basis	Competitors	Suppliers
Importance	Gaining a competitive edge over competitors is important for a business to survive.	The success of a business depends on how effectively a business manages its suppliers.
Factors to be considered for a successful business	(i) Who are our competitors? (ii) Level/size of competitors. (iii) The areas of strengths/ weaknesses of the competitors. (iv) Financial standing of competitors. (v) Overall image of competitors' products in the market. (vi) Operational capacity of the competitors.	(i) Multiple sources of suppliers. (ii) Cordial relationship with suppliers to ensure supply of the product in times of shortage. (iii) Payment to suppliers should be made on time.

6 'Customer is the king'. Do you agree? Justify your answer. **CBSE TBQ**

Ans Yes, I agree that 'customer is the king'. As Charles G Mortimer rightly said, "Instead of trying to market what is essential for us to make, we must find out much more about what the consumer is willing to buy... we must apply our creativity more intelligently to people and their wants and needs, rather than products".

As is brought forward by the above statement, it can be safely concluded that the most influential force which rules the market is the consumer. A business exists only because of its customers.

Therefore, customer satisfaction is the foundation stone of a successful business. Business has to produce goods and services according to the needs of the customers.

This factor is the most important factor of the external micro environment, as demand from consumers directly affects an enterprises

(i) Profitability
(ii) Reputation and goodwill
(iii) Expansion plans

7 Briefly discuss the following characteristics of a good marketing information.

(i) Relevant
(ii) Clarity
(iii) Completeness
(iv) Objective
(v) Punctuality

Ans Refer to text on page 115.

8 What role is played by marketing research? **CBSE TBQ**

Ans Marketing research plays an important role in today's competitive market, fast moving technological developments and changing consumer needs and expectations.

Role Played by Marketing Research Refer to text on page 115 and 116.

9 Explain the term secondary forces. What are external environment comprise of ? Explain with suitable examples. **CBSE TBQ**

Ans Secondary forces refer to factors which affect a business in general. These forces are outside the business and are generally a part of macro environment.

External Environment Refer to text 'macro environment' on page 112 and 113.

For example, an airline is planning to expand over the next 5 years. The following would be some of the macro environment factors it should consider

(i) **Political** It includes political unrest, terrorism, landing rights in foreign countries.

(ii) **Economic** It includes oil prices, exchange rates, taxation (e.g. VAT on fuel), economic boom or depression.

(iii) **Social** It includes change in population size, fashion (e.g. increasing willingness to go on short breaks).

(iv) **Technological** It includes engine efficiency, new aircrafts, better and cheaper video conferencing.

(v) **Ecological** It includes concern about the impact of carbon emissions from jet engines, noise, resistance to airport expansion.

(vi) **Legal** It includes health and safety regulations, consumer legislation (e.g. compensation for cancelled flights), safety and security legislations.

10 Differentiate between the micro and macro environment. **CBSE TBQ**

Ans The differences between micro and macro environment are as follow

Basis	Micro Environment	Macro Environment
Meaning	Micro environment is made up of factors that are close to the firm and affect it on day-to-day basis. Usually these forces interact with the firm or are involved in the same industry.	Macro environment, also known as general and remote environment refers to factors which affect a business in general.
Further classification	It can be further classified as (i) Micro internal environment (ii) Micro external environment	Macro environment comprises of only external factors.
Factors comprising of environment	The internal environment comprises of (i) Value system (ii) Vision, mission and objectives (iii) Management structure and nature (iv) Internal power relationship (v) Human resources (vi) Company image and brand equity miscellaneous factors The external environment comprises of (i) Customers (ii) Competitors (iii) Suppliers (iv) Marketing intermediaries (v) Producers	The external factors affecting macro environment are as follows (i) Demographic forces (ii) Economic factors (iii) Technological forces (iv) Political forces (v) Natural factors (vi) Cultural forces
Degree of control	The internal environment is controllable whereas the external environment is controllable to some extent.	The macro environment is uncontrollable.
Interdependence	The micro environment is dependent on macro environment.	Macro environment is independent.
Example	A new competitor entering in the market.	Government introduces GST.

11 State the main steps involved in marketing research. **CBSE TBQ**

Ans The main steps involved in marketing research are as follows

Step 1 Defining the marketing problem to be tackled and identifying the marketing research problem involved in the task.

Step 2 Specifying the information required.

Step 3 Developing the research design and research produce, i.e. determining whether such information is already available or whether it is to be collected.

Step 4 Select the research instrument to be used and select sample type and size.

Step 5 Analyse and interpret the information in terms of the problem being tackled.

Step 6 Summarise the findings.

Step 7 Preparing research report.

12 Of what help is a marketing mix for an entrepreneur? **CBSE TBQ**

Ans Marketing mix is helpful for an entrepreneur as it helps him to take various decisions regarding product, price, place and promotion.

(i) Marketing mix helps an entrepreneur to take following decisions regarding the product

(a) It is designed according to the needs of the customers.

(b) It is of saleable quality.

(c) Improving the quality.
(d) Attractive designing and packaging.
(e) After sales service.

(ii) It helps an entrepreneur to take following decisions relating to the price of the product
(a) Determination of price according to the paying capacity of customers.
(b) Fair pricing of the product.
(c) Credit facility.
(d) Discount and allowance.

(iii) It helps an entrepreneur to take following decisions relating to the distribution of the product
(a) Availability at the right place.
(b) Availability through convenient outlets.

(iv) It helps an entrepreneur to choose from amongst the following elements of promotion
(a) Advertising. (b) Sales promotion.
(c) Personal selling.

13 Write a brief note on components of product mix.

Ans Refer to text on page 119.

14 Determination of the price of a product is very crucial decision. Why? Support your answer with reasons. **CBSE TBQ**

Ans Pricing is undoubtedly one of the most important decision areas of marketing, since it has a direct bearing with the revenue of the business. Determination of a perfect price by a firm decides not only the marketing strategy but also a firm's market standing in future.

Importance of Pricing Refer to text on page 121.

15 'Sugar-on' is a company engaged in the production of sugar. While deciding on the price per kg of sugar they totally disregarded the regulations laid down by the government regarding this product. The government had fixed a price-ceiling on this product @ ₹ 28 per kg, but 'Sugar-on' decided to sell it for ₹ 32 per kg.

(i) Which factor related to determining the price of the product has been overlooked by the company?

(ii) Mention all the other factors of this category.

Ans (i) The factor of price overlooked by the company is 'Government regulations related to pricing'.

(ii) External factors which exercise influence on pricing are
(a) Market characteristics
(b) Nature of economy
(c) Nature of competition
(d) Bargaining power of major consumers
(e) Bargaining power of major suppliers
(f) Competitors pricing policy
(g) Government controls/Regulations on pricing
(h) Societal or social considerations

16 Name the methods used for pricing. Define marketing mix. Draw a chart showing the components and sub-components of the mix. **CBSE TBQ**

Ans **Methods Used for Pricing** Refer to text on page 121.

Marketing Mix Refer to text on page 117.

Components and sub-components of marketing mix

Elements of Marketing Mix

Product	Price	Place	Product
• Quality	• List price	• Advertising	• Channels of distribution
• Design	• Margins	• Personal selling	• Order processing
• Features	• Discounts	• Sales promotion	• Storage transportation
• Brand	• Credit terms	• Public relations	• Inventory control
• Name	• Pricing objection		
• Packaging	• Pricing strategies		
• Labelling			
• Sizes			
• Services			
• Warranties			

17 What is meant by indirect channels of distribution? Explain any two indirect channels of distribution. **CBSE TBQ**

Ans Indirect channels of distributions are those in which producers supply their products through one or more intermediaries. Two indirect channels of distribution are as follows

(i) **Producer-Retailer-Consumer** (One-level channels) Under this type, producer sells the product to the retailer, who in turn sells to the consumer. This chain is generally witnessed in the 'white goods' market where producers of refrigerators, washing machines, etc, sell their products to retailers, who then sell the same to consumers.

Producer → Retailer → Consumer

(ii) **Producer-Wholesaler-Retailer-Consumer** (Two-level channels) This is the most common channel of distribution. Under this channel, two intermediaries, *viz.* the wholesaler and retailer are involved between the producer and the consumer. Some popular products distributed through this channel are sugar, soaps, ghee, grains, etc.

Producer → Wholesaler → Retailer → Consumer

18 Explain briefly the place mix and its components. **CBSE TBQ**

Ans Refet to text on page 122.

19 Anuj opens a grocery store. To advertise his shop in the local market, he announces free coupons worth ₹ 100 and ₹ 200 on a purchase of goods ₹ 1,000 and above. Which element of promotion mix is being used by Anuj? Also, explain other two tools of promotion mix.

Ans Element of promotion mix used by Anuj is sales promotion.

Other Tools of Promotion Mix Refer to text on page 123 and 124.

20 What do you mean by sales promotion? Explain its featues and advantages.

Ans Refer to text on page 124.

21 Explain the advantages of personal selling and public relations.

Ans Refer to text on page 123 to 125.

22 Mr. Rahul wants to become a good salesman. He consults his friend Shyam to guide him for the same. Shyam expalined to him different qualities in this content. Explain different qualities of a good salesman which can be possessed by Rahul as advised by Shyam. Also, explain element of promotion mix which is referred in the above paragraph.

Ans (i) Rahul can become a good salesman by possessing the under mentioned qualtities

(a) A good salesman should always has a smile on his face.

(b) A good salesman should possess the sufficient degree of patience.

(c) He should try to find out his limitations and make constant efforts to overcome them.

(d) A good salesman should possess good health, attractive appearance and impressive voice.

(e) A good combination of mental qualities like imagination, sound judgement etc. should be possessed by a good salesman.

(f) He should be polite and courteous towares his customers.

(ii) Element of promotion mix referred here is personal selling.

Personal Selling It is an art to induce people to buy the product. It is an effort to win the everlasting confidence of the consumers through directy interacting with them.

23 Discuss briefly the factors affecting the marketing mix.

Ans Refer to text on page 125.

24 There has been a lot of debate in identifying the list of marketing mix elements. The traditional marketing mix by McCarthy (1964) has regrouped Bordens (1965) 12 elements and has comprised to four elements of product, price, promotion and place.

A number of researchers have additionally suggested adding people, process and physical evidence decisions (Booms and Bitner, 1981; Fifield and Gilligan, 1996). The other suggested Ps are personnel, physical assets and procedures (Lovelock, 1996; Goldsmith, 1999); personalisation (Goldsmith, 1999); publications (Melewar and Saunders, 2000); partnerships (Reppel, 2003); premium price, preference of company or product, portion of overall customer budget and permanence of overall relationship longevity (Arussy, 2005); and 2P+2C+3S formula (Otlacan, 2005), therefore personalisation, privacy, customer service, community, site, security and sales promotion.

Source *By Chai Lee GOI, Curtin University of Technology, Malaysia*

(i) Which concept is highlighted in the above paragraph?

(ii) Explain different components of marketing mix.

Ans (i) Marketing mix.

(ii) Refer to text 'marketing mix variables' on page 118.

CHAPTER ASSESSMENT

Objective Type Questions (1 Mark)

1 The word 'market' is derived from the Latin word
(a) marcatus (b) markitus
(c) marcus (d) None of these

2 .... concept of market was prevalent in the 'pre-industrial revolution' era.
(a) Traditional concept (b) Modern concept
(c) Scientific concept (d) None of these

3 Which concept of market follows the adage 'market means people'?
(a) Traditional concept (b) Modern concept
(c) Scientific concept (d) Emerging concept

4 Emerging concept of market is also referred to as ....

5 .... environment is made up of factors that are close to the firm and affect it on a day-to-day basis.

6 Under e-business, there is less risk in payments. State true or false.

7 The success of business depends on how effectively a company manages its suppliers. State true or false.

Short Answer Type I Questions (2 Marks)

8 Discuss briefly the traditional concept of market.

9 How did Clark & Clark and Peter Drucker explain the modern concept of market?

10 What is meant by perfectly competitive market and imperfect competitive market?

11 Mention any two factors of internal micro environment.

Short Answer Type II Questions (3 Marks)

12 Differentiate between e-business and e-commerce.

13 Write a short note on 'marketing intermediaries'.

14 How is pricing important for a business? Explain any three points.

15 Explain in detail emerging concept of market or e-commerce.

16 Explain demographic forces of macro environment.

Long Answer Type Questions (5 Marks)

17 Explain political forces of macro environment.

18 Explain indirect channels of distribution.

19 Explain the process of marketing research.

20 What do you mean by marketing mix? Explain briefly its components.

For explanations scan the given QR Code

CHAPTER 06

Business Finance & Arithmetic

In this Chapter...

- Unit of sale, unit cost and unit price
- Concept of cost
- Break-even analysis (For a single product or service)

Unit of Sale, Unit Cost and Unit Price

Measurement is essential and crucial in any business. It is important to measure sales, costs and profits. Therefore, let us understand how these are measured.

Unit of Sale (For a Single Product or Service)

Unit of sales can be defined as the measure of the products/services being sold. It is a unit on the basis of which a customer is billed.

e.g. a lawyer bills his client by number of hours he/she has worked for the client, then 'time' will be the unit of sale for him/her. In the example of selling shoes, a pair of shoes will be the unit of sale.

To understand this further, a list of some businesses alongwith their respective unit of sale is shown below

Business	Item being Sold/Serviced	Unit of Sale
Fruit Vendor	Apple	Kilogram
Grocer	Rice	Kilogram
Dairy	Milk	Litre
Grocer	Oil	Litre
Garment shop	T-shirt	Piece or Number
Textile shop	Fabric	Metre (of fixed width)
Real estate developer	Apartment	Square feet (Area)
Plumber	Plumbing service	Time : Hour
Lawyer	Legal advice	Time : Hour
Consultant	Special advice	Time : Hour
Coaching class	Tuition	Time : Hour
Baker	Cake	Kilogram/Pound
Baker	Vegetable puffs	Piece or Dozen

'Unit of sale' is an important tool to understand the **economics of the business** in an easy and standardised manner and for tracking the past with the future, so as to be able to take corrective action.

Unit of Sale – As a Tool of Control

For any business, it is very essential to know what one's unit of sale is. Unit of sale will aid the business in determining the direction in which it is heading.

e.g. if the number of units sold in the first three months is 9,000 units and the number in the next three months is 10,000 units, then it indicates that the business is doing better in terms of sales. But, on the other hand, if the units sold in the next three months are 7,000 units, then it means that the volume of sales has fallen and therefore, some corrective actions should be initiated to achieve the former level.

Unit Cost (For a Single Product or Service)

Unit cost can be defined as the cost incurred by a company to produce, store and sell one unit of sale of a particular product or service. Here, the unit cost refers to the variable cost like raw material, packing material, sales commission, freight, etc. Unit cost is also known as cost of goods sold.

Let us understand this concept with the help of an example of a tea vendor.

For a tea vendor, the sum of cost (per cup) of milk, sugar, tea leaves as well as cooking fuel used and disposable cups make up the **variable cost/unit cost**. While calculating the unit cost, the wastage aspect must also be counted.

Here, 1 litre milk and 2 litres of water may not give 30 cups of 100 ml (3 litres), but less, say 28 or so, due to evaporation, spoilage, etc. Thus, evaporation or spillage is a wastage aspect for a tea vendor. For him/her, one cup (of 100 ml) is the unit of sale and the total of the variable costs (such as milk, sugar, tea leaves, wastage aspect, etc.) per cup is the unit cost.

In order to calculate per unit cost, calculate the cost of milk, sugar, tea leaves as well as cooking fuel used and the cost of disposable cups for, say 100 cups and divide by the total quantity. Also add the labour of the person making the tea to the unit cost, if it is variable in nature.

Unit Price (For a Single Product or Service)

Unit price is the price at which one unit of product is sold. For the survival of the business, unit price of a product is required to be fixed at more than its unit cost.

There are many factors that influence the price which an entrepreneur fixes for its product, but ultimately, it is the consumer who determines the price, at which the transaction will take place.

Taking the above example of the tea vendor, if the unit cost is ₹ 6 and the vendor decides to sell it for ₹ 8 and the consumer is also willing to purchase it at this price, then ₹ 8 is the unit price.

Gross Profit

Excess of unit price over unit cost is known as the unit gross profit or unit gross margin. This represents the business's profit from selling a product or providing service before deducting fixed expenses such as salaries, rent and other expenses.

Formula

Unit Price – Unit Cost = Gross Profit per Unit

In the example discussed above,

The unit price is ₹ 8 per cup.

Unit cost, which includes milk, sugar, tea leaves, etc, for one cup is ₹ 6.

The gross profit per unit (one cup) would be

$$= (8 - 6) = ₹\ 2$$

Note *If unit cost exceeds unit price, then, it is referred to as 'Gross loss'.*

Concept of Cost

Cost is an important concept for any form of business. But before delving further in this concept, let us try to understand the difference between expenditure, expense and cost.

Expenditure

It is basically a payment or disbursement and is equated to outflow of money (whether in cash or in the form of cheque payment). The expenditure may be for the purchase of an asset like buying machinery, paying dues for items bought on credit, a distribution to the owners, buying raw material, paying for advertising, salaries, etc.

In other words, expenditure is the amount spent or liability incurred for acquiring assets, goods or services.

Expenditure may further be categorised as follows

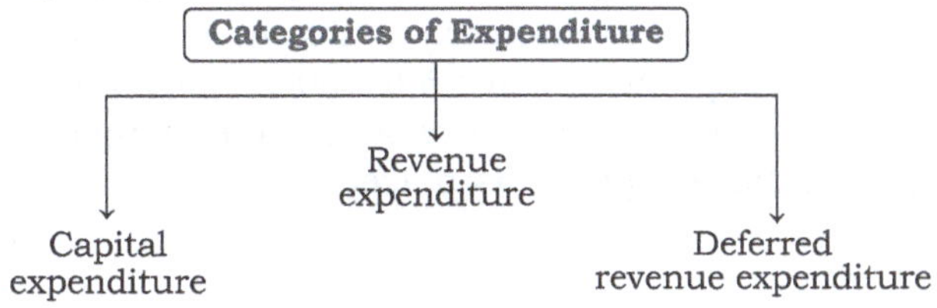

1. **Capital Expenditure** It is an expenditure incurred to acquire assets or improve the existing assets, so that the earning capacity of the business is increased. e.g. purchase of machinery to manufacture goods, purchase of furniture or computers to carry on business, etc.
2. **Revenue Expenditure** It is the expenditure incurred, the benefit of which is consumed or exhausted within the accounting period. e.g. cost of goods sold, salaries, rent, etc.
3. **Deferred Revenue Expenditure** It is basically a revenue expenditure in nature, but is written-off in more than one accounting period. e.g. large advertising expenditure that will give benefit for more than one year.

Expense

It is the value of the resource that was used up or was necessary in order to earn the revenues during the time period.

According to **RN Anthony**, "Expense is a monetary measure of inputs or resources consumed".

Expense may be in the following forms

- Cash payments such as salaries, wages, rent, etc.
- Writing-off a part of fixed asset (depreciation).
- An amount written-off out of a current asset (say bad debts).
- Cost of goods sold.

Note *Expense is basically revenue expenditure.*

Difference between Expenditure and Expense

Expenditure is the outflow of money for the purpose of making various payments. Expenses are a subset of expenditures made specifically for consuming goods and services.

So, expenditure is a broad concept and expense is a narrow concept.

For instance, when a business acquires a machine, it would be called expenditure, while when the business pays for electricity for running the machine, this would be called an expense.

Here's one example to illustrate the difference between an expense and expenditure. A company makes an expenditure of ₹ 5,00,000 to purchase equipment. The expenditure occurs on a single day and the equipment is placed in service. Assuming the equipment will be used for 10 years; part of the original expenditure in buying the equipment will be reported as depreciation expense of ₹ 50,000 per year for the next 10 years.

So, in this example, ₹ 5,00,000 is the expenditure and ₹ 50,000 is an expense.

Another example is in the area of buying raw materials. Because of price consideration, minimum order quantity or economic order lot, etc., the company buys and pays for 1,000 tonnes of raw material at ₹ 6,000 per tonne.

Thus, the expenditure on that particular day is ₹ 60,00,000. During the month, 400 tonnes of raw material was used upto produce and sell company's products.

Thus, ₹ 24,00,000 was the expense (or cost as you will see it later) for producing the saleable end product which generates revenue. Balance of ₹ 36,00,000 stays in the inventory.

Cost and Expense

These terms are differentiated as per their common usage. Generally, costs are derived while expenses are incurred.

Cost is a derived value of money consumed to produce a current or future outcome. Costs are expressed as a value measured in relationship to a casual volume of consumption and provide management a decision supporting view to improve business economics.

An expense is a specific accounting event related to outflow of cash. Expense simply records the event and is used to understand what happened from an accounting perspective.

The following examples will help to understand the difference between expense and cost

- In a factory, there are three products being manufactured. Production unit of each is separate—occupying 50%, 30% and 20% space respectively. The rent of ₹ 50,000 per month being paid for the factory is an **expense**. This amount is then allocated between the three products in proportion to the area occupied i.e. ₹ 25,000, ₹ 15,000 and ₹ 10,000. These amounts represent the **space cost** for each of the product to be used in determining what it costs to produce the product. (Here, cost is allocated).

- A business pays ₹ 1,20,000 at the beginning of the year as the insurance premium. This is an **expense** (in accounting jargon, it is a prepaid expense). Every month ₹ 10,000 is charged as insurance premium before arriving at the business profitability. This is the cost of insurance per month. (Here, cost is derived).

It is quite likely that we will be using the words 'expense' and 'cost' interchangeably as they are quite closely linked.

All expenses ultimately end up as cost — either directly and immediately or indirectly (through allocation and derivation) and with a time lag.

Types of Costs

Costs incurred to start and run a business can be classified into two broad categories, which are as follows

- Start-up costs.
- Operational costs (which will include both fixed as well as variable costs).

1. Start-up Costs

It is the cost which is incurred initially to start a business. It consists of expenses for acquiring assets as well as acquiring initial raw material and other related items of initial expenses, till such time the cash flow from the business can provide for these.

This component of the start-up cost is referred to as working capital.

The following is a list of some of the start-up costs to be incurred

(i) **Land** Acquiring land to set-up a business.
(ii) **Building** Constructing building to start the business.
(iii) **Computers** Purchasing computers.
(iv) **Equipments** Investing money in purchasing equipments.
(v) **Machinery** Buying and installing machines.
(vi) **Vehicles** Buying vehicles to be used for transportation purposes.
(vii) **Vessels** The vessels which will be used in case of catering business.
(viii) **Software** The software needed to be installed in computer.
(ix) **Registration** For registering the company.
(x) **Inauguration Ceremony** Expenses incurred at the time of inaugurating the business.
(xi) **Raw Materials** Purchasing raw materials for a manufacturing business.
(xii) **Salary** Paying advance salary to attract talented persons during initial period.
(xiii) **Rent Advance** Money to be paid in advance to the landlord.

2. Operational Costs

These costs are for carrying out the day-to-day operations of the business or enterprise.
They are further classified as below

(i) **Fixed Costs**

These are the ones which an entrepreneur has to incur by virtue of the fact that one has started a business and is operating it. These are ongoing costs which are not affected by changing sales volume. The fixed costs are not dependent upon the level of output.

It is important to remember that these costs are 'fixed in nature' and not necessarily 'fixed in amount'. e.g. telephone bill may vary slightly month to month, depending upon the usage. However, this variation is not linked to the sales volume directly.

Following is a list of some items on which expenses will remain fixed in nature

- Consultancy charges
- Travel
- Salary
- Wages
- Rent
- Telephone
- Water
- Office lighting
- Office stationary
- Employee welfare
- Advertising
- Insurance premium

(ii) **Variable Costs**

Variable costs are those which vary as a total cost of the organisation when output (number of items-goods and services-produced) varies. In other words, it varies with the change in number of units produced. When output changes, these costs also change. Thus, when output will be zero, variable cost will also be zero and will increase with the increase in output.

An example of a variable cost for a bakery would be the cost of flour, sugar, baking power, etc.

Following is a list of some items for which the costs incurred are variable

- Raw materials
- Packing material
- Freight inward and outbound

– Sales commission
– Royalty
– Factory power
– Piece rate wages (wages based on production)

For all the above items, the cost incurred will be more if the sales are more and will be less if the sales are less.

Classification of a Cost as Fixed or Variable

For classifying a particular expense/cost as either fixed or variable, it is important to know for which industry or type of business it is related to.

e.g.

- Telephone bill is generally a fixed expense, except when it relates to a 'call centre'.
- Paper bill in an office or shop would be fixed, but in a printing business, it would be a variable cost (like raw material).
- Fodder to the cows is variable, because more cows means more milk.
- Water in the office is fixed, water in a soft drink factory is variable.
- Stationary in a coaching class is variable because more students means more stationery, but stationary in an office is fixed.

The most important point to remember is, not to get trapped in classifying an expense in one or the other category, without knowing which business it refers to.

Need for Classification of Costs

The purpose and objective of every business is to earn profit. For doing this, an entrepreneur needs to price his/her product or service appropriately after treating different costs in an appropriate manner.

What a business has spent on machinery cannot be recovered from the production in one month. But raw material used in a product must be recovered from that product only.

So, the costs should be classified clearly so that their recovery is possible.

CHECK POINT 01

1. What do you mean by 'Unit of sale'?
2. What does excess of unit price over unit cost known as?
3. What is expense?
4. Give one example of revenue expenditure.
5. Why is water in the office considered as fixed cost?

Break-even Analysis (For a Single Product or Service)

Break-even analysis is an important tool in the hands of entrepreneurs which helps them to assess that volume of business which will help them to recover all their costs.

Calculating the break-even point (through break-even analysis) can provide a simple yet powerful quantitative tool for managers.

In its simplest form, break-even analysis provides insight into whether or not revenue from a product or service has the ability to cover the relevant costs of production of that product or service.

Entrepreneur can use this information in making a wide range of business decisions, such as

- Setting prices
- Preparing competitive bids
- Applying for loans
- Profit planning
- Goal setting

Break-even Point

A business's break-even point is the amount or level of sales or revenue that it must generate in order to equal its expenses. In other words, it is the point at which the company neither makes a profit nor suffers a loss, i.e.

At the break-even level,

$$\text{Total Revenue} = \text{Total Expenses}$$

The formula for calculating break-even level is

$$\text{Break-even Volume (Per month)} = \frac{\text{Fixed Cost (Per month)}}{\text{Gross Margin per Unit}}$$

Note *Gross margin per unit is also referred to as contribution per unit and can be calculated as : Selling Price per Unit – Variable Cost per Unit.*

Let us understand this further through a simple example of Ram and his tea vending business, considering the following facts or assumptions

- Ram, who was earlier working in a restaurant, has now decided to start a tea vending business. He was getting ₹ 300 per day as his wages, while working in the restaurant.
- Ram is thinking in terms of a mobile hand cart for his tea vending business, which he will take around to the various construction sites in the given locality during day light only.
- Before starting the business, he needs to buy vessels, cart, stove, fuel, strainer, thermos flask, etc., for which he needs ₹ 12,000.

- He will need to buy the initial supply of milk, sugar, cups, tea leaves for which he will need around ₹ 1,000.
- Ram had ₹ 1,000 which he used for buying various consumable items. He borrowed ₹ 12,000 from a friend and agreed to pay him ₹ 4 per day as interest (which comes to 12% per annum).
- The cost of producing tea from 1 litre milk is as shown below

One litre milk	= ₹ 30
Two litres of water	= ₹ 2
Sugar (300 gm)	= ₹ 30
Tea leaves (100 gm)	= ₹ 20
Fuel	= ₹ 2
Total	= **₹ 84**

- Now, we also have to consider the wastage aspect where there will be evaporation while boiling water and milk, there may be spillage, etc. Hence, the actual number of cups of tea, which can be made from 1 litre of milk and 2 litres of water will be 28 cups of 100 ml each, which means it costs ₹ 3 per cup (84 divides by 28).
- Each disposable cup costs 50 paise.
- So, the unit cost will be ₹ 3.50 per cup.
- Ram has surveyed the locality and finds that all similar vendors are charging ₹ 5 per cup. He also decides to sell his tea at ₹ 5 per cup.
- The gross profit or margin per cup will be ₹ 1.5 = (5.00 – 3.50).
- Ram employs a helper on a daily wage of ₹ 99. He pays no rent but ₹ 10 per day of protection money to be able to do business in that area. He pays interest of ₹ 4 per day. Also, he should be able to recover his own wages of ₹ 300 per day.
- Ram knows that he needs to recover the initial investment of ₹ 12,000 over a period of time. He decided to do this over 5 years or 60 months.

This translates to approximately to

₹ 7 $\left(\frac{12{,}000}{60 \times 30} = 6.67\right)$ per day.

- Therefore, total fixed costs per day for Ram are (300 + 99 + 10 + 4 + 7) = ₹ 420.

From the above mentioned information, calculating the break-even point as

Break-even Volume (Per day)

$$= \frac{\text{Fixed Cost (Per day)}}{\text{Gross Margin per Unit}}$$

Break-even volume (Per day) $= \frac{420}{1.50} = 280$
(For above example)

Break-even level for Ram is 280 cups per day.

Target Setting

Let us assume that Ram has a goal of achieving a daily profit of ₹ 600. What should his sales target be?

- Expected profit per day = ₹ 600
- Fixed cost per day = ₹ 420
- Total = 600 + 420 = ₹ 1,020
- Gross margin per cup = ₹ 1.50

Sales Target/Day

$$= \frac{\text{Fixed Cost (Per day)} + \text{Expected Profit (Per day)}}{\text{Gross Margin per Unit}}$$

Number of cups to be sold = 1020/1.50 = 680 cups per day

CHECK POINT 02

1. What do you mean by break-even point?
2. Give formula to calculate break-even volume.
3. What is the condition of break-even level?
4. If fixed cost of a company is ₹ 1,00,000 and variable cost is ₹ 60,000, then what is the total cost incurred by a company?

EXAM PATTERN EXERCISE

Objective Type Questions (1 Mark)

Multiple Choice Questions

1 .... can be defined as individual items that a company sells. **CBSE TBQ (M)**

(a) Unit price (b) Unit of sale
(c) Unit cost (d) None of these

Ans (b) Unit of sale

2 The cost incurred by a company to produce, store and sell one unit of a particular product is referred to as **CBSE TBQ (M)**

(a) unit price (b) unit of sale
(c) unit cost (d) None of these

Ans (c) unit cost

3 Unit cost refers to the **CBSE TBQ (M)**

(a) variable cost (b) fixed cost
(c) marginal cost (d) None of these

Ans (a) variable cost

4 Gross profit is calculated as

(a) Unit Price – Unit Cost
(b) Unit Cost – Unit Price
(c) Sales – Variable Cost
(d) None of the above

Ans (a) Unit Price – Unit Cost

5 Costs incurred to start and run a business can be classified as

(a) start-up costs (b) operational costs
(c) Both (a) and (b) (d) None of these

Ans (c) Both (a) and (b)

6 Which of the following is not an example of fixed cost?

(a) Salary (b) Rent
(c) Raw material (d) All of these

Ans (c) Raw material

7 Raw material purchased is an example of

(a) fixed cost (b) variable cost
(c) start-up cost (d) Both (b) and (c)

Ans (d) Both (b) and (c)

8 Parag runs coaching classes in Meerut. While assessing the profit of the year, he prepares a Trading and Profit & Loss Account. In this account, stationery expenses should be treated as

(a) fixed (b) variable
(c) semi-variable (d) None of these

Ans (b) Stationery expenses will be treated as variable because more students will result in more expense in stationery.

9 Mahendra manufactures face masks. The selling price of a single face mask is ₹ 55 and the variable cost of making it is ₹ 30 per unit. Mahendra has to bear fixed expenses amounting to ₹ 25,000 per month.
His break-even level of sale will be

(a) 100 units (b) 1,000 units
(c) 2,000 units (d) None of these

Ans (b) 1,000 units

Hint $\frac{25,000}{(55-30)}$

10 At the break-even level, ... is equal to the total expenses. **CBSE TBQ (M)**

(a) total cost (b) total revenue
(c) variable cost (d) fixed cost

Ans (b) total revenue

11 Break-even Volume per month =

(a) Fixed Overheads/Gross Margin per Unit
(b) Variable Overhead/Gross Margin per Unit
(c) Gross Margin per Unit/Fixed Overheads
(d) None of the above

Ans (a) Fixed Overheads/Gross Margin per Unit

12 The business is at neither profit nor loss, when it is at ....

(a) break-even point
(b) maximum profit level
(c) level of full consumption
(d) None of the above

Ans (a) break-even point

13 Which of the following is not a form of expense?

(a) Cash payments such as salaries, wages, rent, etc.
(b) A part of fixed asset written-off
(c) An amount written-off out of current liability
(d) Cost of goods sold

Ans (c) An amount written-off out of current liability

14 **Assertion** (A) Unit of sale is a measure of what products are sold.

Reason (R) It is a unit used to bill a customer.

Alternatives

(a) Both Assertion (A) and Reason (R) are correct
(b) Assertion (A) is correct, but Reason (R) is incorrect
(c) Assertion (A) is incorrect, but Reason (R) is correct
(d) Both Assertion (A) and Reason (R) are incorrect

Ans (a) Both Assertion (A) and Reason (R) are correct

15 **Assertion** (A) Businessman cannot operate for a longer time below break-even level.

Reason (R) At this point, total cost is greater than total revenue.

Alternatives

(a) Both Assertion (A) and Reason (R) are correct
(b) Assertion (A) is correct, but Reason (R) is incorrect
(c) Assertion (A) is incorrect, but Reason (R) is correct
(d) Both Assertion (A) and Reason (R) are incorrect

Ans (b) At this point, total cost is equal to total revenue.

16 Given below is list of some businesses in Column I and their respective unit of sale in Column II. Match them correctly.

Column I (Business)	Column II (Unit of as sale)
A. Fruit vendor	(i) Litre
B. Dairy	(ii) Metre
C. Garment shop	(iii) Kilogram
D. Textile	(iv) Piece or number

Codes

	A	B	C	D		A	B	C	D
(a)	(i)	(ii)	(iv)	(iii)	(b)	(ii)	(i)	(iv)	(iii)
(c)	(iii)	(i)	(iv)	(ii)	(d)	(ii)	(iv)	(i)	(iii)

Ans (c) (iii) (i) (iv) (ii)

17 Given below are some general concepts in Column I and their features in Column II. Match them correctly.

Column I	Column II
A. Unit price	(i) Total profit earned by a business enterprise from selling a product.
B. Break-even point	(ii) The cost incurred by a company to produce, store and sell a product.
C. Unit cost	(iii) No profit and no loss situation.
D. Gross profit	(iv) Price at which one unit of sale is sold.

Codes

	A	B	C	D		A	B	C	D
(a)	(iv)	(iii)	(ii)	(i)	(b)	(ii)	(i)	(iii)	(iv)
(c)	(iii)	(iv)	(ii)	(i)	(d)	(ii)	(i)	(iv)	(iii)

Ans (a) (iv) (iii) (ii) (i)

18 Which concept is highlighted in the given graph by the letter A?

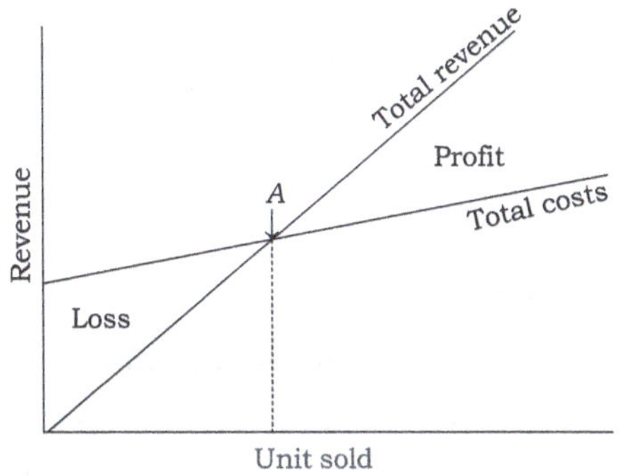

(a) Unit price
(b) Unit cost
(c) Break-even point
(d) None of the above

Ans (c) Break-even point

Fill in the Blanks

19 Ankit owns a dairy business. His unit of sale will be ....

Ans litres

20 XY and Sons makes men's shirt. The unit price of the shirt is ₹ 250 and its unit cost is ₹ 175. The gross profit per unit will be ....

Ans ₹ 75 (250 – 175)

21 .... is the amount spent or liability incurred for acquiring assets, goods or services.

Ans Expenditure

22 According to .... , "expense is a monetary measure of inputs or resources consumed."

Ans RN Anthony

23 Do not fall into the trap of classifying an expense in one or the other category, without knowing which .... it refers to. **CBSE TBQ**

Ans business

24 Operational costs can be further classified as .... and ....

Ans fixed costs, variable costs

25 Quite often the terms 'start-up' and '......' are used interchangeably. **CBSE TBQ**

Ans one-time cost

26 The two types of costs are ... and ... . **CBSE TBQ**

Ans fixed, variable

27 It is important to remember that fixed costs are 'fixed in ....' and not necessarily ' fixed in ....' **CBSE TBQ**

Ans nature, amount

28 Gross margin per unit is also referred to as .... per unit.

Ans contribution

29 Sales target to earn desired profit = ...

Ans Fixed Expenses + Desired Profit/Gross Margin per Unit

30 A business's break-even point is the amount or level of .... that it must generate in order to equal its .... **CBSE TBQ**

Ans sales, expenses

State True or False

31 For a real estate developer, the unit of sale will be square yards.

Ans False. It will be square feet.

32 Unit cost is calculated by adding fixed as well as variable expenses and dividing it by the total number of units produced.

Ans True

33 Excess of unit price over unit cost is known as unit gross profit.

Ans True

34 Pranav has a pav bhaji stall. On a particular day, he sell 50 plates of pav bhaji @ ₹ 35 per plate. The cost of making one plate of pav bhaji comes to ₹ 22 per plate. His gross margin for that day will amount to ₹ 1,750.

Ans False. ₹ 1,750 are total sales revenue i.e. (50 × 35). Gross margin will be ₹ 650 [(35 − 22) × 50].

35 Expenditure is a broad concept and expense is a narrow concept.

Ans True

36 Cost incurred on purchasing computers is a start-up cost.

Ans True. Because it is the cost incurred initially to start a business.

37 $\text{Break-even Volume} = \frac{\text{Fixed Cost}}{\text{Gross Margin per Unit}}$

Ans True

38 Break-even analysis is an important qualitative tool used in decision-making.

Ans False. It is a quantitative tool used in decision-making.

Case Based Questions

39 Read the following article and answer the questions that follow

"Tutor for you" is an online tutoring platform that provides lessons, lectures, notes, questions, sample papers and online audio and video doubt solving to students across India. The company was started by Ram Murthy with an investment of ₹ 50,00,000. Later on, the company changed its vision and entered into the Edtech Industry providing all types of online educational services to all students.

The management decided to provide laptops and systems to full-time tutors who are working from home and incurred expenditure of ₹ 21,00,000 for the same in 2023. The revenue earned by the company in 2022 was ₹ 90,00,000 and the total expenses including telephone bills, sales commission, salary, wages, etc., amounted to ₹ 43,00,000.

The company has saved a lot on cost of operations with the new concept of work from home.

(i) What will be the unit of sale for the services provided by tutors on the platform?

(a) Per student (b) Per video
(c) Per hour (d) Per audio

Ans (c) Per hour

(ii) The expenditure of ₹ 21,00,000 for providing computer systems to tutors will be classified as

(a) fixed (b) capital
(c) variable (d) None of these

Ans (b) capital

(iii) Which of the following correctly defines the investment of ₹ 50,00,000 done by Ram Murthy?

(a) Start-up cost (b) Operational cost
(c) Organisational cost (d) Investment cost

Ans (a) Start-up cost

(iv) What is the net income or profit of the company for the financial year 2022?

(a) ₹ 13,300,000 (b) ₹ 47,00,000
(c) ₹ 40,00,000 (d) ₹ 45,00,000

Ans (b) (90,00,000 – 43, 00,000)

(v) Salary and wages are .... costs.

(a) variable (b) semi-variable
(c) fixed (d) semi-fixed

Ans (c) fixed

40 Read the following article and answer the questions that follow

During the coronavirus pandemic, Vasudha started making handmade face masks of different fabrics with names engraved on each mask. The masks were customised according to the customers who can choose the fabric, colour, and design of their choice as well as the font and colour of their names.

Vasudha incurred ₹ 30 per unit as variable costs and ₹ 12,000 as fixed expenses. She sold a mask for ₹ 60 each.

During the affected year of the pandemic, Vasudha was earning high revenues but after the fear of virus was slowly decreasing, the revenues and expenses were stuck at the same level. Therefore, there was neither any profit nor loss.

Vasudha decided to use social media as a tool to capture audience. She started making videos spreading numbers and facts that proved masks were still necessary. Many health conscious individuals reached her. Vasudha also started giving discounts to customers and free delivery for a month. She also sold her masks to local retailers and stores.

(i) The break-even level of sales is ....

(a) 400 units (b) 200 units
(c) 100 units (d) 300 units

Ans (a) 12,000/(60 – 30)

(ii) What term will be used by the cost incurred on the production, storage and selling of each mask?

(a) Unit price (b) Unit cost
(c) Unit sales (d) Unit margin

Ans (c) Unit sales

(iii) "Therefore, there was neither any profit nor loss." Which of the following concepts is discussed in the above text?

(a) Economic stagnation
(b) Loss of sale
(c) Recession (d) Break-even point

Ans (d) Break-even point

(iv) "Vasudha incurred ₹ 30 per unit as variable costs and ₹ 12,000 as fixed expenses. She sold a mask for ₹ 60 each." ₹ 60 depicts the .... of masks.

(a) unit cost (b) unit price
(c) unit sales (d) None of these

Ans (b) unit price

(v) The fixed cost of ₹ 12,000 incurred by Vasudha is an example of

(a) start-up cost
(b) organisational cost
(c) operational cost (d) None of these

Ans (c) operational cost

Short Answer Type I Questions (2 Marks)

1 'Unit of sale' is an important tool of management. Why?

Ans 'Unit of sale' is an important tool to understand the economics of the business in an easy and standardised manner and for tracking the past with the future so as to be able to take corrective action.

2 'Unit of sale' can be used as a tool of control. How?

Ans Unit of sale facilitates comparison in two time periods and in case of deviations help initiate corrective action.

So, if in a particular month units sold are 2,000 and in next month the units sold are 1,500, then it means that some corrective action should be initiated to achieve the former level.

3 'Teach-one' is a firm providing home tutors, who are expert in their respective subjects. It also provides online teaching services for students of remote areas.

(i) What would be the unit of sale for the firm?

(ii) If 'Teach-one' firm starts consultancy services, then what would be it's unit of sale?

Ans (i) The unit of sale for 'Teach-one' will be 'per hour'.

(ii) In case of consultancy services also, the unit of sale will be 'per hour'.

4 Unit cost is also referred to as 'cost of goods sold'. Why?

Ans Unit cost is referred to as 'cost of goods sold' because it includes variable cost like raw material, packing material, sales commission, freight, etc. It changes with the level of change in the production activity.

5 Give four examples of fixed costs. **CBSE TBQ**

Ans Four examples of fixed costs are as follows

(i) Salary (ii) Rent

(iii) Office lighting (iv) Insurance premium

6 Samiksha, an entrepreneur student, takes up a job in a call center during her summer break. While having a conversation with the accountant of the company and going over the cost records, she is surprised to see telephone charges as being recorded as a variable cost, as she is of the view that they are a part of fixed cost. Is Samiksha's view valid? Comment.

Ans No, Samiksha's view is not valid. Telephone charges in a call centre are a component of variable cost only.

7 In addition of finding the break-even level of a firm, what other use can break-even analysis be put into?

Ans Break-even point analysis can also be used to compute sales target to earn desired profit with the help of the following formula

Sales target to earn desired profit

$$= \frac{\text{Fixed Expenses + Desired Profit}}{\text{Gross Margin per Unit}}$$

8 The following information relates to a company, which produces a single product. **CBSE TBQ**

Direct labour per unit	₹ 22
Direct materials per unit	₹ 12
Variable overheads per unit	₹ 6
Fixed costs	₹ 4,00,000
Selling price per unit	₹ 60

Use the above figures to show that minimum number of units that must be sold for the company to break-even.

Ans Variable Cost per Unit = Direct Labour per Unit + Direct Material per Unit + Variable Overheads per Unit

= 22 + 12 + 6

= ₹ 40 per unit

Selling price per unit = ₹ 60

∴ Gross margin per unit = 60 − 40 = 20

Fixed overheads = ₹ 4,00,000

$$\text{Break-even Point} = \frac{\text{Fixed Overheads}}{\text{Gross Margin per Unit}}$$

$$= \frac{4,00,000}{20}$$

= 20,000 units

9 Mohan, who manufactures a toy car using non-toxic components, wants to compute his break-even point. His fixed expenses in the form of rent, depreciation and salaries of administrative staff amount to ₹ 25,000 per month. He sells the car for ₹ 200 and his variable cost per car is ₹ 150. Find his break-even point.

Ans Fixed expenses per month = ₹ 25,000

Selling price per car = ₹ 200

Variable cost per car = ₹ 150

Gross margin per car = 200 − 150 = ₹ 50

$$\text{Break-even point} = \frac{\text{Fixed Expenses}}{\text{Gross Margin per Unit}}$$

Accordingly,

$$\text{Break-even point} = \frac{25,000}{50} = 500$$

∴ His break-even point is 500 cars.

10 From the following information, ascertain by how much value the sales must be increased by the company to meet their break-even point?

Sales	₹ 3,00,000
Fixed Cost	₹ 1,50,000
Variable Cost	₹ 2,00,000

Ans Break-even Point = $\dfrac{\text{Fixed Cost} \times \text{Sales}}{\text{Sales} - \text{Variable Cost}}$

$$= \frac{1,50,000 \times 3,00,000}{3,00,000 - 2,00,000}$$

$$= \frac{1,50,000 \times 3,00,000}{1,00,000} = ₹\ 4,50,000$$

Hence, sales to be increased by the company to meet break-even point is (4,50,000 – 3,00,000) = ₹ 1,50,000.

11 Break-even point is a point where the cost or expenses and revenue are balanced so there is no loss or gain. In other words, that is the point where the company has neither profit nor loss. In a simple analysis of the break-even point, it can give out the information about whether revenue can cover the cost relevant to the product.

Management can use this information to make various business decisions, including setting prices, preparing competitive bids, and applying for loans. Likewise, with the managerial concept, the break-even analysis seeks to find the appropriate amount of output so that no loss is incurred.

The manager can determine the minimum amount of sales in which the company does not suffer losses. If a product cannot cover its costs, it will reduce the company's profitability.

Source *https://doi.org/10.29121/granthaalayah.v8.i6.2020.502*

(i) Which concept is highlighted in the above paragraph?

(ii) How do you calculate it?

Ans (i) Break-even point.

(ii) When determining a break-even point based on sales. Divide the fixed costs by the contribution margin.

Break-even Point (Sales) = Fixed Costs ÷ Contribution Margin

Contribution Margin = Price of Product – Variable Costs

Short Answer Type II Questions (3 Marks)

1 Explain the types of expenditure.

Ans Expenditure may further be categorised as follows

(i) **Capital Expenditure** It is an expenditure incurred to acquire assets or improve the existing assets, so that the earning capacity of the business is increased. e.g. purchase of machinery to manufacture goods, purchase of furniture or computers to carry on business, etc.

(ii) **Revenue Expenditure** It is the expenditure incurred, the benefit of which is consumed or exhausted within the accounting period. e.g. cost of goods sold, salaries, rent, etc.

(iii) **Deferred Revenue Expenditure** It is basically a revenue expenditure in nature, but is written-off in more than one accounting period. e.g. large advertising expenditure that will give benefit for more than one year.

2 Explain cost, expenses and expenditure. **CBSE TBQ**

Ans **Cost** It is a derived value of money consumed to produce a current or future outcome.

Expense An expense is the value of the resource that was used up or was necessary in order to earn the revenues during the time period.

Expenditure This is the amount spent or liability incurred for acquiring assets, goods or services.

3 Illustrate the difference between expenditure and expense.

Ans Refer to text on page 146.

4 Distinguish between 'unit price' and 'unit cost'. **CBSE TBQ**

Ans Differences between 'unit price' and 'unit cost' are as follows

Basis	Unit Price	Unit Cost
Meaning	Unit price is the price at which one unit of goods is sold.	Unit cost can be defined as the cost incurred by a company to produce, store and sell one unit of goods.
Cash flow	It results in inflow of cash.	It results in outflow of cash.
Importance	Unit price is important from the customer's point of view.	Unit cost holds significance for a manufacturer.

5 M/s 'Urbane Male' is a company engaged in manufacturing shirts for men. The variable cost of production per shirt is given below

Cloth (2m) @ ₹ 125 per metre	₹ 250
Buttons, thread, bukram, etc.	₹ 25
Stiching and cutting charges per shirt	₹ 30
Total variable cost	**₹ 305**

In addition to the above variable costs, the company has to bear certain fixed costs also, such as rent of the factory premises, electricity bill, salary of the administrative staff, etc.

To provide for these costs and also to earn profits, the company decides to sell each shirt for ₹ 400. The company decides to make shirts for children in the age-group of 4-10 years out of the scrap material and distribute it in an orphanage.

(i) What will be the unit of sale for the above company?

(ii) Compute unit cost and gross profit per unit.

(iii) If unit cost exceeds unit price then what does it indicate?

Ans (i) The unit of sale for the above company will be 'per piece'.

(ii) Unit cost is the same as the total variable cost, which amounts to ₹ 305.

Gross Profit per Unit = Unit Price – Unit Cost

= 400 – 305 = ₹ 95

(iii) If unit cost exceeds unit price, then it indicates gross loss.

6 Distinguish between 'expenses' and 'expenditure'. **CBSE TBQ**

Ans Differences between 'expenses' and 'expenditure' are as follows

Basis	Expenses	Expenditure
Meaning	An expense is the value of the resource that was used up or was necessary in order to earn the revenues during the time period.	Expenditure is basically a payment or disbursement and is equated to outflow of money.
Concept	It is a narrow concept.	It is a broad concept.
Example	Rent paid.	Land purchased.

7 What do you mean by start-up cost? **CBSE TBQ**

Ans Start-up cost is the cost which is incurred initially to start a business. It consists of expenses for acquiring assets and acquiring initial raw material and other related items of initial expenses, till such time the cash flow from the business can provide for these.

This component of the start-up cost is referred to as working capital.

Examples of start-up costs are as follows

(i) Acquiring land to set-up a business.

(ii) Constructing building to start business.

(iii) Purchasing computers.

(iv) Investing money in purchasing equipments, etc.

8 Distinguish between 'fixed cost' and 'variable cost'. **CBSE TBQ**

Ans Differences between 'fixed cost' and 'variable cost' are as follows

Basis	Fixed Cost	Variable Cost
Meaning	Fixed costs are incurred by virtue of the fact that an entrepreneur has started a business.	Variable costs are those which vary as a total cost of the organisation, when output varies.
Dependency	Fixed costs are those which are not dependent upon the level of output.	Variable costs are those which are dependent upon the level of output.
Example	Rent of the premises.	Raw material purchased.

9 What is operational cost? Give its classification.

Ans Operational costs are incurred for carrying out the day-to-day operations of the business. They are further classified as

(i) **Fixed Costs** These costs are not dependent upon the level of output. These costs an entrepreneur has to incur for starting a business and also as various administrative expenses.

(ii) **Variable Costs** These costs are those which vary with the total cost of the organisation when output varies. These are related with the production of the product.

10 Write a short note on 'Classification of a cost as fixed or variable'.

Ans For classifying a particular expense/cost as either fixed or variable, it is important to know for which industry or type of business it is related to. e.g.

(i) Telephone bill is generally a fixed expense, except when it relates to a 'call centre'.

(ii) Paper bill in an office or shop would be fixed, but in a printing business, it would be a variable cost (like raw material).

(iii) Fodder to the cows is variable, because more cows means more milk.

(iv) Water in the office is fixed, water in a soft drink factory is variable.

(v) Stationary in a coaching class is variable because more students means more stationery, but stationary in an office is fixed.

The most important point to remember is, not to get trapped in classifying an expense in one or the other category, without knowing which business it refers to.

11 Why is there a need for classification of costs?

Ans The purpose and objective of every business is to earn profit. For this, a business needs to price its goods and services appropriately after treating different costs in an appropriate manner.

What a business has spent on machinery cannot be recovered from the production in one month.

On the other hand, raw material used in a product must be recovered from that product only. Thus, the costs should be classified clearly, so that their recovery is possible.

12 What do you mean by break-even point? **CBSE TBQ**

Ans A business's break-even point is the amount or level of sales or revenue that it must generate in order to equal its expenses.
In other words, it is the point at which the company neither makes a profit nor suffers a loss, i.e.

At the break-even level,

Total Revenue = Total Expenses

The formula for calculating break-even level is

$$\text{Break-even Volume (Per month)} = \frac{\text{Fixed Cost (Per month)}}{\text{Gross Margin per Unit}}$$

where, Gross Margin per Unit = Selling Price per Unit – Variable Cost per Unit

Calculating the break-even point can provide a simple yet powerful quantitative tool for managers by providing them with information whether or not revenue from a product or a service has the ability to cover the relevant costs of production of that product or service.

13 (i) From the following particulars, find out the break-even point

Variables cost per unit	₹ 15
Fixed expenses	₹ 54,000
Selling price per unit	₹ 20

(ii) What should be the selling price per unit, if the break-even point is brought down to 6,000 units?

Ans Contribution per Unit = Selling Price – Variable Cost per Unit

$$= 20 - 15 = ₹\ 5$$

(i) $$\text{BEP} = \frac{\text{Fixed Expenses}}{\text{Contribution per Unit}}$$

$$= \frac{54{,}000}{5} = 10{,}800 \text{ units}$$

(ii) $$\text{BEP} = \frac{\text{Fixed Expenses}}{\text{Contribution per Unit}}$$

$$6{,}000 = \frac{54{,}000}{\text{Contribution per Unit}}$$

$$\text{Contribution per Unit} = \frac{54{,}000}{6{,}000} = ₹\ 9$$

Contribution = Selling Price (SP) – Variable Cost (VC)

$$9 = \text{SP} - 15 \Rightarrow \text{SP} = 9 + 15 = ₹\ 24$$

14 ABC Ltd. is well kown company in Jaipur. It is working hard to build up its reputation in the market. The number of units sold in the first three months is 15,000 units and the number in the next three months is 20,000 units.

What does this tell about its profitability position? What will be the position of the company if it can sell only 12,000 units instead of 20,000 units in the next three months?

Ans If the number of units sold in the first three months is 15,000 units and the number in the next three months is 20,000 units, then it indicates that the business is doing better in terms of sales.

But on the other hand, if the units to be sold in the next three months will be 12,000 units, then it means that the volume of sales has fallen and therefore, some corrective actions should be initiated to achieve the former level.

15 A company makes a product with a selling price of ₹ 20 per unit and variable cost of ₹ 12 per unit. The fixed costs for the period are ₹ 40,000. What is the required output level to market a target profit of ₹ 10,000? **CBSE TBQ**

Ans Selling price per unit = ₹ 20

Variable cost per unit = ₹ 12

Gross Margin per Unit = Selling Price per Unit − Variable Cost per Unit

So, gross margin per unit = 20 − 12 = ₹ 8

Fixed cost = ₹ 40,000

Target profit = ₹ 10,000

Required Output Level

$$= \frac{\text{Fixed Cost} + \text{Target Profit}}{\text{Gross Margin per Unit}}$$

$$= \frac{40,000 + 10,000}{8}$$

$$= \frac{50,000}{8} = 6,250 \text{ units}$$

16 An entrepreneur can use the information generated from break-even analysis in making a wide range of business decisions. What are they?

Ans An entrepreneur can use the information generated from break-even analysis in making a wide range of business decisions, such as

(i) Setting prices

(ii) Preparing competitive bids

(iii) Applying for loans

(iv) Profit planning

(v) Goal setting

Long Answer Type Questions (5 Marks)

1 What do you understand by 'unit of sale'? Explain by giving examples of some businesses alongwith their unit of sale.

Ans **Unit of Sale** Refer to text on page 144.

Examples of Businesses and their Unit of Sale Refer to text on page 144.

2 Explain with the help of examples, the meaning of unit of sale, unit cost, unit price and gross profit.

Ans Refer to text on page 144 and 145.

3 How much profit can we earn?

Ans Profit is needed by a business to sustain and grow. Also, profit is the main motivating factor that induces an entrepreneur to enter into/or undertake a venture, or it can also be said that the sole reason for the existence of a business is 'profit'.

So, an entrepreneur strives or attempts to earn maximum profits from his venture, but while doing so, he should also keep in mind the interests of the society at large because a business is a part of the society itself.

So, while attempting to maximise profit, an entrepreneur should not

(i) Charge exorbitantly high margin of profit.

(ii) Indulge in unfair trade practices such as using inferior quality raw material, fraudulent weights, etc.

(iii) India follows a mixed economy in which certain sectors are given full freedom of operations, i.e. they can charge any percentage of profit for their products. But there are certain other sectors also, which work under the control and supervision of the government and therefore, their profit can be regulated by the government.

4 What is start-up cost? Identify the areas for requirement of start-up costs. **CBSE TBQ**

Ans **Start-up Costs** Refer to Q. No. 7 of short answer type II questions (3 Marks).

Area for Requirement Refer to text on page 147.

5 Rajat is planning to open a retail shop selling high-end customised furniture. As a cost manager, advise Rajat on the costs required to transform his plan into a successful venture.

Ans Rajat will have to incur the following costs

(i) **Start-up Costs** These costs are necessary to start a business. Various costs in this heading, required to be incurred by Rajat are as under

(a) Securing a shop to start his store.

(b) Furnishing and renovating the shop.

(c) Purchasing computers.

(d) Expenditure incurred in getting his shop registered.

(e) Purchasing raw materials.

(ii) **Operational Costs** These costs are incurred for carrying out the day-to-day operations of the business.

They can be further classified as

(a) **Fixed Costs** These costs are not dependent on the level of operations. Some of the expenses belonging to this category which Rajat will be required to bear are as under

- Salary of administrative staff.
- Rent of the shop.
- Electricity and telephone bill, etc.

(b) **Variable Costs** These costs vary with the level of production activity.

Costs which Rajat will bear on this head are as under

- Raw material purchased.
- Labour charges of carpenters, designers, etc.
- Carriage inward, etc.

6 Define the term 'break-even'. **CBSE TBQ**

Ans The concept of break-even can be explained with the help of the graph given below

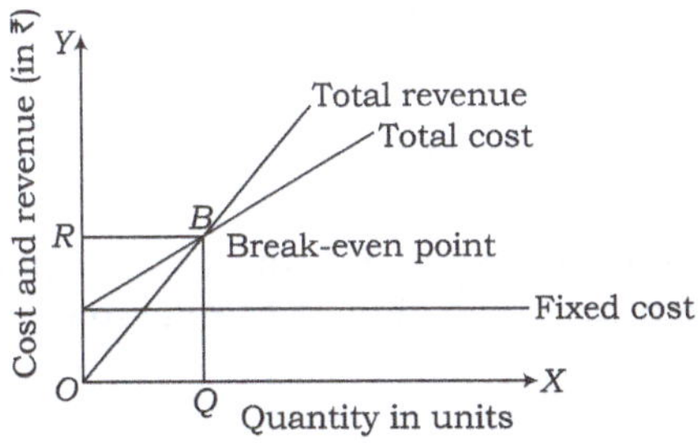

In the graph given above, B is the break-even point at which a firm's total revenue equals total cost. OQ is the quantity produced at this level and OR is the revenue generated which also equals total cost.

For meaning of break-even point, refer to Q. No. 12 of short answer type II questions (3 Marks).

7 From the following particulars, calculate

(i) Break-even point in terms of sales value and in units.

(ii) Number of units that must be sold to earn a profit of ₹ 90,000

Fixed factory overhead cost	₹ 60,000
Fixed selling overhead cost	₹ 12,000
Variable manufacturing cost unit	₹ 12
Variable selling cost per unit	₹ 3
Selling price per unit	₹ 24

Ans (i) Break-even Point

$$= \frac{\text{Fixed Cost}}{\text{Selling Price per Unit} - \text{Variable Cost per Unit}}$$

Variable cost per unit = 12 + 3 = ₹ 15

Total fixed cost = 60,000 + 12,000 = ₹ 72,000

$$\text{BEP} = \frac{72{,}000}{24-15} = 8{,}000 \text{ units}$$

(ii) Number of untis that must be sold to earn a profit of ₹ 90,000

$$= \frac{\text{Fixed Cost} + \text{Profit}}{\text{Selling Price per Unit} - \text{Variable Cost per Unit}}$$

$$= \frac{72{,}000 + 90{,}000}{24-15} = \frac{1{,}62{,}000}{9} = 18{,}000 \text{ units}$$

8 Variable costing has now arrived of a period and is providing to be an exceptionally important tool in planning and controlling operations in many large industrial companies. However still not as broadly working as absorption costing, it is progressively gaining popularity in use.

In variable costing, product costs contain only those manufacturing costs which are directly related to the product and vary with production volume. Under absorption costing all manufacturing costs, direct and indirect, are included as cost of manufactured goods. This article discusses variable costing that is used only for internal reporting and analysis and its applicability in the manufacturing situation.

Variable and absorption costing are not commonly exclusive. Accountants find that variable costing more effectively meets internal requirements because it provides better insight into cost relationship while the absorption costing method meets external reporting requirements.

Source *International Scholar Journal of Accounting and Finance, 5(1), 2015, 1-12*

(i) Which concept is highlighted in the above paragraph?

(ii) Explain all types of costs.

Ans (i) Variable cost.

(ii) Refer to text on page 147 and 148.

CHAPTER ASSESSMENT

Objective Type Questions (1 Mark)

1 .... is also known as unit cost.

(a) Cost of goods sold
(b) Expenditure
(c) Start-up cost
(d) None of the above

2 Profit = ... – Total Sales Expenses.

(a) Unit Cost (b) Total Sales Revenue
(c) Both (a) or (b) (d) None of these

3 Unit price has to be more than the ....

(a) unit cost (b) fixed cost
(c) total sales expenses (d) None of these

4 Unit of sale is an important tool to understand the ....

5 .... cost is a cost that changes with the change in the level of output.

6 Income statement does not show cash transactions. State true or false.

7 Break-even point is a situation where profit margin is less than loss. State true or false.

Short Answer Type I Questions (2 Marks)

8 How is unit of sale considered as a tool of control?

9 Explain any two types of expenditure.

10 Mention any two forms of expense.

11 List any two items for which the costs incurred are variable.

Short Answer Type II Questions (3 Marks)

12 Explain the concepts 'unit price' and 'gross profit'.

13 Write a short note on start-up costs.

14 The following information relates to a company, which produces a single product

Direct labour per unit = ₹ 25; Direct materials per unit = ₹ 10 ; Variable overheads per unit = ₹ 8 ; Fixed cost = 10,00,000; Selling price per unit = ₹ 50

Use the figures given above to show the minimum number of units that must be sold for the company to break-even.

Long Answer Type Questions (5 Marks)

15 Discuss in detail various operational costs.

16 Differentiate between expenditure and expense.

17 Define unit of sale and unit cost. Explain the concept with the help of an example.

For explanations scan the given QR Code

CHAPTER 07

Resource Mobilisation

In this Chapter...

- Meaning of resource
- Planning effective 'resource mobilisation'
- Types of resources
- Physical resources
- Human resources
- Financial resources
- Material resources
- Intangible resources

Meaning of Resource

An economic or productive factor required to accomplish an activity, or as a means to undertake an enterprise and achieve the desired outcome is referred to as 'resource'.

Therefore, 'resource' refers to tangible or non-tangible means required to support the activities of an organisation to achieve pre-determined organisational goals. These resources are the life blood of any economic activity.

Human, financial, physical and knowledge are the basic factors that provide a business, the means to perform its business processes and are therefore referred to as **business resources**. Their successful and timely identification, procurement and utilisation ensure the success of an organisation.

The resources needed by an organisation can be grouped as

1. **Basic Resources** Which are needed by all the organisations and usually comprise of
   - Land
   - Labour
   - Capital
2. **Other Resources** Which vary from enterprise to enterprise, but commonly comprise of
   - Entrepreneurship
   - Energy
   - Expertise
   - Information
   - Management
   - Machines
   - Materials and Methods

Procurement of Resources : Mobilisation

A very important function of entrepreneurs is the arranging and procuring of business resources. Resource mobilisation is the process of getting resource from the resource provider, so that the organisation's work can be initiated and pre-determined organisational goals are achieved on time. It deals in acquiring the needed resources in a 'timely cost-effective manner'.

Resource mobilisation advocates upon having the right type of resource, at the right time, at right price and making right use of acquired resource, thus ensuring optimum utilisation of the same.

Planning Effective 'Resource Mobilisation'

Resource mobilisation is quite often equated with fund raising, but it should be remembered that fund raising is just a part of resource mobilisation as in addition to liquid assets, a business needs many other resources also.

It includes building valuable contacts and networks and garnering the interest, support and in kind contributions, important for an organisation. It should also be kept in mind that the success of any enterprise lies in the capacity and ability of the entrepreneur to

- Mobilise the resources.
- Organise the resources.
- Manage them efficiently and effectively as they are always scarce with reference to their demand.

So, organisations should make adequate preparations for resource mobilisation to be effective and138 should ensure that they are maximising all opportunities.

An organisation's resource mobilisation plan should be closely integrated with organisational goals and be chalked out step-by-step as follows

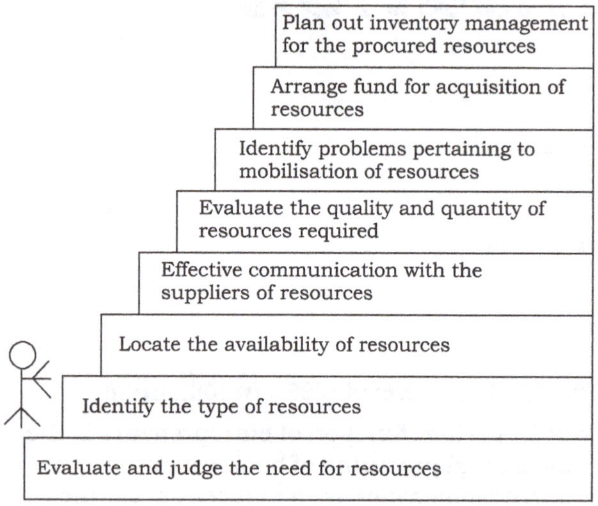

A resource mobilisation plan must follow closely, the vision, mission and goals of the organisation.

Factors Affecting the Resources Required for a Business

A firm's resources, as defined above, are the basic inputs into the production process, combined in different ways so as to provide a firm, a capacity to achieve superior performance.

Different firms need different resources, depending upon

- Nature of activity
- Size of activity
- Product specification
- Type of business activity
- Business strategy pursued by them

According to **Johnson and Scholes**, "Strategy is the direction and scope of an organisation over the long-term, which achieves advantage for the organisation through its configuration of resources within a challenging environment, to meet the needs of markets and to fulfil stakeholder, expectations".

Types of Resources

There are certain basic resources that are required by all forms of business.

These resources can be grouped as

– Physical – Human – Financial
– Material – Intangible

A brief discussion of these resources is given below

Physical Resources

These resources are those that are made by humans through their abilities and skills. The category of physical resources covers a wide range of operational resources concerned with the physical capability of the enterprise, encompassing mainly

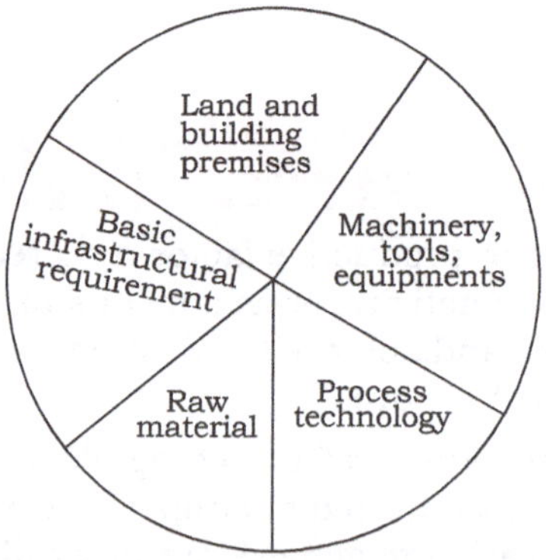

1. Land and Building Premises

The first and foremost concern for the entrepreneur is to finalise the **place** where the enterprise is going to be established. A careful analysis of the following allied issues is essential before taking the final decision related to 'place'

- Capital cost
- Access to other resources
- Transport and communication cost
- Availability of manpower and its cost (wages, salaries)
- Cost of production
- Availability of other utilities like water, gas, fuel, etc
- Access to market for both raw material and finished goods
- Pollution concerns involved
- Degree of legal requirements like taxes, registration fees etc

2. Other Physical Resources

The other physical resources like machinery, tools, equipments, process technology, raw material, etc., too require a thorough investigation as they will have bearing on

- Short and long-term cost of the project.
- Durability and utility (usefulness) expected from these assets.
- Possibility of growth potential.
- Market needs help to decide the range of products and the type of technology.
- Market size to be covered will indirectly help to assess the size/capacity of plant.
- Quality concerns.
- Feasibility for transfer of technology, i.e. is it possible to acquire and implement the technology/technique so selected.
- Feasibility for training of manpower, i.e. is it possible to provide the required training to the workers on the selected technology.

All the above factors should be carefully analysed and evaluated before making the final selection.

CHECK POINT 01

1. Define resource.
2. State five types of resources.
3. Which is the first and foremost concern for the entrepreneur?
4. State any one factor to be analysed and evaluated before making the final selection.
5. Name any one physical resource.

Human Resources

Human resources may be thought of as "The total knowledge, skills, creative abilities, talents and aptitudes of an organisation's workforce as well as, the values, attitudes and benefits of an individual involved".

These are the most important assets that a firm must have and that the management must be most concerned with, because in the absence of these resources, other non-living resources are useless.

Herbert G Hicks and C Ray Gullet have rightly observed that, "The people working in a firm make it what it is". An organisation's performance and resulting productivity are directly proportional to the quantity and quality of its human resource.

A rich and continuing supply of qualified people/personnel is the best assurance an enterprise can have that it will flourish.

'Right man at the right job at the right time'—is the mantra for successful enterprises because it

- Ensures benefits of specialisation to the firm.
- Minimises wastages of resources.
- Reduces inefficiencies.
- Reduces labour turnover ratio and rate of absenteeism.
- Saves cost of production.

Factors to be Considered for Building up Efficient Human Resources

In order to build up loyal, efficient and dedicated personnel, the entrepreneur needs to assess the following

1. What Kind of People Does He/She Need?

To carry on its work, each organisation needs personnel with the necessary qualifications, skills, knowledge, work experience and aptitude for work.

The entrepreneur must clearly know 'what kind of persons should be selected'.

Kind/Type refers to specific qualifications, skills, experience, age, etc., to be possessed by the proposed employees. The type of manpower required, depends upon the nature of business activity and therefore, varies from business to business. It demands a careful planning, persistence and control.

This process demands first of all the determination of the tasks which comprise the job and the skills, knowledge, abilities, responsibilities, duties required of the worker for a successful performance of the job.

While assessing the kind/type of manpower required, entrepreneur should not forget a policy to appoint women, persons from backward communities and people with special abilities.

e.g. Hindustan Lever had for themselves drafted exemplary 'organisation charts', to determine: how many people, at what level, in what positions and what kind of experience and training would be required to meet its objectives.

Manning Table

To develop manpower for the whole organisation is not an easy task. This important economic resource is required to create, design, develop, manage and operate the enterprise, therefore an enterprise needs to exercise extreme diligence in its selection.

For developing manpower, the total work to be done is divided and grouped into packages called 'jobs'. A job is a group of homogeneous tasks performed by an employee in exchange for a pay. It consists of duties, responsibilities and tasks that are defined, specific and can be accomplished, quantified, measured as well as related.

In an organisation, each person would have different position, duties, responsibilities, etc., making it imperative for an organisation to have a wide range of personnel ranging from managers, supervisors, administrators, engineers, technical, skilled and unskilled workers.

What kind of person to recruit and for what qualities that person should be tested needs a very careful, systematic, scientific and organised planning.

Manning table is an important tool which facilitates this process. It is a survey chart or inventory for scheduling manpower requirements in an industrial plant, typically showing each operation with number of workers and time required, each worker classified as to job, experience, handicaps and the minimum time for training a replacement.

The human resources required by an enterprise can be broadly classified as follows

(i) **Managerial Staff** This category is like brain box of the enterprise. Framing policies, objectives, goals, etc., for the enterprise, ensuring their implementation and finally getting the work done from workers is the field area of this category.

(ii) **Non-managerial Staff** The real group which effectively converts the raw material into finished goods is 'workers'. Nature of job decides the quality and quantity of workers to be assigned.

(iii) **Trained Technical Manpower** This constitutes of people who have technological expertise and are frequently required for machinery selection, installation, supervision and operation.

(iv) **Administrative Manpower** To run the enterprise, an entrepreneur needs a group of staff which gives support services to managerial, professional and trained staff. They do not contribute to production directly but only provide assisting services in the maintenance of the enterprise.

(v) **Professional Manpower** Chartered accountants, auditors, bankers, lawyers, who are professional experts can be outsourced by the entrepreneur if required. Small enterprises cannot afford them on their regular payrolls.

The 'manning table' for all these is given below

Manning Table

Larger the enterprise complicated is the classification, while smaller the unit restricted manpower is required.

TOP	MIDDLE	LOWER
Board of Director		
President	Marketing Manager	
Chair person	Production Manager	First Line Inspectors Superintendents
General Director	Human Resource Manager	Supervisors
CEO	Financial Manager	Foremen

(A) Managerial Staff

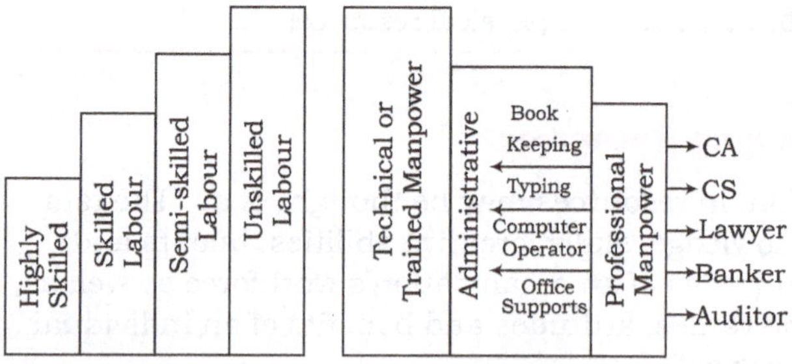

(B) Non-managerial Staff **(C) Others**

2. How Many of People Does He/She Need?

This is the second important question which deals with the number of personnel of each kind required by an enterprise and is affected by the following

- Finding out the total amount of work to be done and then dividing it into different sets of activities.
- The total number of tasks and jobs required to be accomplished under different activities.

- How much work can an average person do in a specified period of time?
- Level of absenteeism expected.
- Level of labour turnover.
- The present number of employees.
- The future plans for expansions, diversification and growth.

Efficient Utilisation of Human Resource

The human resource required should be efficiently managed to ensure optimum utilisation. The efficient utilisation of human resources is only possible if the entrepreneur is able to decide

- the total work to be done.
- the right type of people who can do the work.
- employing right man at right job.

Selection of Personnel

Selecting the right number and right kind of people with appropriate skills at the right place and at the right time to do the work requires a comprehensive, careful, in-depth and scientifically evolved strategy, on the part of entrepreneur, comprising of

- Efficient tapping and scientific selection.
- Appropriate and cost effective training.
- Proper induction, orientation and familiarisation with the organisation and its climate.
- Periodic performance appraisal.
- Feedback and scope for development.
- Proper motivation and remuneration schemes.
- Ensuring scope for the participation in management.
- Ensuring adherence to certain statutory requirements governing the compensation and welfare of measures of employees, such as Factories Act, Provident Fund and Miscellaneous Provision Act, etc.

Expert Professional Assistance

Today is an era of specialisation. Even the most successful companies have realised that

- They cannot do justice to all aspects of business-production, distribution, marketing, legal, researching, etc.
- They do not have adequate expertise, resources, time and energy in their hands to meet out the never ending requirements of the enterprise. Thus, either outsourcing or availing of professional services from outside the firm, has become a major trend in human resources over the past decade.

Although, there is no single legal definition of professional services, but it can be referred to as a calling, occupation or business that

- involves specialised education, knowledge, labour, judgement and skill.
- is predominantly mental or intellectual.
- has professional workforce.
- has good capital resources intensity.
- has proven expertise in the field.
- expects compensation in return for the work done.

Therefore, it is an industry of technical or unique functions performed by independent contractors and consultants, whose occupation is the rendering of such service.

Availing professional expertise as and when need arises or on a regular basis will assist the entrepreneur to have a better cost efficiency through

- Reduced wastages.
- Savings of time, cost and energy.
- Higher efficiency and effectiveness because of professionally proven expertise in the concerned field.
- Focus on the core areas/activities of the enterprise.
- Availing of qualified quality service in time bound frame and at a fraction of cost.
- Lowering the chances of risks.
- Savings on additional fixed investment required in creating infrastructure for providing these facilities on one's own.
- Enhancing business due to others' expertise and experience in the defined field.
- Access to new and growing markets.

Outsourcing 'Non-core' or 'Routine' Functions

This is an emerging trend where enterprises try to concentrate on their core business and outsource non-core or routine activities to outside firms. This has been driven by the need to improve flexibility, increase responsiveness, decrease labour costs and allow the organisation to focus on what it does best.

Therefore, in order to achieve specialisation in work, the entrepreneurs should try procuring/ arranging for following types of qualified resources as per their requirement

- Professional accountants
- Lawyers
- Auditors
- Bankers

- Transporters
- Public relation professionals
- Researchers
- Copywriters
- Appraisers
- Warehouses
- Advertisers
- Couriers
- Customer support services
- Financial accounting services
- Business consultants
- Law firms
- Architects
- Attorneys
- Business development managers, etc

Ways to Procure Professional Services

Now-a-days, these services are not limited to licentiates (i.e. individuals holding professionals licenses), they may run to partnership, firms, or corporations as well as to individuals.

It is for the entrepreneur to analyse and evaluate the extent, nature and type of resource required. Commonly, one can arrange for these through

- Contractual arrangement
- Third party arrangement
- Lease basis
- Captive unit arrangement
- Part time arrangement
- Regular basis

The selection of an independent contractor or consultant providing professional services usually depends on skill, knowledge, reputation, ethics and creativity and price.

Some of them charge fixed rates for projects while other define the price only after assessing the work involved. It is quite common to hire professionals on the basis of an hourly fee or estimated length of project.

CHECK POINT 02

1. What is the most important asset that a firm must have?
2. What is the mantra for a successful enterprise?
3. What kind of people are included in non-managerial staff?
4. Who are included in professional manpower?
5. Mention any two ways of procuring professional services.

Financial Resources

Finance is one of the important pre-requisites to start an enterprise. It is the availability of finance that enables an entrepreneur to bring together personnel, machines, materials, methods, land and convert a dream into reality.

It will not be incorrect to elucidate finance as 'lubricant to the process of production' or 'life blood of enterprise' or 'whoever has the gold makes the rule'. As a part of financial resourcing, an entrepreneur must work out the following

1. How Much Finance is Needed?

First of all, an entrepreneur should try to assess as accurately as possible the requirement of funds for a venture. Excess funds, if raised, will prove to be a burden for the business and shortfall of funds will hinder the smooth functioning of the business. So, the right amount of capital required should be assessed.

2. Term for Which Finance is Required

The next question to be addressed by the entrepreneur is regarding the term for which finance is required.

Generally, finance is required for

(i) **Long-term** It is generally a period of 5 or more years for
- Procuring fixed assets.
- Meeting out expansion or diversification plans.
- Conducting research work.

(ii) **Short-term** It is generally a period of up to 1 year. To meet working capital requirement, short-term finance is to be raised.

(iii) **Medium-term** A period, where finance is required for more than 1 year but less than 5 years, is called medium-term requirement. To meet especially modernisation requirements, finance is required for medium-term.

3. Sources for Generating Finance

The next decision which the entrepreneur needs to take is regarding the source from where finance can be generated. Funds can be arranged either through the owner himself/ herself or he/she can borrow from outsiders. Most entrepreneurs invest small capital from their own funds and remaining from outside. The sources of finance are given below

(i) **Owner's Fund** This is that part of capital that belongs entirely to the entrepreneur in the form of
- Equity capital
- Preference capital
- Margin money/seed money

(ii) **Borrowed Funds** Entrepreneur can if required raise capital from outside through
- Issue of debentures
- Loan from financial institutions
- Loan from banks
- Private lenders of money

It should be kept in mind that in general, banks and financial institutions require physical asset as security to release loans.

The assets mortgaged with these institutions for the sanction of a loan are called **collateral security**.

So, loans raised can either be

(a) **Secured** Against which certain security is offered.

(b) **Unsecured** Against which no security is offered. These are released under various government schemes.

While selecting the source of funds, a proper balance should be struck between owner's funds and borrowed funds.

Factors to be kept in Mind before Selection of Suitable Source of Business Finance

The factors that need to be considered while choosing an appropriate source of finance are

Factors to be Kept in Mind

- Cost
- Tax benefits
- Control
- Purpose and time period
- Financial strength
- Risk involved

(i) **Cost** Before deciding about the source of funds to be used by an organisation, it is important to consider cost of procurement of funds and cost of utilising the funds.

(ii) **Tax Benefits** Tax benefits should be evaluated in terms of utilisation of various financial resources. Interest on debentures and loan is deductible from the total income before calculating tax while dividend payable to shareholders is not deductable.

(iii) **Control** Business firms should choose a source keeping in mind the extent to which they are willing to share their control over business. e.g. issue of equity shares may mean dilution of the control.

(iv) **Purpose and Time Period** This is the very important factor to be kept in mind before selecting a suitable source of business finance. A short-term requirement can be fulfilled through borrowing funds at low rate of interest. Similarly, the selected sources should match with their use/purpose appropriately.

(v) **Financial Strength** Financial strenght of business organisation should be considered before selecting the source. e.g. financially sound business can opt for borrowed fund.

(vi) **Risk Involved** Business should also evaluate source of finance in terms of risk involved in it. There is less risk in equity as the share capital has to be repaid only at the time of winding up.

Material Resources

Whether a business enterprise markets a product or a service, certain operations are essentially carried out combining raw material, processing and assembling machines, tools, power etc.

A deep insight into the production process is essential for effective utilisation of resources. To successfully convert raw material into finished products with value addition, a wide array of arrangements needs to be worked out by the entrepreneur.

Some of the important decisions are regarding
- Size of the unit and its installed capacity.
- Identifying machinery and the technical know-how required.
- Technical training involved.
- Quality control systems required.
- Type of technical staff required.
- Maintenance cost.
- Availability of spare parts and support services (after sale services).
- Wear and tear rate of assets.
- Type of raw materials required.
- Suppliers of the raw material, their number and location.

Intangible Resources

These resources are much ignored by the business enterprises. These resources are those which can neither be seen nor touched, but enables a business to continue to earn a profit that is in excess of the normal basic rate of profit earned by other business of similar type.

This category generally comprises of the following resources

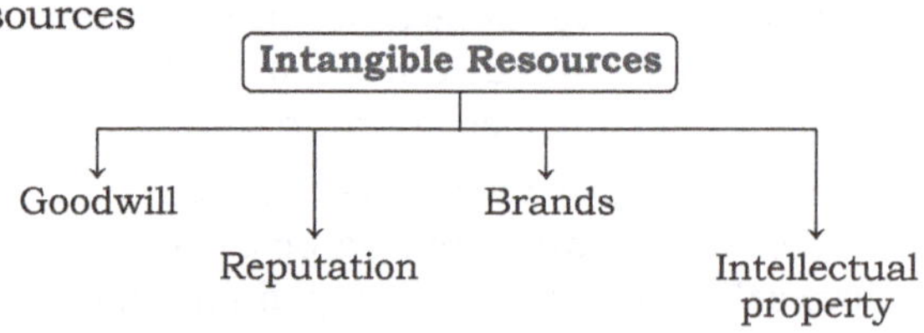

1. **Goodwill** Goodwill of a business is the difference between the value of tangible assets of the business and the value which one is ready to pay for it, i.e. actual value of business. Goodwill generally does not exist in case of a new business.

   But, if an existing business takes in a new partner, then the goodwill of the business will be enjoyed by the new partner.
2. **Reputation** A business's reputation is also an intangible resource which help it to gather necessary support from employees and suppliers.

   It depends upon the track record of delivering on business's strategies and objectives.
3. **Brands** Strong brands are often the key factor in whether a growth strategy is a success or failure.

   Being associated with strong brand, an entrepreneur can command and sustain higher margin.
4. **Intellectual Property** Key commercial rights protected by patents and trademarks may be an important resource for an entrepreneur.

CHECK POINT 03

1. Availability of .... enables an entrepreneur to bring together personnel, machines, materials, methods and land.
2. What is the time duration for short-term finance?
3. Define collateral security.
4. State any one factor to be kept in mind before selecting a suitable source of finance.

EXAM PATTERN EXERCISE

Objective Type Questions (1 Mark)

Multiple Choice Questions

1 Requirement of resources depends upon
(a) natue of business (b) size of business
(c) types of business
(d) All of the above

Ans (d) All of the above

2 The first step in the resource mobilisation plan is to
(a) identify the type of resources
(b) evaluate and judge the need for resources
(c) locate the availability of resources
(d) arrange funds for acquisition of resources

Ans (b) evaluate and judge the need for resources

3 .... resources are those that are made by humans through their abilities and skills.
(a) Physical (b) Human
(c) Financial (d) Material

Ans (a) Physical

4 Mr. Dinesh Batra is the marketing manager of Batra Publications. He is working at
(a) top level
(b) middle level
(c) lower level (d) None of these

Ans (b) middle level

5 .... resources have unlimited potential for improvement and development.
(a) Physical (b) Human
(c) Intangible (d) None of these

Ans (b) Human

6 Mr. Anil is working in a well known company in New Delhi. He is responsible for providing assistance services such as book keeping, typing office support etc. He is a part of ....
(a) managerial staff
(b) trained technical manpower
(c) administrative manpower
(d) professional manpower

Ans (c) administrative manpower

7 Selecting the right number and right kind of people with appropriate skills requires a .... strategy.

(a) comprehensive (b) scientifically evolved
(c) Both (a) and (b) (d) None of these

Ans (c) Both (a) and (b)

8 Mrs. Rameshwari Devi was working as an auditor in a well known firm in Pune. She is not an employee here but gives advisory services in exchange of consultancy fees. She is a part of ....

(a) professional manpower (b) managerial staff
(c) administrative manpower
(d) None of the above

Ans (a) professional manpower

9 .... is a survey chart or inventory for scheduling manpower requirements in an industrial plant.

(a) Resource mobilisation
(b) Manning table
(c) Job chart (d) None of the above

Ans (b) Manning table

10 The source(s) of finance is/are

(a) owner's fund (b) borrowed fund
(c) Both (a) and (b) (d) None of these

Ans (c) Both (a) and (b)

11 Analysis of which of the following issues is not essential before taking final decision related to place?

(a) Availability of manpower and its cost
(b) Availability of utilities like water, gas, etc.
(c) Access to market for both raw material and finished goods
(d) None of the above

Ans (d) None of the above

12 **Assertion** (A) Resource mobilisation is not a single activity.

Reason (R) It involves a series of steps to get optimum utilisation of resources.

Alternatives

(a) Both Assertion (A) and Reason (R) are correct
(b) Assertion (A) is correct, but Reason (R) is incorrect
(c) Assertion (A) is incorrect, but Reason (R) is correct
(d) Both Assertion (A) and Reason (R) are incorrect

Ans (a) Both Assertion (A) and Reason (R) are correct

13 **Assertion** (A) A business reputation is an intangible resource of business.

Reason (R) It helps business to gather necessary support from employers and suppliers.

Alternatives

(a) Both Assertion (A) and Reason (R) are correct
(b) Assertion (A) is correct, but Reason (R) is incorrect
(c) Assertion (A) is incorrect, but Reason (R) is correct
(d) Both Assertion (A) and Reason (R) are incorrect

Ans (a) Both Assertion (A) and Reason (R) are correct

14 Given below are types of resources in Column I and their meaning in Column II. Match them correctly.

Column I	Column II
A. Physical Resources	(i) Comprises goodwill, brands, reputation etc.
B. Human Resources	(ii) Funds required to bring together personnel, machines, material etc.
C. Financial Resources	(iii) Comprises whole workforce of organisation.
D. Intangible Resources	(iv) Created or produced by humans by using their skills.

Codes

	A	B	C	D		A	B	C	D
(a)	(iv)	(iii)	(ii)	(i)	(b)	(ii)	(i)	(iii)	(iv)
(c)	(iii)	(iv)	(ii)	(i)	(d)	(ii)	(i)	(iv)	(iii)

Ans (a) (iv) (iii) (ii) (i)

15 Which concept is highlighted in the given picture?

(a) Human resource
(b) Intangible resource
(c) Financial resource
(d) None of the above

Ans (a) Human resource

Fill in the Blanks

16 .... refers to tangible or non-tangible means required to support the activities of an organisation to meet pre-determined organisational goals.

Ans Resource

17 .... deals with acquiring the needed resources in a timely cost effective manner.

Ans Resource mobilisation

18 According to Johnson and Scholes, "........... is the direction and scope of an organisation over the long-term, which achieves advantage for the organisation through its configuration of resources, within a challenging environment, to meet the needs of markets and to fulfill stakeholders expectations."

Ans strategy

19 ....resources comprise of land, building, plant etc.

Ans Physical resources

20 .... is a type of non-managerial staff.

Ans Semi-skilled labour

21 The consultancy of .... help the entrepreneur to have cost efficiency in different areas.

Ans professionals

22 .... are the most important assets that a firm must have, because in the absence of these resources, other resources are useless.

Ans Human resources

23 A .... is a group of homogeneous tasks related by similarity of functions.

Ans job

24 Outsourcing is an emerging trend where enterprise outsources .... activities to outside firms.

Ans non-core

25 XYZ Ltd. is lacking in the resources which cannot be seen, touched or preserved but can affect the profitability of the business. XYZ Ltd. is lacking in .... resources.

Ans intangible

State True or False

26 A resource mobilisation plan should closely follow the vision, mission and goals of the organisation.

Ans True

27 Kamal wants to start a business in catering. His father advices him that first he should arrange for land, labour and capital as these are the basic resources required for any business.

Ans True

28 Johnson and Scholes have said, "the people working in a firm make it what it is."

Ans False. The above observation was made by Herbert G Hicks and C Ray Gullet.

29 Human resources comprise of all the poeple or individuals engaged at different levels in an organisation.

Ans True

30 Entrepreneur can raise capital from outside through issue of debentures.

Ans True

31 A period, where finance is required for more than one year but less than 5 years, is called short-term finance requirement.

Ans False. It is called medium-term finance requirement.

32 New enterprises have goodwill.

Ans False. New enterprises do not have goodwill.

33 Goodwill and intellectual property rights are tangible resources.

Ans False. They are intangible resources.

Case Based Questions

34 Read the following article and answer the questions that follow

Sumit is a manager of Alexis Co. Company decided to expand in a nearby city and he was been given a task to manage the new production unit in a different city. Sumit first developed a plan for arranging all the needed resources that would be required to operate the production unit. Sumit studies the market of the new city and suggested an area in which the company can start the production unit.

The management assessed the possibilities and came in a contract with the land owner for giving the land on lease.

The construction of production unit was started and was estimated to be completed in 2 months. Till then, Sumit was focused on finding and selecting the right employees for the unit.

The unit will require more than 60 workers at all levels when it is operational. Therefore, Sumit was keen to collect data about suitable candidates from various sources.

He collected all the required data and screened out around 100 candidates that will be called and invited to work once the unit was operational. For financial assistance, the company decided to borrow funds from CVB bank. As the company was known and reliable in the eyes of the bank, it was easy to get funds for the new unit. The work was done with proper efficiency and effective planning and the company is confident that the unit will be fully operational in around 3 months.

(i) "Sumit first developed a plan for arranging all the needed resources that would be required to operate the production unit."

Which concept is highlighted in the above text?

(a) Resource mobilisation
(b) Resource allocation
(c) Both (a) and (b)
(d) None of the above

Ans (a) Resource mobilisation

(ii) Which of the following factors should Sumit consider while mobilising resources?

(a) Plant capacity
(b) Nature of operations
(c) Size of operations
(d) All of the above

Ans (d) All of the above

(iii) "As the company was known and reliable in the eyes of the bank, it was easy to get funds for the new unit."

Which of the following intangible resources is highlighted in the above text?

(a) Patent (b) Popularity
(c) Reputation (d) All of these

Ans (c) Reputation

(iv) The land taken on lease by the company is considered as a .... resource.

(a) physical (b) material
(c) human (d) financial

Ans (a) physical

(v) Sumit is working at which level of management?

(a) Top-level (b) Middle-level
(c) Senior-level (d) Lower-level

Ans (b) Middle-level

35 Read the following article and answer the questions that follow

Anjali is a self-made entrepreneur making various types of hair extension products and selling them through e-commerce. She works from the convenience of her home, but now the sales have increased and the scale of operation needs to be expanded. So, she decided to rent a building for making it her office. She visits various places to find a suitable place and finally chooses one near the center market of Delhi.

Anjali was working with her mother to make the products when the business was at its starting point. But now she has to employee around 10 people to help in the work load. The workers will have to make the final products as directed by Anjali. She will first train the people and then start actual production with them. Anjali's brand is very famous across all social media because of the fact that she uses real hair for making her extensions. That is why, the sales have increased by a huge percentage since last year.

(i) Which of the following factors should be considered by Anjali while selecting the right place for her office?

(a) Availability of utilities
(b) Capital cost
(c) Legal requirements (d) All of the above

Ans (d) All of the above

(ii) "But now she has to employee around 10 people to help in the work load."
Which type of resource is discussed in the above sentence?

(a) Human (b) Physical
(c) Material (d) Financial

Ans (a) Human

(iii) Which type of staff is desired by Anjali for her venture?
(a) Managerial (b) Non-managerial
(c) Administrative (d) Professional

Ans (b) Non-managerial

(iv) "Anjali's brand is very famous across all social media because of the fact that she uses real hair for making her extensions." Which of the following resources is highlighted in the above text?
(a) Financial (b) Personnel
(c) Material (d) Production

Ans (c) Material

(v) Anjali and her mother are .... staff.
(a) non-managerial
(b) managerial
(c) administrative
(d) All of the above

Ans (b) managerial

Short Answer Type I Questions (2 Marks)

1 What factors help in determining the resources required? **CBSE TBQ**

Ans The factors which help in determining the resources required as follows
(i) Nature of activity
(ii) Size of activity
(iii) Product specification
(iv) Type of business activity

2 What basic resources are required to commence any enterprise? **CBSE TBQ**

Ans The basic resources required to commence an enterprise are
(i) Physical resources
(ii) Human resources
(iii) Financial resources
(iv) Material resources
(v) Intangible resources

3 Name any four factors to be kept in mind while selecting physical resources. **CBSE TBQ**

Ans Four factors to be kept in mind while selecting physical resources are
(i) Durability and utility of the assets
(ii) Quality concerns
(iii) Feasibility for transfer of technology
(iv) Feasibility for training of manpower

4 What are physical resources? Give two examples. **CBSE TBQ**

Ans These resources are those that are made by humans through their abilities and skills. The category of physical resources covers a wide range of operational resources concerned with the physical capability of the enterprise.
Examples of physical resources are
(i) Land and building
(ii) Plant and machinery

5 Efficient utilisation of human resources is only possible if the entrepreneur is able to decide on certain factors. State those factors.

Ans Efficient utilisation of human resources is only possible if the entrepreneur is able to decide
(i) The total work to be done.
(ii) The right type of people who can do the work.
(iii) Employing right man at the right job.

6 To achieve specialisation, entrepreneurs outsource certain services. State any two of these services.

Ans In order to achieve specialisation in work, the entrepreneurs outsource the following services, as per their requirement (any two)
(i) Accounts related services to professional accountants
(ii) Legal services to lawyers
(iii) Transport related services to transporters

7 Professional services can be outsourced through a number of methods. State those methods.

Ans Professional services can be outsourced through
(i) Contractual arrangement
(ii) Third party arrangement
(iii) Lease basis
(iv) Captive unit arrangement
(v) Part time arrangement
(vi) Regular basis

8 Enlist any four expert professional assistance required to start a school. **CBSE TBQ**

Ans Four expert professional assistance required to start a school are as follows
(i) Professional accountants
(ii) Bankers
(iii) Advertisers
(iv) Public relation professionals

9 In order to build up loyal, efficient and dedicated personnel, the entrepreneur needs to address two questions, what are they?

Ans In order to build up loyal, efficient and dedicated personnel, the entrepreneur needs to address the following questions

(i) What kind of people does he/she need?

(ii) How many people does he/she need?

10 Mr. Ram Sharma was working in MNC in Gujarat as a purchase manager and was fulfilling all the managerial activities in a company. At which level of management was he working? Mention other two managerial staff of the same level.

Ans Mr. Ram Sharma was working at middle level management. Other two managerial staff of middle level management include

(i) Executive officer (ii) Sales manager

11 Professional accountants in business play crucial roles identifying and addressing unique challenges facing mid-sized enterprises in strategic management, corporate governance, risk management and internal control, financial reporting and accounting and other areas.

IFAC's Professional Accountants in Business Committee commissioned financial journalist Eric Krell to conduct a series of interviews with 10 leading professional accountants in business on their experiences in mid-sized enterprises.

Although those interviewed are from different mid-sized enterprises from all over the world, they deal with similar issues and their solutions point in the same direction.

Source *https://www.iaasb.org/system/files/publications/files/the-crucial-roles-of-pro*

In the light of the above article, state the importance of professional accountants in a business.

Ans A professional accountant is important for an organisation as he/she assists and helps the business to reduce the costs as well as financial risk involved in the business. He/She also helps top management to analyse, create and communicate the required financial information to all the stakeholders.

Short Answer Type II Questions (3 Marks)

1 State the factors affecting the resources required for a business.

Ans Refet to text on page 162.

2 'Place' is an important physical resource and many factors need to be considered before making the final selection of this resource. What are they?

Ans The factors to be considered before making the final selection regarding 'place' are

(i) Capital cost

(ii) Access to other resources

(iii) Transport and communication cost

(iv) Availability of manpower and its cost

(v) Cost of production

(vi) Availability of other utilities like water, gas, fuel, etc

(vii) Access to market for both raw material and finished goods

(viii) Pollution concerns involved

3 With reference to utilisation of resources, state any four moral responsibilities of the entrepreneur. **CBSE TBQ**

Ans Since resources are scarce in relation to their needs, therefore, the moral responsibility of the entrepreneur arises to use them

(i) In an efficient and effective way.

(ii) In a way so that their optimum utilisation is ensured.

(iii) In a way such that wastage is minimised.

(iv) In a way so that recycling or reuse is encouraged.

4 Why does an entrepreneur need expert professional services? **CBSE TBQ**

Ans An entrepreneur needs expert professional services because they have realised that

(i) They cannot do justice to all aspects of business-production, distribution, marketing, legal, researching, etc.

(ii) They do not have adequate expertise, resources, time and energy in their hands to meet the never ending requirements of the enterprise.

5 Why should entrepreneurs ensure that there is a 'right individual at the right job'? **CBSE TBQ**

Ans 'Right man at the right job at the right time' is the mantra for successful enterprise because it

(i) Ensures benefits of specialisation to the firm.

(ii) Minimises wastages of resources.

(iii) Reduces inefficiencies.

(iv) Reduces labour turnover ratio and rate of absenteeism.

(v) Saves cost of production.

6 It will not be incorrect to elucidate finance as "lubricant to the process of production" or life blood of enterprise" or "whereas has the gold makes the rule".

To which type of resources does the above statement refer? Explain it.

Ans The above statement is referred to financial resources. Finance is one of the important pre-requisites to start an enterprise. It is the availability of finance that enables an entrepreneur to bring together personnel, machines, materials, methods, land and convert a dream into reality.

It will not be incorrect to elucidate finance as 'lubricant to the process of production' or 'life blood of enterprise' or 'whoever has the gold makes the rule'.

As a part of financial resourcing, an entrepreneur must work out the following

(i) How much finance is needed?

(ii) Term for which finance is needed.

(iii) Source of generating finance.

7 Briefly mention about sources available for generating finance.

Ans The sources of finance are given below

(i) **Owner's Fund** This is that part of capital that belongs entirely to the entrepreneur in the form of

(a) Equity capital

(b) Preference capital

(c) Margin money/seed money

(ii) **Borrowed Funds** Entrepreneur can if required raise capital from outside through

(a) Issue of debentures

(b) Loan from financial institutions

(c) Loan from banks

(d) Private lenders of money

It should be kept in mind that in general, banks and financial institutions require physical asset as security to release loans. The assets mortgaged with these institutions for the sanction of a loan are called **collateral security**.

8 Briefly state any three factors required to be considered while selecting a suitable source of finance.

Ans The factors that need to be considered while choosing an appropriate source of finance are

(i) **Cost** Before deciding about the source of funds to be used by an organisation, it is important to consider cost of procurement of funds and cost of utilising the funds.

(ii) **Tax Benefits** Tax benefits should be evaluated in terms of utilisation of various financial resources. Interest on debentures and loan is deductible from the total income before calculating tax while dividend payable to shareholders is not deductable.

(iii) **Control** Business firms should choose a source keeping in mind the extent to which they are willing to share their control over business. e.g. issue of equity shares may mean dilution of the control.

Long Answer Type Questions (5 Marks)

1 Prem is planning to start a three-star hotel in the city of Jaipur. For this, he needs to mobilise various resources. Give him the step-by-step process to mobilise resources.

Ans For step-by-step process of resource mobilisation, refer to text on page 162.

2 The number of personnel of each kind, required by an entrepreneur is affected by various factors. State those factors.

Ans The number of personnel of each kind, required by an enterprise is affected by

(i) Finding out the total amount of work to be done and then dividing it into different sets of activities.

(ii) The total number of tasks and jobs required to be accomplished under different activities.

(iii) How much work can an average person do in a specified period of time.

(iv) Level of absenteeism expected.

(v) Level of labour turnover.

(vi) Present number of employees.

(vii) Future plans for expansions, diversifications and growth.

3 What is said to be an 'efficient utilisation of human resources'? **CBSE TBQ**

Ans Efficient utilisation of human resources means getting maximum output from an employee in an effective manner.

Different categories of employees have to be managed differently for their efficient utilisation as given below

(i) **Managerial Staff** This category is the brain box of the enterprise. Framing policies, objectives, goals, etc., and ensuring their implementation is the key function of this category.

(ii) **Non-managerial Staff** This category of workers effectively converts raw material into finished goods. Nature of job decides the quality and quantity of workers to be assigned.

(iii) **Trained Technical Staff** This category of workers have technical skills and are required for machinery selection, installation, supervision and operation.

(iv) **Administrative Staff** This category of workers give support services to managerial, professional and technical staff.

(v) **Professional Staff** Chartered Accountants, lawyers, auditors, etc., belong to this category.

For efficient utilisation of the above staff, the entrepreneur should be able to decide

(i) The total work to be done.

(ii) The right people who can do the work.

(iii) Employing right man at the right job.

4 Selection of a personnel requires a comprehensive strategy comprising of various factors. State those factors.

Ans Selecting the right number and right kind of people with appropriate skills at the right place and at the right time to do the work requires a comprehensive, careful, in-depth and scientifically evolved strategy, on the part of entrepreneur, comprising of

(i) Efficient tapping and scientific selection.

(ii) Appropriate and cost effective training.

(iii) Proper induction, orientation and familiarisation with the organisation and its climate.

(iv) Periodic performance appraisal.

(v) Feedback and scope for development.

(vi) Proper motivation and remuneration schemes.

(vii) Ensuring scope for the participation in management.

5 Give the importance of professional assistance for an entrepreneur.

Ans Availing professional expertise as and when need arises or on a regular basis will assist the entrepreneur to have a better cost efficiency through

(i) Reduced wastages.

(ii) Savings of time, cost and energy.

(iii) Higher efficiency and effectiveness because of professionally proven expertise in the concerned field.

(iv) Focus on the core areas/activities of the enterprise.

(v) Availing of qualified quality service in time bound frame and at a fraction of cost.

(vi) Lowering the chances of risks.

(vii) Savings on additional fixed investment required in creating infrastructure for providing these facilities on one's own.

(viii) Enhancing business due to others' expertise and experience in the defined field.

(ix) Access to new and growing markets.

6 Discuss the various types of resources needed by a business.

Ans Following resources are required by a business

(i) **Physical Resources** These resources are those that are made by humans through their abilities and skills.

The category of physical resources covers a wide range of operational resources concerned with the physical capability of the enterprise.

(ii) **Human Resources** Human resources may be thought of as "The total knowledge, skills, creative abilities, talents and aptitudes of an organisation's workforce as well as, the values, attitudes and benefits of an individual involved".

These are the most important assets that a firm must have and that the management must be most concerned with, because in the absence of these resources, other non-living resources are useless.

(iii) **Finance Resources** Finance is one of the important pre-requisites to start an enterprise.

It is the availability of finance that enables an entrepreneur to bring together personnel, machines, materials, methods, land and convert a dream into reality. It will not be incorrect to elucidate finance as 'lubricant to the process of production' or 'life blood of enterprise' or 'whoever has the gold makes the rule'.

(iv) **Material Resources** Whether a business enterprise markets a product or a service, certain operations are essentially carried out combining raw material, processing and assembling machines, tools, power etc. A deep insight into the production is essential for effective utilisation of resources.

(v) **Intangible Resources** These resources ane much ignored by the business enterprises.

These resources are those which can neither be seen nor touched, but enables a business to continue to earn a profit that is in excess of the normal basic rate of profit earned by other business of similar type.

7 Write a short note on other physical resources.

Ans The other physical resources like machinery, tools, equipments, process technology, raw material, etc., too require a thorough investigation as they will have bearing on

(i) Short and long-term cost of the project.
(ii) Durability and utility (usefulness) expected from these assets.
(iii) Possibility of growth potential.
(iv) Market needs help to decide the range of products and the type of technology.
(v) Market size to be covered will indirectly help to assess the size/capacity of plant.
(vi) Quality concerns.
(vii) Feasibility for transfer of technology, i.e. is it possible to acquire and implement the technology/technique so selected.
(viii) Feasibility for training of manpower, i.e. is it possible to provide the required training to the workers on the selected technology.

All the above factors should be carefully analysed and evaluated before making the final selection.

8 Hindustan Lever had for themselves drafted examplary 'organisation charts'; to determine how many people at what level, in what positions and what kind of experience and training would be required to meet its objectives. For what purpose does Hindustan Lever do such preparations? Explain it in detail alongwith its factors.

Ans Hindustan Lever had made such charts for building up efficient human resource.

For meaning of human resource, refer to Q.No. 6 (ii) of long answer type questions (5 Marks).

For factors to be considered for building up efficient human resources, refer to text on page 163 and 164.

9 What are 'material resources'? While planning, state the important decisions to be made by the entrepreneur. **CBSE TBQ**

Ans Refer to text on page 167.

10 Define 'intangible resources'. What do they generally comprise of ? **CBSE TBQ**

Ans Refer to the text on page 167 and 168.

11 Resource mobilisation is the process of getting resource from resource provider and using different mechanisms to implement the organisation's work for achieving the pre-determined organisational goals. It deals in acquiring the needed resources in a timely cost effective manner.

Resource mobilisation advocates upon having the right type of resource, at the right time, at right price with making right use of acquired resources thus ensuring optimum utilisation of the same.

Source *January 2017 International Journal of Multicultural and Multireligious Understanding 3(6):1DOI:10.18415/ijmmu.v3i6.5*

(i) Which concept is highlighted in the above paragraph?
(ii) Write a short note on procurement of resources.

Ans (i) Resource mobilisation.
(ii) Refer to text on page 161.

CASE STUDIES

Interesting Realisation Rahul Sharma, founder-owner of a five star hotel, engineer from Benaras Hindu University has come a long way. Hailing from a family which had three generations of businessman, Rahul, had to virtually start from scratch to struggle his way up in life.

His forefathers were well settled at Batala in Punjab, where they had foundries, non-ferrous rolling mills and machine tool units.

In 1957, Rahul's father decided to separate from his family and shift to Bhandara, near Nagpur to start a metal unit, in partnership with a local businessman for manufacturing of non-ferrous utensils.

In 1968, Rahul took over his father's business, only to find that the income from the business was barely enough to sustain his large family of four brothers and two sisters.

Rahul critically reviewed the whole business situation— the companies structure, overheads, raw materials, suppliers, etc., to evaluate where the things were going wrong.

It was here he realised, that, on one hand, their basic raw material like brass scrap, copper and zinc, was not only costly but the transportation cost heavily affected their working capital as this all came from the Western region of Maharashtra, mainly from Mumbai and Pune and on other hand, the major chunk of their finished products, i.e. brass utensils were also sold in these regions. This fact came as the turning point.

Easy availability of raw material and closeness to the market acted as the key agents to make him shift to Pune. Since then, there was no looking back. This not only resulted in saving the transportation cost but brought down, significantly, their overall cost of production.

1 Which material resources were used by Rahul's business?

Ans The material resources used were brass scrap, copper and zinc.

2 Which basic factor regarding this resource was neglected by Rahul's father?

Ans Excess transportation cost of material resources was not considered by Rahul's father.

CHAPTER ASSESSMENT

Objective Type Questions (1 Mark)

1 Resources that are made by humans through their abilities and skills are called
(a) physical resources
(b) human resources
(c) intangible resources
(d) All of the above

2 Mantra for successful enterprise is
(a) more profit more time survival
(b) right man at the right job at the right time
(c) Both (a) or (b)
(d) All of the above

3 Intangible resources comprises of
(a) goodwill (b) brands
(c) reputation (d) All of these

4 To develop .... for the whole organisation is not an easy task.

5 .... is like brain box of the enterprise.

6 Professional service refers to a calling, occupation or business that has proven expertise in the field. State true or false.

7 Finance is considered as life blood of enterprise. State true or false.

Short Answer Type I Questions (2 Marks)

8 Define human resources.

9 Differentiate between managerial and non-managerial staff.

Short Answer Type II Questions (3 Marks)

10 Write a short note on 'selection of personnel'.

11 Explain 'expert professional assistance' in detail.

Long Answer Type Questions (5 Marks)

12 Explain in detail outsourcing 'non-core' or routine functions.

13 Discuss sources for generating finance.

14 What do you mean by material and intangible resources?

15 Discuss all the factors to be considered before selecting a suitable source of business finance.

For explanations scan the given QR Code

PROJECT WORK

Title of the Project	Case study on Cafe Coffee Day and interview with the man behind – V.G. Siddhartha
Company Chosen for the Project	Cafe Coffee Day
Name	....
School	....
Year	....
Class	XI
Submitted to	....

CONTENTS

Acknowledgement

I would like to express my profound gratitude towards many individuals, as without their kind support, it would not be possible forme to complete this project report. I would like to extend my sincere thanks to my teacher, who gave me the golden opportunity in enhancing my hidden capabilities.

Unfortunately, I addresssed several difficulties in coordinating the activities of the project but I am highly indebted to Mrs .... for her guidance and constant supervision, as well as for providing necessary information regarding the project and also for her support in completing the project.

I would also like to express my gratitude towards my parents and subject teacher for their kind co-operation and encouragement as they helped me a lot in completion of this project.

I would love if you appreciate the quality and performance of this work.

At last, I end up by thanking all who helped me in finalising the project within the limited time frame.

About Cafe Coffee Day

Introduction

I had always enjoyed hanging out with my friends at Cafe Coffee Day (CCD) and had felt awed by the success of this brand in India as well as in abroad. So, for this project, I decided to be face-to-face with my role model VG Siddhartha, the man behind this brand.

A low profile entrepreneur, he shies away from limelight, but his coffee shops cover that up for him. He started Cafe Coffee Day with one outlet in Bengalore in 1996 and presently Cafe Coffee Day is the largest chain of coffee shops in India, a nation known for its obsession for tea.

Back in the 1990's, when the internet was still in its infancy stage, the access to internet was limited to posh places and cafes and Cafe Coffee Day offered the perfect solution with its tagline, 'A lot can happen over coffee'. People would enter his cafe to surf the internet and as a bonus, they would even sip their favourite coffee. But during that time, drinking coffee was not much popular in India.

So, Siddhartha targeted his promotional activities towards the youth. He wanted young boys and girls to taste his brew during their hangout parties, get-togethers, etc. He wanted them to taste their choice of coffee, cakes and sandwiches, watch music videos, check their e-mails etc. He had his vision clear; if coffee is going to become popular, it would be the young to do it. And the success of Cafe Coffee Day over the years has proved him right.

Before having my final face-to-face encounter with him, I collected the following information regarding Cafe Coffee Day which I would like to share with you.

Statistics Related to Cafe Coffee Day

Type	Private
Industry	Coffee shop
Founded	1996
Founders	VG Siddhartha
Headquarters	Bengaluru, India
Number of locations	1,620 (3rd March, 2015)
Area served	India, Austria, Czech Republic, Dubai, Malaysia, Cairo and Egypt
Key people	VG Siddhartha (Chairman)
Products	Coffee Tea Pastries Frappuccino beverages Smoothies
Revenue	1,150 crore (2014)
Owner	Amalgamated Bean Coffee Trading Company (ABCTCL) now known as Coffee Day Global Ltd
Number of employees	5,000 +
Subsidiaries	Cafe Emporio Coffee Day Fresh 'n Ground' Coffee Day Xpress Coffee Day Take Away Coffee Day Exports Coffee Day Perfect Coffee Day Beverages
Website	www.cafecoffeeday.com (http://www.cafecoffeeday.com/)

Menu of CCD

- Espresso
- Espresso Americano
- Cappuccino (Hot coffee)
- Kenyan safari (International coffee)
- Cold coffee
- Ice cream
- Pizza, Samosa, Puff, etc.

A cup of coffee at Cafe Coffee Day

Sandwich, Coffee and Tea served at Cafe Coffee Day

Dont' they look Yummy.

A veg burger at Cafe Coffee Day

Cafe latte at Cafe Coffee Day

In Conversation with VG Siddhartha

Student A very good day sir! I am Kamakshi Batra of Class XI from St. Joseph's Convent School, Bengaluru. Thank you for taking time out from your busy schedule and enlightening us about your entrepreneurial journey.

VG Siddhartha The pleasure is all mine!

Student Sir, please can you start by telling us about your childhood and your family?

VG Siddhartha I was born in Chikmangaluru district of Karnataka. My family had been planting coffee for over 140 years. So, you can say that I have coffee in my blood. I am married and have two children.

Student And your education?

VG Siddhartha I have a degree in Masters in Science in Economics from Mangalore University, Karnataka.

Student What other businesses you tried your hands in, before venturing in the business of coffee shops?

VG Siddhartha After completing my Master's degree, I went to Mumbai and joined JM Financial Services as a management intern on the Indian stock market, under Mr Mahendra Kampani. After two years, I returned to Bengaluru, because I felt tied up in the job that I was doing. My father gave me money to start a business of my choice. I bought a stock market card for ₹ 30,000 alongwith a company called Sivan Securities, which was renamed in 2000 as Way 2 Wealth Securities Ltd with a vision to set 'new standards in the retail financial services in India'. Its venture capital division is known as Global Technology Ventures and is a highly successful investment banking and stock broking company today.

Student	So, sir what motivated you to enter the retail coffee business in India?
VG Siddhartha	I had a chat with the owners of Tehibo, the leading coffee chain in the world today and they helped me to understand the basics of coffee business. The world grows around 120 million bags of coffee bean every year which costs around $ 7 billion approximately. But when the same bean is retailed as a cup of coffee, the value becomes $ 100 billion. I did not wanted to chase the $ 7 billion mark with my coffee plantation business. I wanted to aim for the $ 100 billion figure. So, keeping this in mind, I opened the first Cafe Coffee Day outlet on 11th July, 1994 at Brigade Road in Bengaluru.
Student	So, how was your initial experience with your venture? Did you face any problems or setbacks? Did education helped you to overcome those setbacks?
VG Siddhartha	The initial problem that I faced was that Indians, and that too North-Indians loved their tea. So, to draw them away from their favourite beverage was a tough job. Also, the general perception of coffee being expensive was also a problem. I tackled the above problems by identifying my target customers–the youth, and designing my promotional programmes to woo them. Education definitely helps to tackle problems as it broadens a man's perception.
Student	What do you think is more important for success–education or experience?
VG Siddhartha	I think that for an entrepreneur experience is more important for success, though being educated no doubt helps.
Student	Do you have a mentor who was your guiding light to success?
VG Siddhartha	My father-in-law Mr SM Krishna, who is the former Chief Minister of Karnataka, had been my mentor. His advice on various matters has helped me to sail through distress waters.
Student	What have been your achievements so far?
VG Siddhartha	Today Cafe Coffee Day has achieved enormous success. The Cafe Coffee Day chain has 1,534 outlets in 135 cities across 28 states in India. We also have outlets in Karachi, Vienna, Dubai and Prague. I was awarded 'Entrepreneur of the year' title in 2003 by Economic Times for crafting a successful pan Indian brand for a commodity business and giving Indian consumers a new life style experience that is within the reach of a common man. In 2011, Cafe Coffee Day was named 'most popular hangout joint amongst youth' at 3rd youth marketing forum and India's 'most popular coffee joint' at Indian Hospitality Excellence. I have been credited with bringing 'coffee revolution' in India.
Student	How have you been able to adapt your business according to the changing times?
VG Siddhartha	I have been able to assess the market trends and respond to them in a swift manner. Also, my experience in coffee plantation helped me to stride forward in this sector.
Student	What are your future plans for expansion?
VG Siddhartha	I have taken 1.85 million hectares of Amazonian forest land on a 30-year lease from the Republic of Guyana in South America to start a furniture business in India.
Student	Any decision of yours which you would like to change?
VG Siddhartha	Presently, I am very much satisfied from what I have achieved. So, there are no regrets.
Student	What according to you, is the reason for your success?
VG Siddhartha	My mantra for success is, "Have the will power to persist and simply refuse to give up".
Student	In the end, a few words of motivation for the young entrepreneurs.
VG Siddhartha	Do not be afraid to dream and more important, follow your dreams.
Student	Thank you sir for your precious time and providing insight on your entrepreneurial journey so far.
VG Siddhartha	The pleasure was all mine.

Sample Paper 1

A Highly Simulated Sample Question Paper for CBSE Class XI Examination

Entrepreneurship

General Instructions

Read the following instructions carefully and follow them

1. This question paper contains 34 questions. All questions are compulsory.
2. This question paper is divided into four sections—Section A, B, C and D.
3. Section A : Questions number 1 to 18 are Multiple Choice Type Questions. Each question carries 1 mark.
4. Section B : Questions number 19 to 24 are Short Answer Type-I Questions. Each question carries 2 marks. Write answer to each question in 30 to 40 words.
5. Section C : Questions number 25 to 29 are Short Answer Type-II Questions. Each question carries 3 marks. Write answer to each question in 50 to 70 words.
6. Section D : Questions number 30 to 34 are Long Answer Type Questions. Each question carries 5 marks. Write answer to each question in 120 to 150 words.
7. There is no overall choice. However, an internal choice has been provided in Section B, C and D of question paper. A candidate has to attempt only one of the alternatives in such questions.

Time : 3 hours **Max. Marks : 70**

Section-A

1. Mr. Kumar is working in a well-known company in Gujarat. He is responsible for providing assistance services such as book-keeping, typing, office support, etc. He is a part of (1)

   I. managerial staff
   II. trained technical manpower
   III. professional manpower
   IV. administrative manpower

   Codes

   (a) I and II (b) Only IV
   (c) I and IV (d) I, II and III

2. Talk-talk is a local mobile company. It is using the same technology as big company to manufacture its products. It is an example of (1)

   (a) drone entrepreneur
   (b) imitative entrepreneur
   (c) innovative entrepreneur
   (d) social entrepreneur

3. Anil is the manufacturer of footwear and has a shop in the local market of Aligarh. He manufactures and sells same types of footwear to different retailers.

   The retailers then sell the footwear to customers. The channel of distribution involved in this sale is (1)

   I. direct II. one-level
   III. two-level IV. three-level

   Codes

   (a) Only II (b) I and II
   (c) Only III (d) All of these

4. Shahid considers that starting a business is very easy but it takes a lot of money to finance it. He is not right in his assumption because (1)

   (a) it requires a lot of determination and learning
   (b) it does not take a lot of money to finance a new business
   (c) Both (a) and (b)
   (d) None of the above

5. According to ...., "many new entrepreneurs believe a set of myths about entrepreneurship." (1)
(a) Richard Cantillon
(b) Joseph Schumpeter
(c) JB Say
(d) Guy Kawasaki

6. Rohit Verma is an investor who invests in new and established businesses. He wants to know the details related to products and services to be offered in the business in which he is planning to invest. Rohit is looking into which part of the business plan? (1)
(a) Business finance
(b) Business investment
(c) Business operations
(d) Business venture

7. From the following given information, calculate the gross profit or loss for the company (1)
Unit price = ₹ 80
Unit cost = ₹ 50
(a) ₹ 30
(b) ₹ 130
(c) (–) ₹ 30
(d) ₹ 40

8. Joseph's is a Sushi restaurant located in Connaught Place, Delhi. The restaurant is very famous and serves delicious Japanese sushi. Joseph's is always packed with customers and have high revenues. But during the pandemic time, the business was shut and there was no way of home delivery because the chefs returned to their hometown.
The business suffered a huge loss during the pandemic time and after the pandemic it took almost one year to come to break-even sales. Which of the following market factors affected the business? (1)
I. Economic
II. Legal
III. Technological

Codes
(a) I and II
(b) Only I
(c) Only III
(d) II and III

9. Sona makes decorative items at home and is very talented. She sells her items through Instagram and Facebook.
The resin art nameplate by Sona is the most purchased online. Per piece costs Sona ₹ 300 and she sells it at ₹ 500 each. The fixed costs per month are ₹ 1,000. What is the contribution margin per unit? (1)
(a) ₹ 800
(b) ₹ 500
(c) ₹ 200
(d) ₹ 700

10. **Assertion** (A) The business is neither at loss nor in profit at break-even point.
Reason (R) A business's break-even point is the amount or level of sales or revenue that it must generate in order to equal its expenses. (1)

Alternatives
(a) Both Assertion (A) and Reason (R) are true and Reason (R) is the correct explanation of Assertion (A)
(b) Both Assertion (A) and Reason (R) are true, but Reason (R) is not the correct explanation of Assertion (A)
(c) Assertion (A) is true, but Reason (R) is false
(d) Assertion (A) is false, but Reason (R) is true

11. From the given ways to generate ideas in Column I and their elements given in Column II, choose the correct pair (1)

Column I	Column II
A. Environment scanning	(i) Publications, commercials, reviews
B. Brainstorming	(ii) Lack of innovation
C. Creativity	(iii) In-depth study
D. Market research	(iv) Attribute listening

Codes
(a) A-(i)
(b) B-(ii)
(c) C-(iii)
(d) D-(iv)

12. Which concept is highlighted in the given picture? (1)

(a) Social entrepreneurship
(b) Entrepreneur as a problem solver
(c) Both (a) and (b)
(d) None of the above

13. The pacemaker was invented by (1)
(a) George Crum (b) John Hopps
(c) Percy Spencer (d) Wilhem Roentgen

14. Sonu wants to start his own restaurant in his hometown. He has researched about the tastes and preferences of the target customers. He knows that starting a new venture requires capital investment and funding, but is not aware of exactly what will be the requirement for a restaurant. His father told him that he also needs to know the return on his investment to analyse if the business will be profitable or not.

What would you suggest Sonu to do to know the capital requirements and return on investment of the new venture? (1)
(a) Market feasibility study
(b) Financial feasibility study
(c) Operational feasibility study
(d) Organisational feasibility study

15. Whoops Limited is an ice cream brand selling different types of flavours and variety of ice-creams and smoothies. Most of the outlets of the brand are in high end areas or malls and the target market is high income group's people.

The management of Whoops decided that they should also target the middle-income groups and for this they decided to start a vendor chain and also install their stores in some local areas. The management wants to tap different income groups for increasing its customer base.

Which macro environmental factor is being highlighted in the above case? (1)
(a) Demographic
(b) Economic
(c) Technological
(d) Political

16. Farheen is an enthusiastic marketing intern and is recently been employed in a big company manufacturing and selling a wide variety of products.

After working for several months, the management was very happy with her work and employed her as a full-time employee as the assistant marketing manager. Farheen always had a vision for the company and decided to improve the marketing department. She called a meeting and stated that from now the products should be developed after surveying the market and knowing the tastes and preferences of the customer.

Which of the following concepts is being referenced by Farheen? (1)
(a) Market survey (b) Market demography
(c) Market analysis (d) Market research

17. Stigma Limited manufactures and sells stationary items and toys for all age groups and is operational since 2010. Now, the owner of the firm wants to expand its product line and include kids wear up to 10 years of age in its product line.

The firm came into a lease contract with a land-owner for opening a separate production capacity for the new product line and the capacity will be equipped with all the machinery and material required to manufacture the new products. The lease contract with the land-owner for a place for the production capacity represents .... resources. (1)
(a) material (b) physical
(c) human (d) financial

18. Which of the following is not an example of the micro environmental factors of a market? (1)
(a) Starbucks produces and sells its beverages only to the upper income class customers.
(b) When Coca-Cola launched diet coke, it received a good competition from Red Bull and PepsiCo.
(c) The open advertisement of liquor and tobacco products on television or radio is banned by the government.
(d) Both (a) and (c)

Section-B

19. Sam owns a bakery and has a daily profit target of ₹ 1,000. He incurs ₹ 380 in fixed costs and the gross margin per cake is ₹ 1.80. What will be the sales target per day of the bakery? (2)

Or

The following information is provided by the manufacturer of toy trains for children. The manufacturer wants to know the break-even point of the business.

Rent, salaries and other fixed expenses are ₹ 25,000

Selling price per unit is ₹ 200

Variable cost per unit is ₹ 150

20. XYZ Ltd. is expanding its production capacity and has recently invested a significant amount in purchasing new automated machinery for its factory. The company believes that this will enhance efficiency and improve long-term productivity.

Additionally, it has also acquired new office furniture to provide a better working environment for employees. To ensure smooth installation, the company hired technical experts for set-up and training. The management expects these assets to contribute to the company's growth over several years.

(i) Identify the type of expenditure.

(ii) State two other forms of expenditure. (2)

21. Read the following article and explain any two types of costs incurred by a business.

Variable costing has now arrived of a period and is providing to be an exceptionally important tool in planning and controlling operations in many large industrial companies. However, still not as broadly working as absorption costing, it is progressively gaining popularity in use.

In variable costing, product costs contain only those manufacturing costs which are directly related to the product and vary with production volume. Under absorption costing, all manufacturing costs, direct and indirect, are included as cost of manufactured goods.

This article discusses variable costing that is used only for internal reporting and analysis and its applicability in the manufacturing situation. Variable and absorption costing are not commonly exclusive.

Accountants find that variable costing more effectively meets internal requirements because it provides better insight into cost relationship while the absorption costing method meets external reporting requirements. (2)

22. Steps in the Entrepreneurial Process

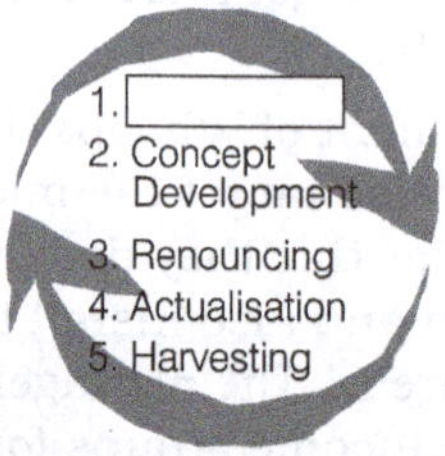

(i) Identify the missing step in the given figure.

(ii) Explain the step identified in (i) in detail. (2)

Or Mention any two features of an enterprise.

23. Why is feasibility study important? Explain any two points. (2)

24. How can unit of sale be used as a controlling tool? (2)

Or What are start-up costs? Explain.

Section-C

25. Yusuf is a young entrepreneur and operates his own business of spare parts. He wants to hire some staff for the store because he is planning to expand his scope of operations. He has contacted few people to get some human resource but is not sure about a suitable way for the same.

As a human resource consultant, advise Yusuf some ways to procure professional services for his store. (3)

26. The break-even point is an important tool of financial management. In this article I will describe a concept and basis for analysis that is quite different from the usual technique.

In order to determine the portion of each expense that is fixed and the portion that is variable, which is the basis for calculating the break-even point, we will use linear regression analysis, a technique based upon the relationship between two variables. Detailed monthly operating statements are required for a complete departmental analysis using this technique; however, for the purpose of this article I have taken a shortcut and used only monthly sales and operating expenses. The amounts are taken from the monthly operating statements of a 352-room suburban hotel.

Source *International Journal of Hospitality Management, Volume 2, Issue 3, 1983*

(i) Which concept is highlighted in the above paragraph?

(ii) Write a short note on the given concept. (3)

27. Anupama loves gardening. Her garden is the envy of the whole neighbourhood. Her neighbours, relatives and friends are constantly asking her for shoots of various plants that she has in her collection.

She decides to turn her hobby into a profession and decides to open a nursery dealing in organic plants only. She also initiates a plantation drive in her locality.

(i) Identify the source of Anupama's business idea.

(ii) In addition to the above source, state any two more source of business idea. (3)

28. "It is often stated that the scientific concept of market widens the area of market".

In the light of this statement, explain how the scientific concept widens the area of market. (3)

Or

Which major concerns are being faced by the business in the natural environment?

29. Procurement of physical resources is not easy. Giving reasons state what is required to be planned for this procurement? (3)

Or

"The real group which effectively converts the raw material into finished goods is workers."

In this context, define the type of staff mentioned above. Also list the type of personnel included in this staff.

Section-D

30. Kareena Kapoor Khan is shown using 'Head and Shoulders'shampoo for dandruff problem.

(i) Which source of attitude does this point to?

(ii) What is attitude?

(iii) Explain other source of attitude. (5)

31. 'Fresh Bakes Pvt. Ltd.' is a new bakery chain specialising in organic and gluten-free products.

The company invested heavily in setting-up its state of the art production facility with advanced baking equipment and a modern interior for its retail outlets. To ensure a smooth launch, it spent significantly on advertising, branding and licensing.

Once operational, the company had to cover recurring expenses like rent for its retail stores, salaries of employees and maintenance of baking machinery.

To keep its pricing competitive, 'Fresh Bakes Pvt. Ltd.' monitored its ingredient costs closely, which varied depending on seasonal availability. The company also adjusted production volumes based on daily customer demand to avoid wastage.

Quoting lines from the above text, identify and explain the three types of costs incurred by 'Fresh Bakes Pvt. Ltd.' while operating its business. (5)

32. What is the role of technology and social media in today's business? Explain. (5)

Or

What is the difference between e-business and e-commerce?

33. Entrepreneurship is a source of innovation, job creation and economic growth, as such it is pivotal to attract the young and the educated to become entrepreneurs.

Undergraduates are an important source of nascent entrepreneurs in the future and consequently it is interesting to explore their intention for opportunity entrepreneurship.

However, there is intellectual disagreement whether entrepreneurs are born or made. This is a post-positivist study, cross-sectional and the level of analysis is individual.

Hierarchical regression analysis shows that family business background and gender explained largest and significant incremental variance in students' entrepreneurial intention.

Consequently, the findings from this study lend support to the notion that entrepreneurs are more likely born.

Knowledge generated from this study is valuable in the design of entrepreneurship education, training and development policy to promote opportunity entrepreneurship.

Source *International Journal of Entrepreneurship and Small Business, January, 2015*

(i) Which concept is highlighted in the above paragraph?

(ii) Describe the need for entrepreneurship. (5)

Or An entrepreneur identifies a need that no existing businesses addresses and determines a solution for that need. Entrepreneurial activity includes developing and launching new businesses and marketing them, often with the end goal of selling the business to turn a profit. An entrepreneur who regularly launches new businesses, sells them and then starts new businesses is a serial entrepreneur. Additionally, although the term 'entrepreneur' is often associated with start-ups and small businesses, any founder of a successful household-name business began as an entrepreneur.

(i) Which concept is highlighted in the above paragraph?

(ii) Explain any three functions of an entrepreneur.

34. Consider the following data of a company

Sales = ₹ 40,000; Fixed cost = ₹ 7,500

Variable cost = ₹ 17,500

Find the following

(i) Contribution (ii) Profit

(iii) BEP (iv) Margin of safety (5)

Answers

1. (b) Only IV **2.** (b) imitative entrepreneur

3. (a) Only II **4.** (c) Both (a) and (b)

5. (b) Joseph Schumpeter

6. (d) Business venture

7. (a) ₹ 30 **8.** (b) Only I

9. (c) ₹ 200

10. (a) Both Assertion (A) and Reason (R) are true and Reason (R) is the correct explanation of Assertion (A)

11. (a) A-(i)

12. (b) Entrepreneur as a problem solver

13. (b) John Hopps

14. (b) Financial feasibility study

15. (a) Demographic **16.** (d) Market research

17. (b) physical **18.** (d) Both (a) and (c)

19. 767 cakes per day

Or 500 toy trains

34. (i) ₹ 22,500 (ii) ₹ 15,000

(iii) ₹ 1,333.33 (iv) ₹ 26,666.67

Sample Paper 2

A Highly Simulated Sample Question Paper for CBSE Class XI Examination

Entrepreneurship

General Instructions

Read the following instructions carefully and follow them

1. This question paper contains 34 questions. All questions are compulsory.
2. This question paper is divided into four sections—Section A, B, C and D.
3. Section A : Questions number 1 to 18 are Multiple Choice Type Questions. Each question carries 1 mark.
4. Section B : Questions number 19 to 24 are Short Answer Type-I Questions. Each question carries 2 marks. Write answer to each question in 30 to 40 words.
5. Section C : Questions number 25 to 29 are Short Answer Type-II Questions. Each question carries 3 marks. Write answer to each question in 50 to 70 words.
6. Section D : Questions number 30 to 34 are Long Answer Type Questions. Each question carries 5 marks. Write answer to each question in 120 to 150 words.
7. There is no overall choice. However, an internal choice has been provided in Section B, C and D of question paper. A candidate has to attempt only one of the alternatives in such questions.

Time : 3 hours **Max. Marks : 70**

Section-A

1. Mrs. Rameshwari Devi is the marketing manager at Gyan Publications. She is working at (1)

I. top-level II. middle-level
III. lower-level IV. senior-level

Codes

(a) Only I (b) II and III
(c) Only II (d) Only IV

2. Which of the following entrepreneurs uses traditional methods and refuses to upgrade to modern technology? (1)

(a) Drone entrepreneur
(b) Induced entrepreneur
(c) Innovative entrepreneur
(d) None of the above

3. When Sharad opened the door on hearing the doorbell, a person was standing who was selling 'Booster World Encyclopedia'.

Here Booster World is using which type of promotion method? (1)

I. Personal selling II. Advertising
III. Sales promotion IV. Branding

Codes

(a) Only I (b) I and II
(c) II and III (d) Only III

4. Samratbhai launched 'Coolxtream' fridge in 2004. This fridge is made from terracotta and runs without electricity. Which entrepreneurial function has been preformed by him? (1)

(a) Innovation (b) Risktaking
(c) Both (a) and (b) (d) None of these

5. Which amongst the following is/are the disadvantage(s) of entrepreneurship? (1)

(a) Irregular income
(b) Independence
(c) Work schedule (d) Both (a) and (c)

6. Aman is planning to venture into a business of manufacturing ventilators to cash on demand generated due to the outbreak of Covid. What will be the plan size for his venture? (1)

(a) Medium (b) Small
(c) Large (d) None of these

7. From the following information, ascertain by how much value the sales must be increased by the company to meet their break-even point?

Sales = ₹ 3,00,000

Fixed Cost = ₹ 1,50,000

Variable Cost = ₹ 2,00,000 (1)

(a) ₹ 2,00,000 (b) ₹ 1,50,000
(c) ₹ 3,00,000 (d) None of these

8. Sober Corporations are planning to launch a new product in their existing product line. The top management has made all the strategies and has decided that the price of the new product would initially be set at a low margin to attract customers and gain their confidence.

The pricing strategy highlighted above is/are (1)

I. skimming II. penetration

III. cost-plus IV. None of these

Codes

(a) I and II (b) Only I

(c) Only II (d) III and II

9. The following information relates to a company, which produces a single product.

Direct labour per unit = ₹ 22

Direct material per unit = ₹ 12

Variable overheads per unit = ₹ 6

Fixed costs = ₹ 3,00,000

Selling price per unit = ₹ 6

The variable cost per unit is .... (1)

(a) ₹ 40 (b) ₹ 22 (c) ₹ 18 (d) ₹ 53

10. Refer to the given image.

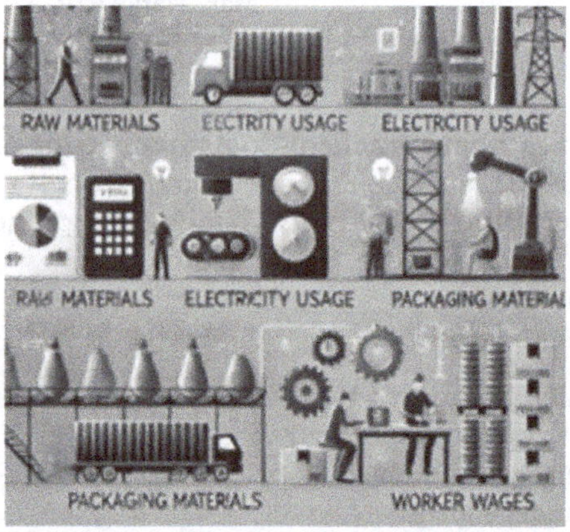

The given image represents which type of costs?

(a) Variable (b) Fixed (1)

(c) Mixed (d) None of these

11. From the given types of feasibility studies in Column I and their descriptions given in Column II, choose the correct pair (1)

Column I	Column II
A. Market feasibility	(i) Legal and corporate structure of the business.
B. Technical feasibility	(ii) How to deliver a product or service.
C. Organisational feasibility	(iii) Identification of funds needed.
D. Financial feasibility	(iv) Description of market trends.

Codes

(a) A-(i) (b) B-(ii) (c) C-(iii) (d) D-(iv)

12. **Assertion** (A) Organising and management are the main functions of an entrepreneur.

Reason (R) Every decision regarding an enterprise is taken by an entrepreneur himself/herself, whether it is related to lines of business to expand or to employ more capital. (1)

Alternatives

(a) Both Assertion (A) and Reason (R) are true and Reason (R) is the correct explanation of Assertion (A)

(b) Both Assertion (A) and Reason (R) are true, but Reason (R) is not the correct explanation of Assertion (A)

(c) Assertion (A) is true, but Reason (R) is false

(d) Assertion (A) is false, but Reason (R) is true

13. The word 'cloud' is used as a metaphor for (1)

(a) internet (b) rain (c) web (d) site

14. Joan is a young entrepreneur and has started her own venture of organic hair dyes named 'Rainbow Dyes'. The product is made by all organic and chemical free ingredients and is available in various colours and shades.

The industry for this type of product is very vast and there are various competitors. Therefore, Joan decided to register on e-commerce platforms and also created business pages on social media platforms.

What was the source of perceiving the idea? (1)

(a) Free association (b) Brainstorming

(c) Attribute listing (d) Focus groups

15. Vibrant Limited is a firm producing and selling a variety of women perfumes with different flavours. It has rented an office building. The production is done in the basement and the marketing, finance and other departments are situated on the upper floors of the building. The business is making a good profit due to which the management decided to purchase the building instead of paying monthly rent as a repetitive cost.

The rent for the office floor to start the business is a .... cost. (1)

(a) operational (b) finance

(c) start-up (d) None of these

16. Neeta runs an online business selling women clothing and accessories of a wide variety. She is generating a good profit from the business and is trying to expand her business and attract more customers. After choosing the right method of doing business, Neeta analysed various elements of the market to make a business plan for acquiring all the necessary materials for the business.

Which of the following factors should Neeta analyse before recruiting the required materials?

(a) Nature of business (b) Size of business (1)
(c) Scale of operations (d) All of these

17. Diversity and inclusiveness in hiring should be a priority. A varied workforce entails a diverse range of viewpoints, concepts and methodologies. This promotes diversity in the workplace, which can enhance the financial performance.

The company's target talent pool should think that when sourcing and recruiting prospects, it does so without prejudice or bias.

The best method to prove this theory is to employ a varied group of workers.

Which resource is highlighted in the above text?

(a) Physical (b) Human (1)
(c) Capital (d) Financial

18. Which of the following is not an example of an e-commerce business? (1)

(a) Bonbon sells a variety of sunglasses and eyewear through its official website.
(b) Rama Ben makes different types of pickles from her village herbs and vegetables and sells them through her daughter's social media page.
(c) Jackson and Sons operates a big store in the central market selling a variety of stationary products.
(d) All of the above

Section-B

19. Refer the given image.

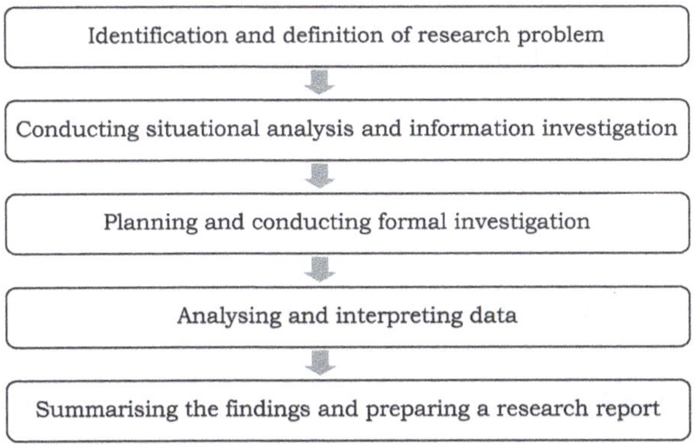

(i) Identify the concept highlighted in the given picture.
(ii) List any two primary instruments of research. (2)

Or State and explain any two classifications of markets.

20. The purpose and objective of every business is to earn profit. For doing this, an entrepreneur needs to price his/her product or service appropriately after treating different costs in an appropriate manner.

(i) State the different types of costs involved in a business.
(ii) State the different between cost and expense. (2)

21. The main purpose of Amazon market research is to identify 'winning' products, or those that may produce high sales, by examining market trends.

The goal is to look for goods you can purchase at a bargain and then resell for a profit at pricing that is competitive.

For instance, you could be able to sell pairs of shoes for 10 per piece, but if the quality isn't that great, your consumers will complain and you'll wind up with low sales. You must therefore seek out those 'winning' products that not just sell well and garner favourable evaluations.

After reading the above article, explain what is market research and why is it vital? (2)

22. Explain any two advantages of being an entrepreneur. (2)

Or

What is the role of marketing in entrepreneurship?

23. "The process of generating ideas starts from where ideas come from, ways to generate ideas and the role of structured approach, analysis and intuition in the ways to generate ideas."

In this context, mention any two sources of ideas. (2)

24. Beetles Corporations incurred the following costs in the current month

Particulars	Costs (₹)
Sales commission	40,000
Land	10,00,000
Salaries	2,00,000
Royalty	1,50,000
Rent	52,000
Registration	1,00,000
Raw material	2,00,000

Determine the variable cost for the corporation. (2)

Or

If the variable cost per unit of production for producing 100 units of a product is ₹ 50 and the selling price per unit are ₹ 90. What will be the contribution per unit?

Section-C

25. In an organisation, each person would have different position, duties, responsibilities, etc. making it imperative for an organisation to have a wide range of personnel ranging from managers, supervisors, administrators, engineers, technical, skilled and unskilled workers.

What kind of person to recruit and for what qualities that person should be tested needs a very careful, systematic, scientific and organised planning. Therefore, Amit, the manager of Collpuff Limited has developed a structured tool that helps in making survey charts and scheduling operations.

(i) Identify and explain the tool developed by Amit.

(ii) State the meaning of resource. (3)

26. Explain variable costs and its types. (3)

Or How variable costs differ from fixed costs?

27. Kartar wants to start a business after completing his studies. However, he does not have any business idea. He thinks that a great idea related to a business venture will appear out of nowhere.

(i) Is Kartar justified in his thinking? Discuss.

(ii) State any two misconception related to a business idea. (3)

28. What do you mean by e-business? How does it differ from e-commerce? (3)

29. What is meant by intangible resources? State and explain the intangible resources used by a business. (3)

Or

What are professional services? Explain the ways to procure professional services.

Section-D

30. 'Bright Future Innovations' is a start-up founded by Anil Verma, an aspiring entrepreneur with a vision to develop affordable solar-powered lamps for rural households. Aware of the challenges, he thoroughly researched the market and studied the electricity shortage in remote villages.

Based on his analysis, he designed an efficient and cost effective lamp that required minimal maintenance.

Despite financial constraints, Anil took a bold step by investing his savings and securing a small loan to launch his venture. He faced multiple challenges, including convincing villagers to switch to solar lamps, but his unwavering passion kept him motivated.

He constantly experimented with new designs and sought feedback from users to improve his product.

To ensure his company's growth, Anil personally interacted with his workers, understanding their skills and motivating them to perform better. This helped him create a strong and dedicated team. His innovative approach, risk taking ability and commitment to sustainability made his venture a success.

Quoting lines from the above text, identify five characteristics of an entrepreneur that Anil exhibited while operating his business. (5)

31. Explain the concept of cost in brief. (5)

Or Explain the concept of break-even analysis in brief.

32. Razaq is a native of the beautiful valley of Kashmir. His family owns an apple orchard. During his summer break, he decided to help his family at the orchard. He observed that a lot of time was lost in plucking and picking apples. Being of an innovative mind, he worked on solving the above problem and made a simple plucking device attached with a net and a knife.

This saved considerable time and money.

(i) Identify the role played by Razaq.
(ii) Name any four inventors along with the products they invented. (5)

Or Riya noticed that many underprivileged children in her town lacked access to quality education. Instead of starting a regular business, she established a non-profit organisation that provided free evening classes and skill development workshops for these children. Her initiative gained support from volunteers and donors, allowing her to expand the programme. Riya's primary goal was not profit but social upliftment.

(i) Identify the type of entrepreneur discussed in the case.
(ii) Discuss any three characteristics of entrepreneur identified in (i).

33. In the modern marketing, promotion is the most familiar strategy used by the various business organisations to fascinate the customer. Promotional mix is a critical approach to enhance the sales, that is why companies try to do some more attractive, influencing promotion through various media.

The prime motive of the article is reviewing the promotions mix elements significance (advertising, personal selling, public relations and direct marketing, sale promotion) to brand equity dimensions.
The result endorses that promotional mix component helps to enhance the brand equity.

No doubt, promotion mix elements have a dynamic and significant impact on brand equity, but studies also recommended that monetary promotion might harm brand image which can be a negative effect on brand equity creation.

This article discusses the significance of promotion mix element to brand equity.

Source *International Marketing Strategies of Multinational Fast Food Restaurants in India*

(i) Which concept is highlighted in the above paragraph?
(ii) Discuss its role in an organisation. (5)

34. From the following data, you are required to calculate

(i) P/V ratio
(ii) Break-even sales with the help of P/V ratio
(iii) Sales required to earn a profit of ₹ 4,50,000

Fixed expenses = ₹ 90,000
Variable cost per unit
Direct material = ₹ 5
Direct labour = ₹ 2
Direct overheads = 100% of direct labour
Selling price per unit = ₹ 12 (5)

Answers

1. (c) Only II
2. (a) Drone entrepreneur
3. (a) Only I
4. (a) Innovation
5. (d) Both (a) and (c)
6. (c) Large
7. (b) ₹ 1,50,000
8. (c) Only II
9. (a) ₹ 40
10. (a) Variable
11. (b) B-(ii)
12. (b) Both Assertion (A) and Reason (R) are true, but Reason (R) is not the correct explanation of Assertion (A)
13. (a) internet
14. (a) Free association
15. (a) operational
16. (d) All of these
17. (b) Human
18. (c) Jackson and Sons operates a big store in the central market selling a variety of stationary products.
24. ₹ 3,90,000 *Or* ₹ 40
34. (i) 25% (ii) ₹ 3,60,000 (iii) ₹ 21,60,000

Sample Paper 3

A Highly Simulated Sample Question Paper for CBSE Class XI Examination

Entrepreneurship

General Instructions

Read the following instructions carefully and follow them

1. This question paper contains 34 questions. All questions are compulsory.
2. This question paper is divided into four sections—Section A, B, C and D.
3. Section A : Questions number 1 to 18 are Multiple Choice Type Questions. Each question carries 1 mark.
4. Section B : Questions number 19 to 24 are Short Answer Type-I Questions. Each question carries 2 marks. Write answer to each question in 30 to 40 words.
5. Section C : Questions number 25 to 29 are Short Answer Type-II Questions. Each question carries 3 marks. Write answer to each question in 50 to 70 words.
6. Section D : Questions number 30 to 34 are Long Answer Type Questions. Each question carries 5 marks. Write answer to each question in 120 to 150 words.
7. There is no overall choice. However, an internal choice has been provided in Section B, C and D of question paper. A candidate has to attempt only one of the alternatives in such questions.

Time : 3 hours **Max. Marks : 70**

Section-A

1. Rohit is working in a company which converts raw material into finished goods. He is a part of (1)

I. non-managerial staff
II. trained technical manpower
III. professional manpower
IV. administrative manpower

Codes

(a) I and II (b) Only I (c) I and IV (d) I, II and III

2. Rahul started a business venture because he lost his job. So he is an (1)

(a) drone entrepreneur (b) imitative entrepreneur
(c) induced entrepreneur (d) social entrepreneur

3. Mahesh works in a MNC and gets a monthly salary of ₹ 40,000. He is not happy with his job and wants to start his own venture. His wife is not in favour of this idea and says that there are many disadvantages to this. The disadvantages can be (1)

I. irregular income II. erratic work schedule
III. fewer benefits IV. freedom

Codes

(a) Only II (b) I, II, and III
(c) Only III (d) All of these

4. A buyer buys more during boom than in recession. The buying behaviour of the buyer is being effected by (1)

(a) economic factor (b) technological factor
(c) legal factor (d) tastes and preferences

5. Which amongst the following is commercial function required to be performed by the entrepreneur? (1)

(a) Innovation (b) Detailed investigation
(c) Planning (d) Production

6. ABC Limited wants to diversify its operations. To generate idea related to the product in which to diversify, the CEO of the company, Mr. Raju Verma, called a meeting. In the meeting, an unstructured discussion took place where a number of business ideas were generated by innovating alternative ways of identifying the product and zeroing down to one such product.

The idea here is being generated through (1)

(a) focus group (b) brainstorming
(c) market analysis (d) None of these

7. Sam has a goal of achieving a daily profit of ₹ 600 units. The fixed cost per day is ₹ 420 and the gross margin per cup is ₹ 1.50. What will be the sales target per day? (1)

(a) 680 units (b) 820 units
(c) 180 units (d) 1,020 units

8. Neena is the marketing manager of Stools Limited and is suggesting the company to extend its marketing operations in as many areas as the company can.

Stools Limited manufactures and sells various types of home décor products including indoor plants, flowers, showpieces, etc. The management argued that they should be located only in their place of origin and should not waste resources on building more markets.

Neena explains that a market extends to a region and the whole region is taken as a place of market. The management, after Neena's efforts, agrees to market their products in one more market or area.

Which concept of market is/are highlighted in the above case? (1)

I. Modernised II. Traditional
III. Emerging IV. Scientific

Codes

(a) I and II (b) Only I
(c) Only III (d) III and IV

9. Sham has a tea stall near an office building and sells around 50 cups of tea per day at a price of ₹ 35. The cost of making a cup is ₹ 20. What is the gross margin of Sham's business? (1)

(a) ₹ 1,850 (b) ₹ 1,750
(c) ₹ 750 (d) ₹ 650

10. Given below is list of some businesses in Column I and their respective unit of sale in Column II. Match them correctly (1)

Column I	Column II
A. Fruit vendor	(i) Kilogram
B. Dairy	(ii) Metre
C. Garment shop	(iii) Litre
D. Textiles	(iv) Piece or number

Codes

(a) A-(i) (b) B-(ii)
(c) C-(iii) (d) D-(iv)

11. **Assertion** (A) Enterprise serves as the framework within which decisions concerning what to produce, how much to produce, when to produce and how to produce are taken by the owner.

Reason (R) An enterprise consists of people who work together primarily for the purpose of making and/or selling a product or a service. (1)

Alternatives

(a) Both Assertion (A) and Reason (R) are true and Reason (R) is the correct explanation of Assertion (A)
(b) Both Assertion (A) and Reason (R) are true, but Reason (R) is not the correct explanation of Assertion (A)
(c) Assertion (A) is true, but Reason (R) is false
(d) Assertion (A) is false, but Reason (R) is true

12. Which concept is highlighted in the given picture? (1)

(a) Social entrepreneurship
(b) Entrepreneur as innovators
(c) Both (a) and (b) (d) None of the above

13. Potato chips were invented by (1)

(a) George Crum (b) Percy Spencer
(c) John Hopps (d) None of these

14. Sooraj completed his studies in the field of entrepreneurship and has returned to India. He now has various ideas for starting a venture, but one day after seeing children in the town purchasing and eating sugar candy from street vendors, he had a gut feeling that making a Popsicle candy will be a great idea.

What type of idea generation technique is used by Sooraj? (1)

(a) Brainstorming (b) Intuition
(c) Business intelligence (d) Focus groups

15. Mohan and Sohan are friends since college. They both were students of entrepreneurship class and were very keen to start their own business. They decided to develop a product that would help old people stand straight and designed a prototype for some investors. The investors liked their idea and asked them to produce a lot of 50 samples after which they will final the investment.

Mohan and Sohan withdrew their savings and took some cash from their families as borrowings to make a sample lot. Which resource is highlighted in the above text? (1)

(a) Economic (b) Financial
(c) Material (d) Human

16. Vista Limited is a new start-up developing mobile applications for their clients. The owner of the company is himself a web- designer and sometimes indulges in developing the required application. The company is operational since 2021 but is incurring a wide difference in its revenue and costs of production.

The management analysed the situation and came to the result that the professionals hired for developing the applications are paid a huge amount for each application which is increasing their costs.

What are some other ways in which the company can get affordable professional services? (1)

(a) Contractual basis (b) Regular basis
(c) Lease basis (d) All of these

17. Tim designed a unique type of slime having fragrance and action figures in it.

He decided to develop some samples and sell it in the local markets to test the feasibility of the product. The first lot of 25 units was produced and he started selling it through some local retailers. The product was loved by many children and the demand increased. Tim was on cloud nine and started planning to make more products and start a company.

Which channel of distribution was used by Sooraj to sell his candy? (1)

(a) Zero-level (b) One-level
(c) Two-level
(d) Multi-level

18. Which of the following is not an example of generating entrepreneurial idea through brainstorming? (1)

(a) Ritu plays the role of moderator and asks a group of people to look at a specific product and answer specific questions asked by her.
(b) Delta Limited regularly seats its departmental heads in a meeting room to generate business ideas by solving general problems.
(c) Ram and Mohan came into contact and developed an unstructured discussion which led to the generation of a business idea.
(d) All of the above

Section-B

19. Seema makes resin arts at her home and was not aware of her talent until one of her sisters posted some of her work on her social media channel. She got viral instantly and her sister suggested her to sell her art for a living. Seema started making art on demand at a unit price of ₹ 1,500 per piece and incurred ₹ 800 as costs on making the art. Determine the gross profit per unit for Seema's venture. (2)

Or Determine the total start-up costs from the following costs incurred by a manufacturing business

Particulars	Costs (₹)
Registration	1,00,000
Advertising	50,000
Rent	22,000
Advance Rent	11,000
Employee Welfare	2,600
Insurance Premium	5,000
Land	5,00,000

20. Eastman Kodak, in its film business, has been worrying about the growing competition from Fuji – the Japanese filmmaker. But in reality, Kodak faced a much greater threat from the recent invention of the 'filmless camera' sold by Canon and Sony, which takes video still pictures to be shown on a TV receiver. What greater threat is there to a film business than a filmless camera

(i) Identify the factor of macroeconomic environment highlighted in the above text.
(ii) Explain the factor identified in (i). (2)

21. Read the following article and explain the factors required to build an efficient manpower or human resource.

Herbert G Hicks and C Ray Gullet have rightly observed that, "The people working in a firm make it what it is".

An organisation's performance and resulting productivity are directly proportional to the quantity and quality of its human resource. A rich and continuing supply of qualified people/personnel is the best assurance an enterprise can have that it will flourish. (2)

22.

(i) Identify the concept shown in the above figure.
(ii) State the concept of entrepreneurship. (2)

Or

Explain any two disadvantages of being an entrepreneur.

23. "It is a more in-depth review of business opportunity including market research and due diligence."

In the light of the given statement, write a short note on opportunity assessment. (2)

24. "At every point where a specific commodity is concentrated for sale, a market is found."

Identify the concept of market highlighted in the statement and explain it. (2)

Or

List and explain any two roles of e-commerce in entrepreneurship.

Section-C

25. Amit runs a garments shop in Lajpat Nagar, Delhi. The shop is a high quality, designer showroom for wedding and party wear clothes. Lajpat market is very busy on all days of the week and the revenue is good for the businesses. Amit has built a good reputation and goodwill among his customers and others; therefore, the shop is always full of customers and generated highest revenue among all the other shops.

Amit has decided to reach a particular sales target this month and his accountant has suggested that they should first estimate the break-even analysis to compute sales target and earning desired profits.

(i) State the meaning of break-even analysis.
(ii) As an accountant, explain the use of break-even analysis in computing sales target to earn desired profits. (3)

26. Explain the concept of financial resources for entrepreneurs. (3)

Or Explain any two sources of generating finance.

27. Samir has decided to open a new business of supplying sports equipments to Sports Authority of India. He decided to charge least possible price for his products and to source them from small-scale units. He tried to urge Sudhakar to join his business. Before giving his final answer, Sudhakar wants to know about the business.

(i) Which part of business plan should Sudhakar look into?
(ii) Explain two elements of business plan. (3)

28. What do you mean by market environment? State the elements of market environment. (3)

29. What are material resources? (3)

Or While planning, state and explain the important decisions to be made by an entrepreneur.

Section-D

30. Prabhakar runs a company that manufactures affordable mobile phones by utilising the same advanced technology employed by big manufacturing companies. Instead of innovating new products, Prabhakar focuses on replicating existing technologies to produce cost effective alternatives for budget conscious consumers.

His strategy has made technology more accessible to a larger audience, but it also raises questions about innovation versus replication in entrepreneurship.

(i) Identify Prabhakar's classification as an entrepreneur based on C. Danhof's typology.
(ii) Explain the characteristics of entrepreneurs belonging to the same category as Prabhakar.
(iii) Describe two other types of entrepreneurs classified by C. Danhof, with examples. (5)

31. 'The Bakery Shop for All' is a growing bakery chain specialising in organic and preservative free baked goods. To expand its reach, the company analysed consumer preferences and identified a rising demand for healthy eating habits. It decided to introduce a new range of whole-grain and gluten-free bread at an affordable price.

To maintain profitability, 'The Bakery Shop for All' focused on controlling costs by sourcing raw materials in bulk at discounted rates. The company also optimised its production process to minimise waste and ensure consistent product quality.

To attract price sensitive customers, it set its product prices competitively while maintaining a reasonable profit margin.

Additionally, to track its financial performance, the company regularly measured the number of bread loaves sold daily, the cost incurred per loaf and the price at which each loaf was sold. This helped the company analyse sales trends, manage expenses and maximise profitability.

Quoting lines from the above text, identify and explain the terminologies that help in measuring sales, costs and profits. (5)

32. What are social entrepreneurs? Give examples. (5)

Or What are the characteristics of social entrepreneurs?

33. Faced with an increasingly changing business environment, being flexible and more innovative has become an obligation for organisations.

To better innovate and remain competitive, organisations must use all their knowledge, proficiencies and abilities of people to consistently create new creative products and services.

Our work is centered on the beginning of the innovation process, commonly referred to as 'Fuzzy Front End' focusing on idea generation for new product development.

The current paper presents a qualitative approach for managing idea generation stage within an innovation management process in order to ensure an improved quality of the first draft of idea generation stage outputs.

This paper presents a theoretical construct, defined as a qualitative approach to manage the emergence of idea that aims to support activities of the Front End of innovation.

We first present the global context of this work, the life-cycle and the core concepts adopted for the idea generation. Next, we explore and discuss based on a set of defined characteristics some of existing creativity techniques.

Then, we provide an overview of the quality concept in order to guide our research on developing a qualitative approach to support the idea generation stage.

Source *Conference International Conference on Management Sciences and Innovations (ICMSI), Barcelona, Spain, 14th-15th October, 2015*

(i) Which concept is highlighted in the given paragraph?

(ii) Discuss its different ways. (5)

Or This article aims to understand the extent to which Social Entrepreneurship (SE) contributes to the construction of a collective dimension linked to Social Innovation (SI). We aim to propose new ideas that can deliver insights into the SE phenomenon. This research is also distinct from entrepreneurial ecosystems as its development already requires some successful entrepreneurial action and to do it, the structuring and consolidation of an entrepreneurial ecosystem, constitutes a real challenge for the development of SI.

This work has been based on a participant observation of eight major events dedicated to social entrepreneurship or the shared economy. In-depth interviews with Tunisian social entrepreneurs were also conducted in order to enrich our corpus.

The results show the necessary cooperation of social entrepreneurs for a sustainable and responsible social innovation.

Indeed, the analysis emphasises that the viability and sustainability of a social innovation rests essentially on a collective construction, beyond common social values.

Source *Journal of innovation and entrepreneurship volume 10, Article number: 14 (2021)*

(i) Which concept is highlighted in the above paragraph?

(ii) Discuss some of its characteristics.

34. XYZ Associates has the following details

Fixed cost = ₹ 40,00,000

Variable cost per unit = ₹ 200

Selling price per unit = ₹ 400

Find

(i) The break-even sales quantity

(ii) The break-even sales

(iii) If the actual production quantity is 60,000, find

(a) Contribution

(b) Margin of safety (5)

Answers

1. (b) Only I
2. (c) induced entrepreneur
3. (b) I, II and III
4. (a) economic factor
5. (d) Production
6. (b) brainstorming
7. (a) 680 units
8. (b) Only I
9. (c) ₹ 750
10. (a) A-(i)
11. (b) Both Assertion (A) and Reason (R) are true, but Reason (R) is not the correct explanation of Assertion (A)
12. (b) Entrepreneur as innovators
13. (a) George Crum
14. (b) Intuition
15. (b) Financial
16. (d) All of the above
17. (b) One-level
18. (a) Ritu plays the role of moderator and asks a group of people to look at a specific product and answer specific questions asked by her.
19. ₹ 700 *Or* ₹ 6,11,000

34. (i) 20,000 units (ii) ₹ 80,00,000
(iii) (a) ₹ 1,20,00,000 (b) ₹ 1,60,00,000